Mom and Dad
Are Divorced,
But I'm Not

Mom and Dad Are Divorced, But I'm Not

Parenting After Divorce

Hal W. Anderson
and Gail S. Anderson

Caroline Thurston Fox, ACSW, *Consultant*

Nelson-Hall nh Chicago

This book is affectionately dedicated to Renelle, Jay, Orin, Wendelyn, Weston, Jonathan, Keira, Marisa, Samara, Genina, Briana.

LIBRARY OF CONGRESS CATALOGING IN PUBLICATION DATA

Anderson, Hal W
  Mom and dad are divorced, but I'm not.

  Includes index.
    1. Divorce—United States—Psychological aspects.   2. Children of divorced parents—United States.   3. Separation (Psychological)   4. Stepparents—United States.   5. Parenting—United States.   I. Anderson, Gail S., joint author.   II. Title.
HQ834.A69   306.8'9   80-27602
ISBN 0-88229-522-5 (cloth)
ISBN 0-88229-777-5 (paper)

Contents

Foreword by Caroline Thurston Fox   vii
Preface   xi
1. You Are Not Alone   1
2. Despair and Hope   5
3. Children Need to Know   13
4. Children Are Not Possessions   37
5. How Children React to Divorce   55
6. Parenting Under Stress: The Early Months   75
7. Creating the Single-Parent Family   91
8. Part-Time Bachelor Parent   119
9. Long-Distance Parent   139
10. Pitfalls and Problems   157
11. Dating and Remarriage   183
12. Stepparenting   201
13. Yours, Mine, and Ours: The Blended Family   221
14. Re-Creating Family Life After Divorce   245
Bibliography   255
Index   257

Foreword

The fact that divorce is common in the United States and that it affects many individuals is well known. Over a million couples are divorced each year with millions of children thus affected. However, how individuals and families respond to painful separation and attain successful readjustment following divorce has not been studied adequately.

As a clinical faculty member at the University of Denver Child Study Center for sixteen years, I have been concerned about how to understand and to treat children and parents reacting to divorce. With clinical responsibilities as co-director of the clinic, intake worker, and supervisor of graduate students, I had the opportunity to know hundreds of families affected by divorce. In fact, over half the children referred for clinic services were living in divorced families including both single-parent and regrouped families. Children from these homes are referred for many reasons, including poor academic progress, aggressive behaviors, withdrawn behaviors, or sometimes a combination of difficulties. Generally, these children are showing symptoms of loss and grief associated with the separation of their parents and other changes in their lives. Not only are they mourning the loss of previous relationships, but at the same time they also may be facing the need to adapt to new relationships with a former parent, stepparents, and stepsiblings.

Many issues are involved in the process of divorce, and professionals need to understand these issues in order to assist individuals in handling them. Why do some parents and children move through divorce in a constructive way while others fall into serious difficulties? How can both parents and children be helped to deal with their confusion of sad and angry feelings following divorce? How can single parents be supported in the difficult task of rearing children by themselves? What new ways can our society find to assist children and parents? What problems are common to all children affected by divorce, and what problems are affected by such factors as individual differences in the child's own personality and the timing of the divorce?

Useful books have been written on divorce, and potentially valuable clinical studies regarding the effects of divorce on children and post-divorce treatment are underway. However, clinical knowledge about divorce problems and treatment is still limited. The divorce rate has increased so rapidly that professionals have tended to focus on individual cases while ignoring the flood of family changes engulfing millions of individuals.

Married for thirty-five years and a parent, I have experienced how difficult it is to rear children even in stable circumstances, and I have considered how overwhelmingly difficult it is for parents torn by their own stresses to meet the critical needs of children who are reacting to divorce. I have responded to these parents' guilt and depression, their difficulty in coping effectively, and their tentative hope for readjustment of their troubled lives. I have sought more clinical knowledge and have felt the need for appropriate books to share with parents.

When my divorced friends, Gail and Hal Anderson, commented, "Someone ought to write a book," I challenged them, "Why don't you?" On New Year's Day several years ago, Hal and Gail explored all the books they could find related to divorce in the Denver Public Library and decided to write one themselves. They recognized the need for a book written in a clear and encouraging fashion to help parents and children through the agonizing process of divorce and its aftermath.

As a professional consultant to Gail and Hal, I have joined them in the stimulating search for identification of issues related to children and divorce. We have spent many Saturdays together, questioning how to assist parents and children come through divorce in a way that can be growth-producing. Although this book is written in an informal, and even almost entertaining way, it contains sound principles of mental health.

Hal and Gail used their experiences as professional educators in writing the book, but most importantly, they responded as parents using their own family experiences and feelings in the book. Their home, in which eight children live full-time and three children visit, is a rich laboratory for observing children of different ages and past experiences as they form a new family group. Gail and Hal are not perfect parents. They sometimes yell at their kids, the front porch is a cluttered maze of wheeled toys and papers waiting to be delivered, and often the children's needs have been postponed while their parents finished one more page of the book.

Their children flourish, however, because their parents treat them with respect and have concern for their total growth. The philosophy of facing problems and then moving actively to do something about them is prominent in their home as well as in the book. I salute Hal and Gail for their constructive modeling of happy family life following divorce. They live what they teach!

Caroline Thurston Fox, ACSW

Preface

While writing this book we were continually confronted with the problem of gender in the English language. We wanted the book to be useful to both mothers and fathers, but we found it awkward to constantly say "he or she" and "her or him." And you can't very well write an entire book using only the impersonal plural, "they"! Although we struggled, we did not resolve this dilemma. Instead, we settled on a compromise: in situations where females predominate in our society (custodial parent, for example), we used the feminine gender; in situations where males are most common (non-custodial parent), we used the masculine gender. Of course we realize that there are many exceptions; as you read, shift "he" to "she" or vice versa as it is applicable to your life.

Related linguistic frustrations cropped up when we talked about children. As long as we used the ambiguous third person plural, we were fine. But as soon as we wished to discuss an individual child, we were thrust back to the complicated and intrusive "he or she" form. Most often, therefore, we simply gave up and adopted the so-called impersonal or neuter "he," realizing, however, that the use of the masculine form as neuter is a practice which many people today find deplorable. We sympathize, but we have no linguistic solutions to offer.

Completing this book has been satisfying as well as surprising. If we had known ahead of time what it would involve—time-consuming research, the frustration of trying to put ideas clearly into words, the cost of paying for overdue library books and necessary supplies (reams of paper!), the expense of eating out after a full day at the typewriter, juggling to make sure that all our children were occupied for a few hours on Saturday or Sunday so that we could retreat to our attic and type — we would probably have written the book anyway! We wanted to share with others what we had learned about parenting after divorce, both from our own personal experiences and from the experiences of others.

We extend our deepest thanks to all the people who have contributed in various ways to shape this book: Marcia Helland, our friend, who passed on a virulent case of writing dreams along with her seven-year accumulation of writers' magazines (as well as assurance that both of us had writing in our ascending moon in the house of Jupiter — or a similar astrological revelation); Synva Hoffman, our friend who believed in dreams and encouraged us from the birth of the idea to the finished product; Jeanne Benet, our grammarian and literary critic, who spent countless hours going over the manuscript to find our dangling participles, awkward phraseology, and other semantic slips, and whose contributions have greatly enriched this book; Aurelia Lujan, our faithful typist, who never complained as she valiantly worked with copy made illegible by marginal scrawlings and coffee stains; and the numerous parents and their children who through interviews and conversations shared with us bits and pieces of their lives — tales of success, frustration, joy, pain, and love.

Most of all, we wish to thank Caroline Thurston Fox, our good friend and consultant, whose faith in us as parents and authors encouraged and sustained us. Not only did she unsparingly contribute her professional experiences and clinical knowledge, but even more, she shared her wisdom and common sense, her insights and understanding, and her deep dedication to helping parents find joy and fulfillment in parenting their children.

And we give heartfelt thanks to all our friends and family whose love and loyalty made this book possible: our many friends who offered support and sympathy over the months, particularly Carolyn Lupe and Albert Aguayo, whose help we deeply appreciate; our children's grandparents, who although initially overwhelmed by the implications of our divorces and subsequent remarriage, have come to accept our blended family and love all our children as their grandchildren; Lynn Reser, our children's aunt who was always on hand, helping with assorted projects, providing special treats and excursions for the children, and filling in for us while we were working; and, of course, the children themselves who had to temporarily forgo many hours of being parented while we were writing about parenting! Without them, we would never have written this book.

Childhood is a gift the gods give children. It is as precious as the rubies they give the earth and the sun they give the spheres. It is each child's absolutely; as rare as a unicorn or a phoenix. One childhood to every child. No two childhoods are alike. Childhood is the form that upholds each child's life forever. If a man or a society taints a child's childhood, brutalizes it, strikes it down, and corrupts it with fear and bad dreams, then he maims that child forever, and the judgment on that man and that society will be terrible and eternal.

Ned O'Gorman
The Storefront

1

You Are
Not Alone

Eight years ago, I, my wife, and our eleven children celebrated our second year of being a family by going out to dinner. As funds were limited and appetites hearty, the children rapidly became engaged in a lively exchange, debating what was the best meal for the money. As they chattered, I gradually became aware that an elderly gentleman at the next table was engrossed in the interplay. In the beginning we had been self-conscious about the size of our group—after all, eleven children in a family is not a common sight these days—but by now we scarcely noticed the stir we created. But the old man noticed!

Finally, the waitress brought him his bill. He started for the door. Suddenly, he turned and came back to our table. To my surprise, he patted my shoulder and extended his hand. "Sir," he said to me in a solemn voice, "I don't know what you're doing with so many children, but I'm all for you!" And with that he was gone.

As I looked around the table, I suddenly saw us as the old gentleman had seen us, and I had to laugh. We certainly are not an ordinary family. In the first place, our eleven youngsters span less than a dozen years, and Gail looks too young to have had that many children. (Our youngest was then a year old and our eldest, thirteen.) Furthermore, we have three sets of "twins," and our multi-ethnic family (including "natural" offspring and adopted children) varies widely in looks—from dark to light skin, from curly to straight hair, and from sturdy to fragile builds. No wonder the old man was puzzled, for what he saw was a blend—a "yours, mine, and ours" family.

Gazing fondly at our happy, confident, lively brood, I began to recall some of the joys and sorrows we had all been through together. I was proud of the family I saw before me, remembering that the road had not been easy because this family began with two divorces, each involving five children.

Some marriages end slowly and agonizingly come to a halt. Others erupt suddenly with a violent burst of pent-up anger and resentment. Almost all divorces leave the ex-spouses with feelings of hurt and confusion. Each of our marriages ended explosively — the intensity of our feelings taking each of us by surprise. However, in the midst of our own pain and turmoil, bitterness, guilt and self-doubt, each of us was keenly aware that our children were suffering too. Having been friends for many years and discovering ourselves facing similar challenges, we joined together in a quest for answers to difficult questions. How could we help our children? What could we say to them? How could we give them the reassurance we felt they needed at a time when we felt no solid ground under our own feet?

Desperately, we looked for help. We talked to other divorced people, but — except for a few whose advice we found invaluable — most were as confused as we. We knew from research that children feel profoundly the loss of a parent through death. What does a child feel about divorce? How does he feel when he rarely sees one of his parents — perhaps only for a week or so in the summer? How does a child feel when he acquires a new parent — and perhaps stepsiblings? How do parents and children rebuild and re-create their lives after divorce in meaningful, satisfying ways? We had seen so many divorced parents unwittingly do so much harm to their children. How could we avoid falling into the obvious and not so obvious pitfalls and traps of parenting after divorce?

These, and others, are the questions and concerns with which we grappled. Eventually, we were married, and in time an eleventh child was born. Coping with the varieties of reactions and interactions of our eleven children led us deeper into the search for answers to our problems. We sought help from professional counselors and found their insights and guidelines very valuable — but still we did not have enough *concrete* help.

We went to the public library and read all the books we could find on divorce and remarriage. We discovered, however, that most of them dealt with the problems of the marriage partners themselves with at best only a chapter or two devoted to the problems that children face. Often, the authors seemed to take it for granted that if we, the parents, could pull ourselves through the trauma of divorce without too much personal psychological damage, our children would automatically be all right. Unfortunately, as we and thousands of other concerned parents and child guidance professionals have found, it's not that simple.

Other books which did contain valuable materials were written by professionals for the use of other professionals. The language was often technical, the approach clinical and esoteric, and the material impractical for solving daily problems. They lacked concrete, practical, or usable suggestions. For instance, all the authorities agreed that after divorce parents must reassure their children that they have not been abandoned. But *how*? What does one actually *say*? What does one actually *do*? What were the guidelines?

And thus this book began to take shape. It is written *by* parents *for* parents, but still is firmly based on the experience and knowledge of professionals. Throughout the book we'll give you guidelines and show you how you can use them to understand and solve many problems. We've tried to cover everything: preparing your child for divorce, supporting him through the upheaval and changes, recognizing pitfalls and problems, and helping him find the addition of stepparents and new relatives an enriching experience. We've offered realistic, concrete ideas to help you cope immediately, as well as suggestions for gradually reconstructing your life after divorce.

In this book you will find many personal accounts of parents who have struggled with the challenges of parenting after divorce. We can learn a great deal from the experiences they share with us. The people are real. (Names and minor details have been altered to preserve anonymity.)

As you scan the table of contents or leaf through this book, you will undoubtedly see pieces of yourself and your own situation. Of course, no two people are exactly alike and no two situations are identical. But like ready-to-wear clothes, if the problems and suggested solutions are close enough, you can alter and adapt them to fit. Often recognizing the difficulty — finding the torn seam or the botched up stitches, as it were — can be half the battle. The suggestions we make are basic; use them as needed!

One final thought. Remember, YOU ARE NOT ALONE. Thousands of us have faced divorce and continued to parent effectively. Although we have all suffered and struggled, most of us have made it — sometimes the hard way. This book is for you — so that you can make it more easily.

2

Despair
and Hope

The death of a marriage inevitably involves pain. Although in the past twenty years the stigma of divorce has greatly decreased, the agony of divorce remains acute. Despite legal terms like "no-fault" divorce, most of us still feel that we have failed. We were unable to carry out our marriage vows; we were unable to make our relationship strong and enduring.

With tears in her eyes, Margaret remembers her thoughts as she waited for the divorce proceedings to begin:

> As I stood that morning waiting for my lawyer to accompany me into the courtroom, dozens of images of the past tumbled through my mind. I could see myself, young and bursting with happiness, dressed in my beautiful wedding gown. Standing beside me, I saw Bill, proud and handsome in his rented tuxedo. We were so full of love and confidence, eager to begin our new life together!
>
> In my mind's eye, I could see Bill a year later, blinking hard through tears of joy and pride as the nurse handed him our newborn Billy to hold. And two years later when Jodi was born, we clung together and wept for joy. Those good times were so good!
>
> What happened? Where had all that happiness gone? How could we have become so hateful and destructive toward each other? Ten years ago we stood arm in arm, deeply in love. Today we are antagonists who almost hate each other.

LIVING TOGETHER IN PAIN

After years of sharing affection, cherishing dreams, raising children, and building a life together, Margaret and Bill are separating. With their dreams shattered and feeling angry, bitter, and disappointed, they confront each other in the sterile chambers of a courtroom, hearing the public phrases which legally release them from their commitment to each other. For Margaret and Bill, the road to divorce was long and tortuous, and the final decision to divorce was agonizing. In fact, as Margaret says:

Bill and I made that decision and unmade it half a dozen times. We wanted so much to stay together. We love our children and for their sake especially we wanted to continue being a family. But despite our efforts—and we *did* try—the rift between us grew as great as the Grand Canyon.

Long before divorce was discussed, all members of this family were acutely aware of the problems. Tense and anxious, Billy and Jodi could not help reacting to their parents' growing estrangement. But despite periods of almost unbearable stress, Margaret and Bill continued living together in pain for many years, for as parents who cared deeply for their children, they could not bring themselves to separate.

For generations, parents have been advised by well-meaning friends and relatives to "stay together for the good of the children"— no matter how untenable their marriage. Increasingly, they find that the quality of a child's home life and the degree to which he feels loved and important, secure and worthwhile are the most critical factors in determining how fully the child will mature into adulthood.

THE DAMAGE OF DISCORD AND CONFLICT

When a marriage is seriously flawed, the tensions caused by the parents' constant discord and their growing estrangement may be far more damaging to a child than the experience of divorce. All too often, because of the energies required to cope with their disintegrating marriage, the parents fail to meet the emotional needs of their children.

In her book *Children of Divorce*, Dr. Louise Despert discusses the effect of "emotional divorce" on the development of the children. By the term, "emotional divorce," Dr. Despert means an unhappy (often destructive) marriage which has not resulted in physical separation or legal divorce. As a therapist, Dr. Despert has found that children usually suffered *more* when emotionally estranged parents continued living together than when they expressed their estrangement openly by separating and divorcing. Facing the problem squarely, Dr. Despert contends, is less threatening to children than the anxiety of the unclear situation.

DIVORCE — AN AGONIZING DECISION FOR PARENTS

As co-director of the University of Denver Child Study Center, Caroline Fox deals daily with the problems and confusion of parents and children who seek solutions for their troubled lives. Many of the parents she works with are struggling with the implications of divorce for their children. "Divorce is a crisis for most couples," Caroline Fox explains, "but for parents it is truly a nightmare. Most of them are acutely aware of the suffering of their children."

Some of the parents she sees are contemplating divorce, some are already separated and in the process of obtaining a divorce, while still others are already divorced and perhaps remarried. All are anxiously looking for ways to establish a foundation of security for their children so that they may grow and develop in healthy, productive ways. Over and over, parents facing divorce are tortured by anxieties and questions: What are we doing to our lives? What are we doing to our children? Will their lives be ruined? Will all the anguish and pain of separation and divorce be worth the hope of a better life?

Divorce, especially when children are involved, is a serious decision which involves much consideration. It should never be lightly made, for it is no panacea. It does not magically solve all problems; in fact, it can produce new ones. Prior to divorce (and, indeed, throughout the process) we strongly advise that you seek counseling. In the midst of turmoil you are likely to become so involved with your difficulties that it is almost impossible for you to assess alternatives and priorities objectively. You may need help to make wise decisions for yourself and your children. Getting help to understand yourself and the flaws in your marriage is often the first step toward rebuilding your life. Furthermore, you undoubtedly will need emotional support and understanding during the difficult months of readjustment. A well-trained counselor or therapist can give you that support while helping you help yourself. If *you* are being supported, you will find it much easier to support and guide your children.

Divorce — A Crisis, Not a Catastrophe!

Few of us are so naive as to believe the ancient fairy tale ending, "and so they were married and lived happily ever after." Nor by the same token do we need to blindly accept the converse myth, "and so they were divorced and ruined the lives of their children." Staying together for the sake of the child does not insure the child's emotional health; nor does divorce necessarily doom him to a life of "hang-ups" and suffering. Like marriage, divorce is what we make it. Although undoubtedly divorce is a crisis in your life and your child's life, it need not be a catastrophe. You and your child can profit and gain. Your divorce can bring peace to the family as well as release new energy for living.

Of course the failures are what we hear about — child snatching, court battles, withholding child support, denying visitation. Trouble makes the headlines! We all know of parents who use their children as pawns in their battle to hurt each other. They pull the child back and forth until the helpless youngster is in emotional shreds. These parents, oblivious of their children's needs, behave in appallingly selfish and immature ways. In the end, they lose their children's love and respect; but the real losers are the children themselves. When they are deprived of the love, consideration, and support they require, they frequently become deeply damaged.

Guidelines for Successful Parenting

But what about the millions of other parents and children who not only survive the experience of divorce, but also grow and flourish? How do these parents successfully raise their children? What are their secrets? In talking with them, we discovered that their ingredients for effective parenting after divorce are remarkably similar. Indeed, their suggestions are sound principles for child rearing under any circumstances.

1. *Respect your child.* The parent must respect his child's needs and emotions. During the early months following the breakup of his parents, the child will feel intensely the whole gamut of emotions — love and hate, anger and more anger, disappointment and fear, guilt and despair. He has a right to all his emotions, for he cannot recover

and rebuild his life until he has mourned the passing of his old life as he knew it.

The child also has a right to his individuality. He is a separate person — separate from you and separate from his other parent. He may look somewhat like one of his parents, he may have inherited certain characteristics or traits, but he is not you and he is not your ex-spouse. He is uniquely himself. Appreciate his individuality.

2. *Assure your child that he is a good, lovable, and worthwhile person.* All children need frequent reminders that they are loved and appreciated. Their self-image and self-esteem are very dependent upon how well you regard them. But children of divorce need even more assurance of your love and their worth. Divorce is a scary business for children. Their security is shaken. If one parent leaves, might not the other also go?

The child particularly needs your support at this time. He needs frequent reassurance that the divorce was not his fault. He needs to know that he will be cared for and loved — just as in the past — and that he will not be abandoned. Show him your steadfast love and give him frequent evidence of your approval.

3. *Listen to your child and be honest with him.* Learn to *hear* your child. Listen to the real message behind his words. Understand that behavior often is an attempt to send a message. Communicate straightforwardly and honestly with your child. Don't try to reassure him with empty words or phrases. You and he need to connect in meaningful ways. Don't assume your child is too young to understand explanations about divorce, but at the same time keep in mind his age and stage of development.

4. *Help your child to continue having as strong and as good a relationship as possible with his other parent.* After divorce, it is tempting to want the child to terminate his relationship with his other parent as you have terminated yours with your ex-spouse. Remember that the child needs both his parents and will want to maintain his relationship with both without having to feel guilty or apologetic. When a parent denies the child the opportunity to enjoy a healthy relationship with his other parent, the child suffers.

5. *Learn from the past — don't live in it!* It is appropriate — and even necessary — to mourn after separation, but dwelling on the past is destructive. Self-pity can become poison! Don't be ashamed to get help. The real shame lies in refusing to face the past and analyze mistakes. The failure of a marriage does not mean you have wasted

or ruined your life or your child's life. You can learn from the past and look for a fresh opportunity to begin again.

6. *Believe you can create a better life for yourself and your children.* If you believe that after divorce your life has ended, it will be ended. Don't fear beginning anew, for if you don't try now, you will miss your chance to create a really good life for you and for your children.

When you are freed from the snare of a disintegrating marriage, you release new energies to solve problems and to enjoy life. Ask yourself what you really want for yourself and your children. Obtain counseling in order to clarify your thoughts. Remember that in rebuilding your life you do not have to follow the same plan as before. Dare to dream! Talk to other divorced people who have been successful. Many people have found creative solutions to their problems; you can too.

7. *Set goals!* Rarely does anyone accomplish anything valuable without concrete plans. Decide what you want and plan the steps that will lead you to your goal. For instance, if you want a particular job, you will need to assess what skills you already have and determine what further preparation you will need to attain that goal. Set some goals for parenting. What kind of relationship would you like to have with your children? What experiences would you like to share with them? Break up each goal into smaller pieces—take one step at a time. Don't put off beginning. Start immediately.

8. *Don't blame all mishaps and problems on the divorce.* Problems are a part of living. Mishaps and crises occur all the time to everyone. It is easy to slip into saying (and believing), "If it weren't for the divorce, this wouldn't have happened." Some things would or could have happened regardless of divorce, but most problems have solutions.

Often parents blame all their child's problems or misconduct on the divorce. It is important to remember that no childhood is painless. Growing up is not an easy process; it is full of temporary aches and pains. Divorce intensifies the problems of growing up, but the process of maturation is fraught with stresses and conflicts.

9. *Problems should not be avoided.* Pain should not always be shunned. You, as well as your children, can profit by learning to confront and solve problems. All of us feel justifiably proud when we come through dark days and emerge—a bit scarred, perhaps, but not defeated. Real maturity only comes from facing problems and

meeting challenges. You cannot and should not shield your child from all momentary unhappiness. In doing so you also shield him from growth.

Others have done it — you can too! By following the guidelines listed above, untold numbers of sensitive parents have helped their children through the painful ordeal of separation and divorce. These parents have managed to keep the needs of their children well in mind and have been able to hear and heed their children's pain, even while coping with their own suffering and disorientation.

REMEMBER

Although divorce is the end of your marriage, it is the beginning of a new chapter in your life and in the lives of your children. Your marriage may have failed, but your divorce can be a positive experience. By facing reality and solving problems, you can overcome this crisis. It will not be easy or painless, but it can be rewarding. You and your children can grow in new and exciting ways in the coming years.

3

Children Need
to Know

"I've got to say something about the divorce to Tommy and Missy,"
worries a young mother, "but how can I explain it to them? They're
really too young to understand."

"I can't tell my kids that their father and I are separating," says
another mother. "I'm so upset and depressed, I know I'd just break
down and cry."

And a father asks, "What can I tell the kids? They think I'm the
greatest! Am I to tell them how much I've grown to hate their
mother? Or that I'm in love with another woman? I know I've got to
talk with them, but what can I tell them?"

Each year millions of children are plunged into the emotional
upheaval of separation and divorce. In fact, incredible as it may
seem, many parents never do discuss divorce with their children.
Most often, children of divorce are left adrift — desperately trying to
cope and make sense of their rapidly changing world without the
help and counsel of their parents.

"I've Got to Tell My Child, But . . ."

The decision to separate is rarely easy. Usually it is preceded by
many months or even years of agonizing assessment and introspec-
tion, indecision and self-doubt, bitterness and despair. And when a
couple has children, the decision to divorce is even more painful.
Responsible parents know that their decision is not only personal;
they know that it involves the lives of their children as well. If they
do not understand this initially, they will soon discover that the

decision to divorce is only the first of many difficult, painful decisions to be made throughout the ensuing months and years—
decisions which will affect their children's well-being as well as their
own. Parents wishing to minimize the damaging effects of divorce on
their children must make a firm resolution to keep the lines of communication with their children as open as possible.

Like the parents quoted above, most of us realize how important it
is to prepare our children for the changes in their lives. Especially
when it comes to an emotionally charged subject like divorce, communication with the children is *extremely* important. We *want* to tell
them; we *intend* to tell them. But somehow the days go by and we
don't tell them. Sadly, too many parents find themselves so involved
with their own conflicting emotions and problems that they have
little energy left to cope with the needs of their children. Often they
are overwhelmed by their feelings of guilt and failure and feel totally
inadequate to help their child understand the impending separation
or the separation that has already taken place.

Sara, mother of three school-aged children, confesses, "Making
the decision to separate was awful; telling our relatives and friends
was even worse; but facing my kids with the news was more than I
could manage!" Another mother reports:

> I meant to discuss the divorce with my kids, but each time I
> started, I would get all confused. I'd think maybe Jerry and I
> hadn't tried hard enough. Maybe we *could* make things work.
> Maybe we were exaggerating our problems. I got so hung up
> on the maybe's that I couldn't say a thing to the children.

Some parents reach a mutual decision that divorcing will be best
for all members of the family. But even these parents may falter
when it comes time to discuss their plans with their children. Telling
the children brings into sharp focus the harsh reality of the impending separation. It intensifies our feelings of guilt, anger, and failure.
It is no wonder parents avoid discussing divorce with their children.
It *is* painful and difficult. However, if you truly love your child and
want to help ease his anxiety, you must begin communicating with
him.

Even if you have said nothing to him, your child already knows
there are problems. Children are very quick to perceive and react to
the undercurrents of conflict between their parents. The battlelines
do not have to be openly drawn for them to know they are in the

middle of a battleground; nor is it necessary to have violent arguments in their presence for them to know the atmosphere is crackling with tension. Children are usually very sensitive and aware of the dynamics of interpersonal relationships — no matter how subtle or covert — which exist in their family.

DENYING REALITY COMPOUNDS PROBLEMS

Since children are so aware of the emotional climate of their homes, it is very unwise to attempt to protect them by pretending that everything is all right when it is not. By doing so, you increase their anxiety, for children are apt to feel that if their own parents — whom they see as big, strong "giants" — are afraid to face the truth, the truth must indeed be very terrifying. Melinda, aged ten, an only child, tells how her fears grew during the preseparation months:

> At night, when Mom and Dad thought I was asleep, they'd start arguing. Even though I couldn't hear most of the words, I'd get scared. Once I asked Dad why they were so mad at each other, but he just patted me and told me I was being silly and said I shouldn't worry.
>
> But I couldn't stop worrying because even though they'd pretend nothing was wrong when I was around, I knew something was wrong! I kept thinking they were probably going to get a divorce like my friend Sally's parents. After the divorce, her dad moved to Brazil, so I got scared Dad would leave me and I'd never see him again. And then one day I heard them talking about a boarding school in Connecticut and I figured they were going to send *me* away.
>
> I couldn't stop thinking and worrying about these things but I was too scared to ask any more questions.

By saying nothing to her, Melinda's parents had hoped to shield her from worry. Instead, they greatly increased her anxiety. Melinda did not feel a bit reassured by being told not to worry. She had good reason to worry — the stability of her home as she had known it for ten years was threatened. She knew there was trouble between her parents. Without her parents to help her understand what was happening, Melinda had combined bits of overheard conversations with her own high anxiety and had come to some wrong conclusions. It was true that her parents were considering divorce — and indeed they did separate — but she was not sent to boarding school (they were talking about a distant cousin) nor did her father move to Brazil (most divorced fathers don't go that far!). In fact, after her parents' separation, Melinda's life did not change as drastically as she had feared. She continues to live with her mother in the same New York apartment as before. Her father lives in another apartment some blocks away, and she sees him frequently.

If Melinda had been able to share her fears and anxieties instead of bottling them up, she would not have become so panicky and anxious. Answering her question directly and honestly, her father might have said, "You're right, Melinda. Your mom and I *are* angry with each other and we're not getting along. We're trying to figure out what to do about our problems." With this much information openly given, Melinda might then have felt secure enough to confide her deepest fears—that her parents would separate and she would be sent away. Whether she brought out her fears or not, her father could have been very reassuring. He might have continued:

> Melinda, if Mom and I get a divorce, we'll still love you! You're not going to be sent away. You'll still live with Mom and I will see you often. The one thing your mom and I totally agree about is that we both love you, and want you, and will take care of you. *We* might get a divorce, but *you* won't be divorced! You're our daughter forever!

Fear of the unknown haunts us all. Like Melinda, children are much more afraid of feelings and events which are not out in the open than reality—even if it is painful—which is shared and explained. Remember, *denying reality compounds problems. Pretending creates more stress.* You can't build a foundation of trust on lies and pretense. Only by being straightforward, honest, and sensitive to your child's needs can you retain his faith and confidence.

UNDERSTANDING YOUR CHILD'S FEARS AND CONCERNS

Like Melinda, most children keenly feel stress and tension within their family. Although few children actually voice their concerns, questions and worries plague them: Why are Mom and Dad so angry? Why did Dad leave? Did I make him leave? Will he come back if I'm good? What if Mom leaves too? *What's going to happen to me?*

There are so many questions, but so few answers!

Although most children are aware of problems, they usually do not understand the causes of the problems. They may darkly suspect *they* are the cause of their parents' separation, and they fear that if one parent leaves, the other may go too. Limited by their immaturity, egocentric viewpoint, and lack of information, they become mired in guilt and self-blame.

Over and over, child therapists have found that children who are facing the separation and divorce of their parents share many of the same fears and concerns. Without your help, your child cannot fully understand what is happening. The explanations he formulates are often inaccurate and frightening. Your help and understanding can substantially reduce his confusion, pain, and anxiety during the preseparation as well as the early postseparation months.

Let's look at some of the most common concerns and examine how children get confused when they face their anxieties alone.

WHY CHILDREN HAVE SEPARATION ANXIETY

To understand a child's anxiety about his parents' separation, we must keep in mind how very dependent children are upon both their parents. In our society, parents are almost totally responsible for meeting the needs of their children. To young children, parents are the most powerful, important forces in their lives. They protect them, nourish them, keep them safe, and teach them what it is to be a man or a woman. Above all, parents are the ones who love their children.

The child's greatest fear is that this couple, so essential to his well-being, might leave him. What is worse than being small and unprotected in a large, uncaring world? That indeed is a frightening thought. We see signs of this fear in children's nightmares. It is not at all uncommon for young children (and even older ones) to awaken terrified by nightmares of being lost and alone. When parents separate and one parent leaves the home, the child becomes worried about his own fate. After all, he reasons, if one parent left him, the other might also go away.

WHY CHILDREN NEED EXPLANATIONS ABOUT YOUR DECISION

Because the child perceives the world as revolving around him and his needs, he believes his parents were created expressly for his benefit. When something contradicts this concept, he becomes bewildered, upset, and even outraged. He wonders how his parents dare to contemplate divorce! The child feels that if his parents truly loved him, they would not separate. In her book, *Stepchild in the Family*, Anne Simon points out that death and divorce are both experiences of separation. But, she emphasizes, while death is uninvited, divorce is chosen. Thus divorce "seems to confirm the child's worst suspicion that he is abandoned and therefore is not loved."

From this egocentric position, children are incapable of assessing the state of their parents' marriage and the negative effect that the faulty relationship is having on all family members. Children often view their parents' decision to divorce as proof that they are not sufficiently loved. It is important for parents to explain why the decision has been made, for otherwise a child may feel that his own need for his family to stay together was not taken into consideration. *He needs to know that your decision was not lightly made* — that his needs for support, care, and love will continue to be met.

In the months ahead, in many ways your child will be asking, *What about me? Who will take care of me?* And he needs to hear your answer frequently and clearly: "I will!" or "We will!" if both parents are committed to parenting after separation and divorce.

Why Children Blame Themselves

Children often feel they are very small, helpless, and powerless in a large, confusing world. Paradoxically, however, children also feel supremely power*ful*. They do not easily distinguish reality from fantasy, and they do not have much knowledge or experience with the principle of cause and effect. They rely on magic to explain life's mysteries. Their own magic gives them a sense of power — the feeling that they control people and events.

However, belief in their magical powerfulness creates problems for children because they frequently feel they control events just by their thoughts. For example, imagine this scene: a young child reaches for his fifth cookie and his mother says, "No more!" The child argues and pleads. Mother stands firm. The child then becomes enraged and launches into a tantrum. Frustrated and angry at his controlling mother, he thinks or even shrieks, "I hate you! I hate you!" And probably at this moment he wishes his mother were dead — or at least in Timbuctu! Soon after thinking or voicing his angry thoughts, the child becomes overwhelmed with guilt. He doesn't actually want to lose his parent. He needs his parent's love and support. A few minutes later the child hugs his parent ferociously as if to cancel the potency of his destructive wish.

It takes years for children to realize that no matter how murderous their feelings are, these angry impulses cannot destroy or cause harm to others. Even as adults, we harbor some fear that our "bad" thoughts will cause something bad to happen. Think how we knock on wood to stave off a disaster we have just verbalized!

A child may also feel that his bad behavior is powerful enough to cause his parent to leave. This is especially true when a parent leaves soon after an angry encounter with his child. Sammy, an active five-year-old with mischievous dark eyes and a winning smile, believed he had caused his father to leave. The week before his parents separated, Sammy had been particularly excitable and agitated. His father, a quiet, orderly man, who found Sam's exuberance hard to cope with under the best of circumstances, had spent much of the week imploring Sammy to calm down. Sammy's mother remembers:

> During the weeks before Howard left, Sammy became more and more difficult. His voice was loud and he whined and cried all the time. He couldn't keep still a minute. Howard kept telling him to quiet down, but Sammy was like a penned-up jackrabbit. I guess he was reacting to the trouble between Howard and me.
>
> Anyway, Howard finally lost his temper and spanked Sammy. The next day Howard moved out. I knew Sammy was upset about his dad leaving, but I didn't understand what he was thinking until he started promising he'd be quiet and pleading with me to call his dad and tell him he could come home again.

You need to reassure your child that he is not powerful enough to cause his parents to divorce. He needs to know that it is perfectly normal and natural for both adults and children to have angry thoughts about the people they love. It is helpful for the child to have contact with his absent parent soon after separation so that his fears can be checked. His anxieties are reduced when he sees that nothing bad (like death) has happened to his absent parent and that he has not really been abandoned but continues to have the love and support of both parents.

WHY CHILDREN NEED CONCRETE INFORMATION

Children do not like change—especially change which is thrust upon them suddenly. To leave the safe confines of the known and familiar (even when it is painful) and venture into the unknown and unfamiliar (even when it is hopeful) is a frightening prospect for a well-prepared adult. For a child it is much more ominous.

Limited by inexperience, a child cannot imagine a life substantially different from the life he is living. If all he has ever known is a two-parent home, a one-parent home may seem inconceivable. A young child cannot gain reassurance by imagining how the new situation is going to be. Furthermore, to an inexperienced child, abstract ideas like divorce are incomplete and fuzzy. If you do not tell your child concretely and specifically how his life will be affected by divorce, he will not know and will not be prepared for the changes that divorce inevitably brings.

Your child needs to know what aspects of his life will remain the same and what aspects will change after divorce. The more specific you can be about the arrangements for his care, the more reassured and comforted he will be. Remember that ambiguity raises anxiety and hampers our ability to cope; *predictability and understanding strengthen us and help us prepare for the future.*

WHAT CHILDREN NEED TO KNOW

A group of mothers sat together in a small, comfortable conference room. They had all sought answers at the neighborhood mental health clinic to the problems they were having or were anticipating with their children because of recent separation from their spouses.

"I want to help Jodi understand what is happening," said one distraught mother, "but I don't know how. What should I say to her?"

Another said wistfully, "If only there were some magic words I could use to make my kids feel okay!"

Obviously, there are no words which magically remove hurt and sadness, but there definitely are *messages* you can give your child which will help him negotiate the difficult days and months ahead. Regardless of the age or sex of your child, he needs to hear the following basic messages before, during, and after your divorce.

FIVE BASIC MESSAGES

1. I love you and will continue to love and care for you. My love for you has nothing to do with the divorce.
2. I will always be your parent. Parents can become unmarried, but they can't become unparents.

3. You have a perfect right to feel hurt, angry, and confused. I can understand your feelings for I also have similar feelings. I respect your right to have these feelings.
4. Our divorce is not your fault. You are not powerful enough to make us get a divorce. All children become angry with their parents sometimes, but your angry feelings did not make Dad (or Mom) go away. Sometimes children think that if they are very good, their parents will get back together. But since you did not cause us to separate, you can't make us get back together either. You are not responsible for our separation.
5. I will try to be as honest and open as possible with you so we can help each other adjust to our new lives. Getting used to changes is difficult and takes time. Let's try to help each other by asking questions and sharing our feelings. That way we'll both start feeling better faster.

These messages are important and should be the foundation for communication between you and your child. Of course, we do not suggest that you sit your child down and read the above messages to him. We are providing the messages — the words must be yours. Nor do we presume that a child receives much benefit from receiving these messages only once. Rather, it is imperative that you communicate these basic messages again and again by various words and deeds.

Basic Questions Children Want Answered

In talking with parents and professionals working with children of divorce, we have found that children tend to want answers to many of the same questions. Most of their concerns fall under two broad questions: "Why can't our life be the way it was?" and "What about me?"

Remember that these are some of the questions most children want answered. This does not mean that all children will openly ask questions. As a sensitive, concerned parent, you may need to create situations where you can answer some basic questions even though your child has not asked them directly. You might say to your child, "Many children whose parents are getting a divorce wonder about . . ." followed by "you may be wondering the same thing." Often parents simply sit down with their child in a comfortable, private place and preface their sharing with the statement, "I have some important matters to talk with you about."

Let's look at some of the most common questions and see how they can be answered by weaving in the basic messages noted before.

1. *Why are Mom and Dad getting a divorce?* In answering this question, it is best to be as candid as possible, for as Anne Simon points out, if your child does not "know the truth as his parents see it, he cannot understand the divorce. He must assume that it had no solid base, in which case there was no respect for his childish needs." Most children want their parents to stay together — even when their living together is stressful for the children. If your child doesn't have some understanding of why you are going against his desires, he will believe that your decision was cold and capricious — proof that you do not love and care for him.

However, be prepared for the fact that despite his need for explanations, he does not want to accept your reasons and he will not immediately be convinced that your decision is wise. At this point some parents fall into the trap of debating their decision. *Do not become involved in arguments,* for if your child thinks he can change your mind and reverse your decision, he will undoubtedly feel very powerful and guilty. He does not want to be responsible for a decision as serious as divorce. In fact, it is potentially a situation in which the child can't win, for if you should change your mind and continue to be miserable in your marriage, he is likely to suffer guilt. The decision to divorce should be *your* decision, not your child's.

How should you tell your child? The best way is to explain your reasons briefly and as honestly as possible. Does being honest mean "telling all"? Of course not. You certainly should not expose every intimate detail of your marriage. Some reasons for divorce are within your child's understanding and should be discussed; some reasons (especially sexual problems) are clearly inappropriate and should not be shared. No child needs or really wants a detailed summary of what is wrong with his parents' marriage.

If you are separating because of growing incompatibility — problems of value differences and personality conflicts — you might say something like this to your child:

> Your dad (or mom) and I have been very unhappy together for some time. We have tried hard to solve our problems and get along better, but it is just not working out. We don't agree

about many things and we keep making each other miserable. Because we are so unhappy, we get uptight and sometimes take out our anger on you. We don't mean to, because you are not to blame, but our unhappiness just kind of spills over on to you.

Dad (or Mom) and I started out loving each other, wanting to make a home together, and wanting to share our lives. But people change. They sometimes grow apart. They make mistakes. And sometimes a relationship which started out beautiful and healthy becomes unhealthy and flawed. By separating we are hoping to give each other a new opportunity to grow and be happy.

If the decision to divorce was not mutually agreed upon and you are opposed to the separation, you might add some of the following words:

Actually, I'm opposed to getting a divorce. I don't think we've tried hard enough to solve our problems, but your mom (or dad) does not want to try anymore since she (he) feels that there's no use. Maybe some day I will agree that it was a wise decision, but right now I can't.

And, if you can honestly say it, you might add:

One thing we do agree about is that we both love you and will continue to take care of you. Other things may change, but our love for you will not change.

If you are separating because of problems that evoke social stigma (like infidelity, mental illness, or alcoholism), it is still wise to be as open and honest as possible. It is better for children to receive difficult news from their parents than to hear rumors from relatives or outsiders. Except for the very young child, most children can understand or begin to understand such problems as alcoholism, homosexuality, and emotional instability. Painful as it may be, the child can be told that one of his parents loves another person. In our society today, adultery no longer carries the heavy stigma that it once did. In any case, lying will not work. Your child probably has an inkling of the truth. Lies are usually later refuted, thus weakening your child's trust in you. Some of the following may be helpful:

Your mom (or dad) and I have been unhappy together for some time. We've tried to work things out but we haven't been successful. We just keep making each other unhappy. I've found another woman (man) who makes me very happy. I want to marry her (him) and share my life with her (him). I think that when you have a chance to get to know her (him), you'll like her (him) too. I understand that right now you're feeling too angry and upset to believe me. I'm sorry that our divorce is making your life so sad and difficult. I'm going to continue to see you often because I still love you very much.

You need not go into great detail with your child; he is not your best friend nor your therapist. Actually, he is far more interested in how this divorce is going to affect him. Try as much as possible to focus on his needs and concerns.

2. *What will happen to me?* Because children are very dependent upon their parents and are naturally egocentric, many questions will need to be answered about how the divorce will affect their lives. The more a child is able to imagine and predict what is going to happen, the easier he will find the transition from a two-parent home to a one-parent home. Try to be as specific as possible as you answer questions. If you don't know how things are going to work out exactly, tell your child as much as you do know and assure him that as soon as you know more, you'll discuss plans with him. Some of your answers may have to begin with, "I'm not positive yet, but probably. . . ." The following are some of the most pressing questions your child is likely to have:

Where will I live?

Will I still go to the same school?

Where will money come from?

Will Mom have to go to work (if she has not been employed prior to divorce)?

Will I still see Dad (Mom)?

When will I see him (her)?

How often will I see Dad (Mom)?

Will we kids all stay together?

Will I ever live with Dad (Mom)?

As you answer these as well as other questions, remember the basic message of ongoing love and concern which we discussed earlier. Weave them into your answers. Let your child know that you understand his unspoken fears of abandonment and self-blame and that you realize how hard it is for him to accept change. Reassure him that you will continue to be his parent and that he is not responsible for the divorce.

3. *Will you and Dad (Mom) get back together?* With rare exceptions, children want their parents to stay united. They desperately hope that the separation and unhappiness are only an interruption in their lives and soon everything will be back to normal. Your child loves both his parents and does not wish to be in the position of having to split his time and affections. The dream of parents being reunited takes a long time to fade. A twenty-five-year-old friend was recently getting married. Her parents (who were divorced when she was fourteen) attended her wedding. "You know," she confessed to us sheepishly, "the thought ran through my mind – 'Maybe they'll get back together again!' "

Your child will need to hear you state the finality of your decision. Even if you also harbor a shred of hope of being reunited, we would discourage you from sharing this thought with your child. If a reconciliation does occur, he'll welcome it, but don't raise his hopes – they're already unrealistically high. Say to him:

No, your dad (mom) and I aren't going to live together again. I'm sorry, for I know that makes you very sad and unhappy. I feel a bit the same way, but we can't and won't get back together. But we are still your mom and dad. We both love you and will continue to take care of you.

4. *If I'm good will Daddy (Mommy) come back?* The question behind the question is, of course, "Did I do something to cause the divorce?" And if that's possible, then – "Maybe by being extra good, I can get my Daddy (Mommy) back again." Many children mistakenly feel they are somehow to blame for the divorce. They need to be assured that they are not that powerful. Your child needs to hear this message:

Of course you didn't cause the divorce. Mom and Dad are responsible for the divorce. Since you didn't make us break up, nothing you can do will bring us back together.

5. *How can you stop loving Dad (Mom)? Will you stop loving me?*

Children are limited in their ability to understand relationships. It may seem quite logical to your child that if you no longer love his parent, you may also stop loving him. He needs frequent reassurance that your love for him continues and is not related to how you feel about his other parent. You might say to him:

My love for you is different from my love for my mother and father, my sister or brother, or the love I had for your father (mother). Parents do not love their children the same way they love adults. I still love you very much and will always continue to be your parent just as you will always continue to be my son (daughter). Parents can get unmarried, but they are their children's parents forever – they can't become *un*parents.

FAMILIES WITH POOR COMMUNICATION

We cannot stress sufficiently the importance of communicating openly with your children. Unfortunately, many families have developed ineffective patterns of communication. In fact, children from such families usually have learned *not* to deal openly with emotionally charged issues. They have learned to submerge their feelings or to run away from problems. During the crisis of divorce, these children will have an especially difficult time coping with the emotions that separation and divorce engender.

Children from such families are not likely to talk openly about their feelings. However, a child who does not ask questions outright or express anxiety openly still has concerns and worries. Anxieties don't disappear simply because they are not acknowledged. Quite the opposite. When we do not pay attention to our feelings, they are likely to surface in other ways such as physical illnesses or seemingly unrelated behavioral problems.

Children with problems of communication often react to the crisis of separation and divorce with severe anxiety, depression, confusion, and anger. And because they have had few models for effective communication, they often have problems making others aware of their acute distress. These children too often live with their misery tightly hugged to themselves. Without help, they cannot face and deal with their emotions, and their emotional growth will be impeded.

Even if you have not communicated effectively with your child prior to this time, it is essential that you begin now. If you find it impossible to give your child the help and reassurance he needs, seek professional help. Child therapists and child guidance clinics can help you and your child develop communication patterns which will benefit your child and enhance your relationship with him.

MYTHS THAT MAY STAND IN YOUR WAY

Often parents who want to communicate with their children are hampered by preconceived ideas. A brief examination of some of the most commonly held myths may help you avoid such pitfalls.

MYTH 1 — WAIT UNTIL YOU KNOW FOR SURE HOW THINGS ARE GOING TO TURN OUT BEFORE TELLING YOUR CHILD.

Sometimes parents are unaware that separation is imminent. For many couples an angry exchange of bitter words, a few belongings stuffed hastily into a suitcase, and a slammed door mark the beginning of divorce.

For other parents the decision to separate is preceded by many months (sometimes even years) of indecision. There may be trial separations, reconciliations, and more separations before divorce is finally decided upon.

And still other parents who know their marriage is shaky seek counseling. During the period when they are working on their problems, their relationship may become even more tense and strained than in the past. Sometimes an argument — often over something trivial — precipitates the sudden exit of a husband or wife. Is this separation temporary or final? Will there be a reconciliation or will the separation lead to divorce?

Often parents simply do not know exactly how final the separation will be. Not wanting to worry their children prematurely, they do not discuss matters with them, even when the children have witnessed a fight or seen a parent leaving.

"Wait 'til the dust settles before involving the children," well-meaning friends may advise. But when does the dust settle? How do you know when one chapter of your life is finished and another begins? Life usually does not present itself with clearly defined chapters. If you wait until everything is settled, you'll wait forever. Meanwhile, your child needs information and help *now!*

Like it or not, your child is already involved. He cannot help but be aware (to varying degrees) of conflicts and troubles. If you do not explain what is happening, your child is left to interpret what he has seen and heard. And, as we have discussed, children often *misinter-pret and blame themselves.

Don't procrastinate. Share what you do know. What are the current realities? If there is tension and conflict, tell your child that you are having problems. If you are considering divorce, share that. Telling a child you are thinking of divorce does not commit you to divorce; it merely begins preparing him. If you successfully work out your problems, your child will gladly accept this news. (Of course, you would not want to tell a child frequently that divorce is imminent and then say it is not.) If you and your spouse are having marital problems and are seriously contemplating separation, your child should be made aware of this.

Informing a child that there is trouble makes it open and something which can be handled. It also gives you the opportunity to reassure your child that he is not to blame for your problems. In fact, you might explain that you have been feeling irritable and warn him that in the days to come you may continue to be more grumpy than usual. All of us tend to be more impatient when we are struggling with our own conflicts and turmoil. Telling your child this may lessen his tendency to blame himself for your irritability. In fact, you'll be surprised at how much more understanding and empathetic your children will be when you talk to them in this way. You might say something like this:

> I'm sorry I've been so grumpy and irritable lately, but try to remember that it's not your fault. Your dad (mom) and I are upset and unhappy right now. We may yell at you more than usual, but it's not really your fault. You're okay and we love you. We'll try to work out our problems as quickly as possible.

MYTH 2 — YOU MUST BE CALM BEFORE TALKING WITH YOUR CHILD.

You don't have to be calm before talking with your child. If you wait until you are calm, you might be waiting for months. In fact, you should not hide your feelings from your child. *Emotional integrity is just as important as factual honesty.* Your child needs to know how you feel. He needs to know that he is not alone in his pain. He needs your help now.

By sharing your feelings of anger, worry, and confusion, you allow your child to express his own feelings more freely. He does not have to pretend indifference or bottle up his emotions. A child who is free to cry and storm and protest recovers from shock and begins to adapt to changes more quickly than a child who is not. He does not have to use precious energy keeping his emotions hidden. Furthermore, just knowing what your child is feeling and dealing with is helpful to you. You can allay his anxieties and fears far more effectively when they are openly and clearly expressed. Sharing grief and pain can also create a bond between you and your child. While sharing feelings is healthy, there are wise limits. *Don't share hysteria!* If you are really worried about losing control, by all means ask someone to help you: your spouse, if circumstances permit; a trusted friend, relative, or clergyman; or, if you are in counseling, ask your counselor or therapist for help. Another person's presence and support can help you focus on the important messages your child needs to hear as well as help you answer his specific questions.

Another note of caution: *Don't put your child through a session of mud-slinging!* That may be an honest expression of your feelings but if you indulge in such behavior your child will suffer. Your child needs and loves both his parents. He cannot stand being torn apart by vicious words and slander. Remember that in the midst of separation and divorce, you are not an impartial judge of your spouse's character. It is tempting to try to persuade your child to side with you against his other parent, but doing so not only creates severe emotional conflict for him but it will also weaken his respect for you. Instead, you can say something like this to him:

Obviously Dad (Mom) and I don't see eye to eye. That's why we are splitting up. Right now I am hurt and angry, so I'm not able to see the good in your dad (mom) very clearly. When a person is angry with another person, it's hard to be really fair.

You know both of us pretty well, and you are going to have to decide yourself what you like and don't like about each of us. I hope that over the years you'll be able to use the best in each of us to help you grow up.

MYTH 3 — THERE'S NO USE EXPLAINING TO A YOUNG CHILD: HE CAN'T UNDERSTAND.

Of course a young child cannot fully understand your reasons for separating, but he certainly understands separation. Most babies and young children are quite vocal in their protest against being separated from Mommy or Daddy.

How do you help a young child adapt to separation? What do you say? What do you do? Think about how you handle him when you leave him for a short period with a babysitter. In a warm, yet firm voice, you probably say, "Mommy (Daddy) is leaving now. You're going to stay with Mary. You'll be all right. I'll see you later." Then despite his tears and even tantrums, and despite your own anguish, you leave him. And, of course, you keep your promise—you *do* come back. Little by little your young child learns he can trust you to return. You will not abandon him; even if you leave for a while, you will come back.

The same methods apply when a parent moves out of the home. Tell your youngster you are leaving and that you will see him soon. Don't prolong the agony. Kiss and hug him as usual and then leave. Although it is tempting to leave when the child is napping or away, the best exit is in front of him. Even if your child protests and cries, it is far better for him to see you leave. Emotions *and events* which are out in the open are always easier to deal with in the long run.

Although young children do not understand elaborate explanations, they do understand reassurance and comfort. When Hank left his home, his older children were able to comprehend what he was saying. Three-year-old Johnny knew it was a somber occasion, but he did not understand what was happening until his dad actually picked up his bags and started out the door. Hank describes what happened:

> I was going down the porch steps when Johnny came running out. He was crying and clinging to me. I put down the bags and picked him up, and by that time I was also crying. I didn't know what to do, but I just couldn't drive away leaving him so upset.
>
> I sat down on the steps and out of habit reached in my pocket to get my clippers. Clipping the kids' nails has always been my job. Whenever they need a little extra attention, they come sit on my lap and beg me to clip their nails.
>
> So there I was, sitting on the porch with Johnny on my lap and I was automatically clipping his fingernails. Suddenly, I knew how to help him. I gave him my clippers and I whispered, "Johnny, you keep Daddy's clippers until Saturday. I'll be back Saturday to see you. You keep those clippers for me. Okay?"
>
> It worked like a charm! He gave me a wet little grin. I left him

on the stairs waving to me. The clippers were in his fist. And you know, when I came back that Saturday, Johnny had those clippers in his blue jeans pocket!

To little Johnny, too young to understand verbal explanations fully, the clippers were tangible proof that his father would come back again. With the clippers in his hand, Johnny was able to hold on to a piece of his daddy. The young child may be unable to understand abstract explanations, but he *can* understand messages of love—extra hugs, frequent time on your lap, token objects from the absent parent, and reassurances that he's safe and will be taken care of.

MYTH 4—TEENAGERS ARE LESS AFFECTED BY DIVORCE AND NEED FEWER EXPLANATIONS.

Not true! Teenagers are usually more consciously aware of the tension and friction between their parents than are their younger siblings. They are definitely affected by their parents' separation and divorce and often exhibit more signs of being upset than their parents anticipate. The most important task for the teenager is to negotiate emancipation and separation from the family unit. A shifting family unit leaves the teenager floundering.

Because of their greater maturity, teenagers can and need to understand some of the causes of the divorce. As with all children, they also need concrete details of how their lives are going to be affected. They want to know what changes will occur and what will be expected of them.

Many teenagers are not told enough about the causes of divorce; others are told too much. Don't make the mistake of confiding intimate details of your marriage. Especially avoid airing your sexual problems with your teenager. Although it may be tempting to use your adolescent as a confidant, it is not wise. Disclosures about their parents' sexual incompatibility burden and overstimulate teenagers who are struggling with their own developing sexuality. Their parents' tales only confuse them and add to their anxieties and fears. If you need to "unload" such information, confide in a friend or seek professional help.

MYTH 5—ONCE A CHILD HAS BEEN TOLD, HE'S BEEN TOLD!

Children are not miniature adults! They are unable to comprehend and absorb new information and ideas as easily as adults.

Imagine, for instance, telling a child all there is to know about sex in one afternoon. He is likely to become mentally oversaturated. And, in fact, if some weeks later you hear him relaying the information to a younger brother or sister, you may be surprised to find his story considerably altered from your original explanation.

The same is true of divorce. You cannot expect a child to grasp all the details and implications of your explanation immediately. It takes time — weeks and months, and even longer — for a child to gain real understanding. He will need "refresher" messages from time to time. As a child grows and matures, he brings new, more mature understanding to life situations. James, a sixteen-year-old who has recently fallen in love for the first time, discusses how his understanding of "love" has changed:

> When Mom and Dad got divorced six years ago, they told me they didn't love each other any more. I got real upset and said that people couldn't stop loving each other. They tried to explain that their love for us kids was different from love between adults. They said they could stop loving each other, but they couldn't stop loving us.
>
> None of that made any sense to me. Love was just love — the same for everybody. Dad tried to make it clearer by asking me to compare how I felt about our dog, Princess, with how I felt about loving Mom. But I didn't feel much difference — I really loved Princess!
>
> But now that I'm in love with Pam, it's all different. I know it's not the same as loving Princess! Mom and Dad were right. Love is more complicated than I thought.

Like James, children's concepts grow and change as they experience life more fully. In light of their new understanding, they will reprocess explanations and will ask new questions (or the same questions with a slightly different slant). Encourage your child to discuss his thoughts before you readily provide an answer. Taking a little time to explore his ideas and concerns will help you grasp what new understanding he may be bringing to the question.

There is another reason why your child will return for more answers to questions you thought you had already explained. As we mentioned earlier, children often resist processing the explanations you provide, for they really do not want to accept the changes in their lives. They ask, but they don't seem to hear the answers. Be patient. Explain again, or better yet, *ask them to tell you* why they think Dad left (or whatever the question might be). Again, avoid debating your decision, but allow your child the freedom to ask some of his questions more than once. By asking again, he's not necessarily challenging your answer or being obstinate. He may simply be indicating that he needs more time to accept the new realities in his life.

How Should Children Be Told?

Ideally, both parents should sit down with their children and jointly communicate the news of the impending separation and divorce. The advantages of this approach are obvious. First, it demonstrates the commitment of both parents to continued love and involvement with their children. Second, it minimizes the possibility that in the initial telling, one parent might denigrate the other. In the presence of the other parent, each parent will tend to be more careful about what he says about the other than if he were alone. However, few couples find themselves capable of sitting down together for this type of family session. It is interesting to note that parents who can do this usually have had counseling prior to the decision to separate or divorce.

Roberta and Sid had been in marriage counseling for some time before they came to the mutual decision that they could not bridge the chasms that had come between them. They did, however, pledge that they would both continue to be very involved in the raising of their two children, Naomi, age eleven, and Joey, age six. Naomi vividly remembers the day her parents sat down with them to prepare them for the divorce:

It was January. Joey and I were playing in the snow when Mom and Dad called us in. They said they had something important to discuss with us. I knew it was going to be kind of scary because Mom had that almost crying look like when she told us Grandma died.

First, they asked us if we had noticed they weren't very happy with each other lately. Sure, we knew that. Mom and Dad had been fighting more than Joey and me. They said they were going to get a divorce.

"What's a divorce?" Joey asked. Well, he's only six and he doesn't know as much as me. Daddy looked at Joey a minute and then said, "Joey, do you remember when you and Naomi both got skip ropes last Christmas? Remember how you both decided to tie them together so you could have a longer rope for jumping games with your friends? Well, getting married is kind of like putting those ropes together so you could have one nice, long rope to jump with. Divorce is kind of like when you decided you didn't want to share your jump ropes any more and you untied the knot and each took back your own rope."

Then Daddy explained that when married people are very unhappy together, they sometimes decide to separate and live in two different homes. He told us that even though he and Mom would not be married any more, they would still be our parents and would still take care of us. "But where will *we* be when you get a divorce?" Joey asked. Dad said we'd live with Mom during the week and we would be with him on Saturdays and sometimes on Sundays too.

I had a big lump in my throat and I couldn't even swallow. Mom asked what I was thinking, but I couldn't say a word. I was glad Joey was still asking a bunch of questions because I wanted to know too. He asked where Dad would live and how we would have money for food and a whole bunch of other questions. Dad told him he would send a check to Mom and that we didn't need to worry because he and Mom would still be taking care of us.

Finally, Joey ran out of questions and we were all quiet. Joey started crying. Mom hugged him and asked what was wrong. Then Joey asked the stupidest question of all: "What about Muffy and her kittens? Are they going to be divorced too? Where will *they* live?" That made us all laugh — even me!

Then Dad got up and said he'd better be going. I started crying. I guess I really didn't believe he was really going to leave until he picked up his suitcase. Mom and Joey were crying also and Dad was blinking a lot. He kissed Joey and me and promised he'd call us the next day. I wondered if he was going to kiss Mom goodbye like always or if he was going to shake her hand like a regular grownup. In a way that almost made me laugh. But Dad and Mom just looked at each other and then he left. Mom kept holding us and we were all crying together.

Naomi and Joey were fortunate to have parents who cared deeply for their children and who were able to help them face separation. They did not attempt to hide their own pain, but at the same time they were able to keep in mind their children's needs.

REMEMBER

You can't take away the pain that your divorce will cause your child to suffer, nor should you if you could. His anguish is legitimate and must be faced by *him*. By your pledge of continued love, support, and open communication, however, you can "be with" him during his suffering and help him emerge from the trauma with a minimum of scarring.

4

Children Are
Not Possessions

One day I picked up my three-year-old, gave her a big hug, and said playfully, "You are my baby!"

"No," she said firmly, "I *not* your baby!"

"Are you Daddy's baby?"

"No, I *not* Daddy's baby."

"Well, whose baby are you?"

"I my *own* baby!" she said triumphantly.

How simple, and yet how profound. Of course, she belongs to herself!

My three-year-old grasped an important truth: *No one can own another human being.* We can love someone, want to be with him, share what we have and who we are—but we can never own him, never possess him.

It is easy enough for most of us to give lip service to this concept, but when we are in the process of separating from our spouses and the important issue of custody comes up, we suddenly realize how possessive we can feel about our children. Too often, like the car and the house, the children also become possessions which we each fight to keep.

The Non-Divisibility of Children

Dividing the assets of a marriage equitably between the two partners is a difficult task. Even dividing the accumulated treasures and memorabilia of a marriage (photographs, collections, and trinkets) can be difficult. But dividing the children equitably between the two parents is impossible.

In one of her lighter moments, a friend who was contemplating divorce jokingly suggested that she and her husband each take custody of two of their four children. To make it even more fair, she insisted, they could divide them up according to the number of problems each child had.

For instance, I'll take Mary who is easygoing, but I'll also take Tommy who has an explosive temper. Then Joe can have twelve-year-old Joey who's failing school and Lori who does well in everything. That way Joe and I will have each an equal amount of joys and headaches!

The absurdity of this underlines the real complexities of making custody decisions. Although children—like the car, the furniture, and the house—are tangible products of the marriage, obviously, they are not divisible goods to be parceled out on a "one for you and one for me, even-steven" basis. Children are not possessions to be owned, nor are they objects to be fought over.

WHO SHALL HAVE CUSTODY?

Before you and your spouse separated, you may have looked askance at other separating couples who were deeply engaged in custody battles. How can they be so insensitive to their children's needs, you wondered? But now that you are separated it all seems different. As parents we don't like to admit that we harbor deep feelings of possessiveness or jealousy. However, when we feel close to our children and love them, it is natural to want them to be near us—living with us. Furthermore, our resentment and anger with our spouse color our perceptions, and we often see the other parent as less fit than ourselves to become the custodial parent.

All of us remember the well-known story from the Bible of King Solomon who was asked to judge which of two women was the real mother of an infant. When he proposed to cut the child in two and give half to each woman, the real mother immediately relinquished the child.

This story applies to custody. Each parent may not be able to have his "half" of the child, but parents who truly love their child are able to put the child's needs and welfare above their own selfish desires.

How are custody decisions to be made? Basically, there are only two alternatives: the parents either get together (personally or through their lawyers) and agree who shall be the custodial parent, or the parents can come to no agreement and in that case the court makes the decision.

Court Makes the Decision

There are several problems that arise when a couple throws custody decisions to the court. In the first place, this inevitably results in the use of the terms "winning" and "losing" custody — and no one likes to lose! A loser can't help but feel disgraced and bitter; a winner feels smug and self-righteous.

Second, when a climate of tug-of-war prevails, the child who becomes the prize suffers. Children cannot stand to be fought over or pulled back and forth between warring parents. They can and do adjust successfully to many kinds of living arrangements, but they cannot and do not adjust to being no more than the object of their parents' hostility and endless battles.

Finally, although the court theoretically guards the rights of the children of divorce, many are questioning whether this actually works in practice. Robert and Lawrence Kahn express typical concern for this problem in their book *The Divorce Lawyer's Casebook:* "Unfortunately, in practice, the children's interests are rarely represented. They must take what others dole out." They strongly recommend that "an attorney other than the attorneys representing the husband and wife be appointed to represent the children of the marriage in every divorce proceeding." This is very seldom done at present, however. Judges step in only when they feel that the best interests of the child are clearly not being served by the parents' proposed arrangements.

Parents Make the Decision

When considering the problems of custody decisions made by the court, it is usually better for the parents to make responsible custody decisions. Judges and lawyers do not know your children personally. They know nothing of the intricate and unique balance of relationships within your particular family. You and your ex-spouse who have lived with your children and who love them are obviously in a far better position to assess their needs and desires and to work out *sound* custodial arrangements for them. Furthermore, you and your children's other parent are also in a better position to assess

your own emotional and physical resources and your abilities to deal
with your children's needs.

This puts a heavy responsibility on you. In the emotional turmoil
of divorce, it is extremely important to make responsible decisions;
yet that is precisely when most parents find it difficult to think
clearly. Their objectivity is clouded, and both large and small problems may become equally overwhelming. In their confusion and
hurt, they may not be able to make wise decisions about their
children's welfare. Moreover, parents at this time often have problems keeping their angry feelings about their ex-spouse separated
from the issue of what is best for their children.

Mary, age forty, discusses this problem:

> During the years that Tom and I were married, I was always
> pleased by the attention Tom showed our five children. He was
> a good father — interested and understanding, consistent and
> firm, yet very sympathetic. Often I envied his ease and confi-
> dence with the kids.
>
> After we separated, however, everything seemed changed. I
> didn't see Tom as a good father anymore. He seemed too
> rough, too demanding. I found fault with everything he did or
> didn't do. In the past, I always wanted the kids to spend time
> with their dad; now I found myself inventing reasons to inter-
> fere.
>
> Finally, the children accused me of trying to break up their
> relationship with their dad. I was shocked. I tried to show them
> how bad a father Tom had become, but deep inside I knew the
> kids were right. Tom was the same wonderful father he'd al-
> ways been. I was angry with Tom as a *husband*, not with Tom
> as a *father*. I was getting all mixed up.

Mary's problem is common and understandable. When a couple is
separating, they find it hard to sort out their feelings about each
other. Is it his *wife* that a man wishes to divorce, or is it the mother of
his children? Is a woman angry and dissatisfied with her ex-spouse as
a *husband* or as a father? Feelings of hurt and disappointment about
the marital relationship can easily color our total perceptions of each
other.

That is why lawyers and judges, and indeed all professionals who
are concerned with children of divorce, strongly recommend that
parents seek help of a qualified counselor or therapist before making

final custody decisions. A compassionate — yet dispassionate — professional who has had wide experience and knowledge of children can do much to help you and your spouse examine the various factors, considerations, and alternatives open to you. *Counselors do not have all the answers, of course, but they do have many of the right questions!* Together, you can search for solutions which best suit your individual circumstances. Making custody decisions which keep in mind the needs of the children as well as the needs and desires of the parents can greatly ease the transition and subsequent adjustment from marriage to divorce.

"Should I Live with Mommy or Daddy?"

Sometimes parents who do not want to shoulder the responsibility for making the decision of which parent the child should live with ask the child himself. Asking the child to decide which parent he wants to live with almost always puts the child in deep conflict. No matter which decision he makes, he cannot help but feel disloyal and guilty. Whichever parent he chooses, he feels that he risks losing the other parent's affection and support. The child is deeply dependent upon his parents; he loves and needs them both. He is in no position to make such a far-reaching and important choice.

To a large extent, this is also true of older children. We realize the older child — and especially the teenager — is less dependent and more capable of making independent and responsible decisions. Increasingly, he can be trusted to choose his own clothing, spend his allowance, and plan his free time. It is easy to forget, however, that in many ways he continues to be a child and feels the same conflict at having to choose between his parents as does his younger brother or sister.

The best approach is to take your child's wishes and desires into consideration, but not make your child feel that he is making the ultimate decision. If you are not sure how your child feels, often it is wise to consult a professional who can help determine the child's needs and preferences in such a way that he will not feel guilty or responsible for the final decision of custody.

What Does Custody Really Mean?

What do we mean when we say that a child of divorce is in the custody of his mother or his father? Does the word "custody" mean

that one of his parents *owns* him? Does custody imply imprisonment? Or does it simply mean that the child is "legally in the care of"
one of his parents?

Of course we would all agree on the last interpretation. Legal
custody of a child gives one of the child's parents the right to have the
child live with her or him, as well as the right to make final decisions
about the child's lifestyle, education, recreation, religion, and
health.

However, the custodial parent does not own the child, nor is he
the guard, the "keeper of the keys." A child should not feel that his
custodial parent is keeping him a prisoner. In most cases, he should
not be denied the attention of his other parent. When the custodial
parent denies the child the opportunity to continue his relationship
with the other parent, the child will undoubtedly suffer. Sean, age
nine, is a good example. The social worker who has been seeing this
family reports:

> From the beginning of their separation, Sean's parents have
> fought over custody. After divorce, his mother was granted
> custody, but she often refused to allow Sean's father legal visi-
> tation. On one occasion when Sean's father did have the chil-
> dren with him, he spirited them away to his parents' home in a
> city some miles from their mother until the court ordered that
> they be returned to her.
>
> Confused and withdrawn, Sean was referred to the local
> child guidance clinic for observation and evaluation. During
> this time, he drew a picture which revealed some of his feelings
> about the custody struggle. His drawing depicts three tiny chil-
> dren in the foreground. On one side of the drawing is a large
> woman; on the other side is an even larger man. Both are
> pulling the child closest to each. Behind the figures are two
> separate houses — each with elaborate locks on the doors.

No formal training in psychology is needed to interpret the conflict depicted here! To young Sean, it doesn't matter very much who
has custody — custody means imprisonment!

The custodial parent acts morally as the guardian and safekeeper
of the children when she concentrates on her obligations and responsibilities for her children instead of guarding her right to control their
lives.

GUIDELINES FOR CUSTODY AND VISITATION DECISIONS

As we mentioned, there are many factors which you need to consider when making the decision of who gets custody. But custody should be thought of as only part of the parent-child arrangements. The other part is visitation rights. Seen together as two halves of a pattern, these arrangements formalize the child's relationship to each of his parents. For instance, a child of divorce who lives with his mother but sees his father regularly each week has a different type of involvement with both parents from the child who lives with his mother full-time and sees his father for two weeks during summer vacations.

There is no all-encompassing solution for custody and visitation. There are no simple formulas which can be universally applied. However, there *are* some guidelines. Examine the following questions and try to answer them. This can help you clarify your thinking and enable you to make decisions which are right for your situation.

1. *Who has been the major nurturing parent prior to divorce?* Usually, the parent who has had the major share of the care of the child and who is emotionally the closest to the child should become the custodial parent. In our society, this still tends to be the mother. This was true for Joyce and Ted, who were married for twelve years and have a son, eleven, and a daughter, eight. Joyce reports:

During our marriage I've not had a job, so I've been home with the kids. Ted has hardly ever been home. He's a manufacturer's representative, so he's on the road most of the time. The kids and I learned a long time ago that we couldn't count on Ted's being home for birthdays, anniversaries, or other special occasions. In fact, the kids felt as if they hardly knew their father.

When Ted and I split up, the children naturally stayed with me. It never entered any of our heads for it to be otherwise. Ted was supposed to have the kids with him every other weekend, but time after time, he'd call to say he'd been detained and couldn't make it. In a way, the kids felt relieved. Spending a whole weekend together often made Ted and the children feel bored and uncomfortable.

After a few months of cancellations and a lot of tension, Ted and I finally got together and agreed on some changes. Now Ted sees the children for shorter periods of time, but more frequently than before. For example, last month he took them

out for dinner three times and they spent one Saturday afternoon with him. He calls them when he's in town — kind of spur-
of-the-moment, and if they have nothing else planned, they go
with him. The children and Ted are enjoying these shorter
times together and I enjoy the unexpected free time.

In this situation, what was best for the children was the continua-
tion of their past living arrangement. They were already accustomed
to spending most of their time with their mother since their father
was often away for days or weeks at a time. The revised visitation
pattern reflected the needs and desires of both the father and the
children.

In that situation, Joyce was the obvious choice for custodial parent. However, it is not always the mother who is the chief nurturer in
the child's life. As fathers become increasingly more involved with
the early care of their children, their roles are changing. For Elizabeth, twenty-two, and Mitchell, twenty-four, the father had already
assumed the major nurturing role before the separation. After divorce, he became the custodial parent. Mitchell reports:

Elizabeth and I got married right out of high school and soon
afterwards, Chris was born. Elizabeth and I both worked part-
time so we could go to college. We shared the housework and
shared taking care of Chris.

I really enjoyed Chris. In fact, after he was born, I changed
my major to early childhood education. But Elizabeth really
began to resent being a wife and a mother. Last year she fell in
love with another guy and we agreed to split up. To my surprise, Elizabeth suggested that I take custody of Chris. She
didn't want to be tied down by a baby. I was happy to agree.

Lots of people were shocked by our decision, but things have
worked out well. Chris is now three. While I'm in class, he's at
the University Co-op Pre-School.

Elizabeth sees him from time to time, but she's definitely not
interested in custody. There's a girl I've met recently who loves
kids — Chris especially — and we're thinking about marriage,
but I'm in no hurry. I'm not jumping into anything quickly this
time!

In most cases, mothers tend to desire custody of their children and to gain it — especially when the child is very young. But other factors besides custom need to be considered. If Elizabeth had insisted on assuming custody, even though she resented being tied down and responsible, she would not have been the effective, loving parent that this young child needs. Chris was fortunate to have parents who could look beyond convention to decide what was truly best for them as well as for their son.

2. *What is the mental and physical condition of the parents?* Assuming the role of a single parent is not easy. Having total care for your child or children without another parent coming home to relieve you can be exhausting. When illness or physical or emotional problems lead to the dysfunction of one of the parents, the situation warrants close scrutiny. Such factors as the severity of the problem and its physical effects upon the children and parent must be considered carefully before reaching a decision about custody. Vera and Mike's case represents an extreme but helpful example:

> For years my wife's drinking problem has made life hell for all of us. I've tried to get her to go to Alcoholics Anonymous, but Vera never even admits that she's alcoholic. Finally, last year things got so bad I moved out with the kids.
>
> Because our children are young — their ages are seven, five, and two — Vera was sure she'd be granted custody. Luckily it was easy to prove she couldn't handle the kids since she's usually smashed by ten o'clock every morning. So I got temporary custody.
>
> Vera was supposed to have the kids with her overnight on Saturdays and all day Sundays. A few months ago, after we separated, Martha, the oldest, called me one Sunday when she and the kids were with their mother. Martha was crying and very scared. Her mother had passed out on the floor and the baby and Jamie were both crying. They thought she was dead.
>
> From then on, the kids have not been allowed to spend time with Vera alone. They can see her on Sundays at their grandparents' home — Vera's parents, that is — so there's always someone to take care of them. If Vera ever gets better, visitation might change, but right now this is what's best for the kids.

Vera's hopes of being granted custody were highly unrealistic, for she was obviously not able to assume responsibility for the children. In fact, the children who perceived their father as the nurturing,

secure parent would have been uneasy if they were in the custody of
their mother.

Obviously, most situations are not so clear-cut. Often it is difficult
to judge which parent is more emotionally stable and mature. In
addition, sometimes parents who are facing the crisis of divorce
become temporarily less able to assume the responsibility of caring
for the children.

What happens when a mother who has been close to her children
and wants custody is physically ill? Of course, it depends to some
degree upon the severity of the illness, but in many cases if suitable
arrangements have been made for the children's care, they can often
remain with her. Leonore and Mel faced this problem. Leonore,
thirty-four, has had multiple sclerosis for ten years and for the past
four years has been confined to a wheelchair. Mel reports:

> At first I thought the girls would have to live with me. To be
> honest, I wasn't too happy about that idea. What do I know
> about raising girls? But the girls had other ideas. They didn't
> want to move away from their school and neighborhood, and
> especially they didn't want to leave their mother. Leonore
> agreed that if she could hire a cleaning lady to do the heavy
> work, the girls and she could manage fine. The girls are used to
> helping their mom.
>
> So Leonore has custody and the girls spend every other
> weekend with me. I also pick them up once a week to have
> dinner with me. It's really worked pretty smooth for us.

Even if the children are younger, if help is provided and the parent
can continue to meet the children's emotional needs, the parent's
physical problems need not be the sole factor in custody considerations. Furthermore, custody is never unalterable. If a parent's physical condition worsens, custody arrangements can then be reconsidered.

3. *What are the parents' capabilities?* Try to be as realistic as
possible when you make custody and visitation decisions. Remember that no matter how much we may wish it, even the strongest of us
is not superhuman. It is far better to recognize your limitations and
desires and to deal with them honestly than try to take on responsibilities you will later grow to resent.

Too often, a parent (especially a mother) may feel that society will
criticize her if she does not fight for custody of her children. Dr.

Stephen J. Howard, Clinical Director of the San Fernando Valley Child Guidance Clinic, points out: "Making a decision or taking a stand about custody, based on feelings of pride, anger, rage or guilt, is extremely harmful to all concerned." More important than what you imagine *society* will think is how *you honestly feel* about becoming the custodial parent.

When Mary and Tom separated, Mary kept their five children with her. As we saw earlier, Mary felt threatened by her ex-husband's ease and success at parenting. Deep down she was afraid that the children would prefer to be with their father and that she would lose them. During the months of separation prior to divorce, Mary found herself overwhelmed by the needs of her children who ranged in age from four to sixteen. Her physician, alarmed by Mary's feelings of depression and inadequacy, referred her for therapy. Within a few months, Mary was able to confront some of her most pressing problems:

> I realized how much I had depended on Tom for help with the kids. I found that it was taking all my energy just coping with divorce—becoming a single woman after so many years of marriage. I didn't have enough resources left to manage the older children and give the younger ones the love and support they needed. So I agreed to split up the children and keep custody of the two youngest. Until I remarried, every weekend they were together, either with me or at Tom's. It worked out fine!

In addition, once during the week when Mary did not have the three for the weekend, she had them over for dinner. In this way, the children were able to maintain their close relationship with one another as well as with each of their parents. It is never easy to be a single parent, but in Mary's case the problems were compounded by the number of children involved. Mary was gratified to find that in giving up custody she did not "lose her children." In fact, because she was more energetic and cheerful than before, her relationship with all the children actually improved.

When thinking about custody and visitation patterns, ask yourself: "How much can I handle and still be both an effective parent and an effective individual?" Consider a wide range of alternatives before making any decision. For example, for Mary and Tom, a seemingly

complicated arrangement of custody and visitation actually simpli-
fied their lives, and both the children and the parents gained.

4. *What are the parents' needs and desires?* Because of the women's
liberation movement, there has been some shifting of male-female
roles and expectations in recent years. Many women strongly desire
greater personal fulfillment, and these desires must be considered
when making custody decisions. Cynthia, thirty, married Donald,
also thirty, ten years ago. Within the first five years they had three
boys (now ten, nine, and seven). Cynthia dropped out of college
shortly after her marriage and remained at home caring for her
husband and sons. A year before the divorce, she reentered college
and became very involved with her studies. When the divorce occurred, Cynthia, after lengthy consideration, decided not to ask for
custody of the boys.

> My family, Don's family, and even my friends were horrified
> by my decision, but I realized I couldn't manage the responsi-
> bilities of single parenting and continue my law studies. And I
> could *not* quit school. I knew I'd forever feel cheated and
> trapped by my empty life. So I moved out into a small apart-
> ment close to the campus and close to the public library where I
> work part-time.
>
> The boys spend Sundays with me and during school breaks I
> take them for longer periods. During the week I often take
> them out for a little treat or take them shopping for clothing,
> shoes, or school supplies, so I feel very involved with their
> lives.

Cynthia's unconventional decision has worked well for everyone.
Although initially surprised, Donald has come to feel that it was a
good solution:

> At first I was totally overwhelmed by Cynthia's suggestion that
> she move out and the boys and I "batch it" together. How
> would we manage? How would we get meals, or worse, how
> about the laundry? Actually, we didn't manage very well at
> first, but now with the help of a part-time housekeeper and a
> lot of frozen dinners, we're doing great. In fact, the other day I
> overheard Doug, the oldest, bragging to one of his friends
> about his being a bachelor. Maybe the boys still resent their
> mother's moving out — I know they did at first — but they also

realize that life with their mother wouldn't have been so good while she was pressured by school work.

Originally, this arrangement was to be just until Cynthia took the bar exams, but we all suspect that it will become a permanent arrangement.

The woman who voluntarily gives up custody goes against the expectations of our society, and like Cynthia, she can expect to face harsh criticism. Cynthia reports that when acquaintances first learn that she has given up custody of her children, they sometimes look at her as if to say, "What kind of monster are you?" Just the fact that a woman is a mother, however, does not guarantee that she is well suited for motherhood. Some women intensely feel the need to pursue a career without the restraints of live-in children. If the father desires the child-rearing role, it may be best for everyone to allow him to assume it. After all, an unwilling custodial parent who feels locked into the role cannot be as effective as a parent who accepts the role more freely.

5. *What additional factors need to be considered?* In some situations there are other factors which need to be looked at before making sound custody decisions. These may include the ages of the children, prior relationships, the children's desires, geographic considerations, school choices, and so on. For example, one mother we know has her son with her one school year and her daughter with her the alternate school year. The father lives in Australia and the children take turns staying with him. The children, who are together during school vacations, divide this time between their parents. This seems like a strange arrangement to some (and it is certainly costly), but it has worked out well for the children and for their parents. There will undoubtedly come a time, however, when the children will be reluctant to interrupt their school activities and relationships with friends and will prefer to stay in one place. At that time, new arrangements will have to be worked out to fit the new realities.

In another case, the relationship between two siblings was so explosive that it did not seem wise for them to continue living under the same roof. Agnes reports:

Joe and Vince never did get along real well. But after their dad left, it seemed to get worse and worse. One day I heard the boys fighting in the basement and I got there just in time to see Joe sitting on Vince with a baseball bat mashed against his throat! Vince was actually gasping for air! Well, that was it. I talked with my "ex" and we agreed to have him take Joe to raise. It's worked out great. It's really lowered the tension around here and when the boys see each other now, they actually seem to enjoy it.

In this case the decision of the parents to each assume custody of one of the boys worked out well and actually seemed to improve the relationship between the brothers.

Sometimes, an adolescent may have a severely flawed relationship with one of his or her parents. In that case, it may be foolish to insist that he or she live with that parent full-time. As is well known, in the final analysis, you cannot force an adolescent to live with someone with whom he does not want to live. The wishes of the adolescent must be considered. Sometimes, however, after divorce there is the chance that with some professional guidance, the parent-child relationship may be strengthened. Often the relationship between child and parent mirrors the discord that existed between the two parents.

Increasingly, we are hearing of parents who request joint custody of the children. Usually this means the parents wish to share parenting responsibilities as equally as possible. This arrangement depends heavily on two prerequisites: that the parents have a fairly amicable relationship and can continue to co-parent and that they live close by each other so that the children's daily lives are not unduly disrupted. Although joint custody works for some divorced parents, in our observation we believe that few parents can actually handle it.

When decisions are complicated by additional factors, often it is wise to seek professional guidance. Laying out all the facts and considerations and looking at them with the help of someone knowledgeable about children is a good way to insure a sound decision.

The Check — How Much Is Enough?

Although child support is not a part of custody or visitation as such, it is part of the legal arrangements which concern the children's welfare. In addition, it is often as strongly an emotional issue as is custody! Mention the words "support check" to a parent — either the custodial parent or the non-custodial parent — and you will usually elicit a strong response! From the custodial parent's viewpoint the money is almost never sufficient to cover the needs of the children;

from the non-custodial parent's viewpoint the money sent would be more than sufficient if it were not irresponsibly squandered!

How much money is really enough to support your child? No one but you and your ex-spouse can determine how much it costs to maintain *your* child. Although there are some guidelines, the real issues center around the style of living you want for your child and your ability, as well as your ex-spouse's ability, to meet these financial needs.

First, you must determine as honestly as possible how much money it actually takes to support your child; second, you must assess what proportion of this money will come from each parent.

Think about the following questions:

1. What was the standard of living during your marriage? Do you want your children to continue living that way? Can you afford to continue the same life-style?
2. What opportunities did you want for your child? Travel? Skiing? Nice clothes? Lessons? College? Are those desires operative now? Why or why not?
3. What percentage is each parent capable of contributing? Is fifty-fifty fair? (Only if earning power of each parent is equal!)
4. What percentage will each be able to contribute in one year? In three years? Will this change? Why or why not?
5. What provisions are to be made for the future needs of the child? College? Trade school? Special training? How much will each parent assume? How much do you expect your child to assume?
6. What provisions will be made for changes in circumstances? Cost of living increases? Increased age of child? Changed needs or unexpected expenses like orthodontic work or medical bills? Additional salary raises for you or your ex-spouse?

REALITIES OF CHILD SUPPORT

After divorce, the issue of support often becomes the focal point of hostility, and the child inevitably feels that he is the cause of the fighting. Is there any way to prevent such discord? Probably not entirely. Bearing in mind the following points may help to lessen the conflict, however:

1. *As a divorced parent you continue to be financially responsible for your child.*
2. *It is more costly to maintain two homes than one — that's reality!*
3. *Remember, the money is for your children.* If you are the non-custodial parent, say to yourself as you write out the check: "I am sending this money to my child whom I love." If you are the custodial parent say to yourself as you receive the check: "This money is for my child whom I love."
4. *Remember that you cannot hold the custodial parent accountable for how the money is spent.* Although this may be painful to accept, you are better off recognizing this fact instead of torturing yourself.
5. *As circumstances change, financial support must also change.* A two-year-old boy does not eat the same amount as a fifteen-year-old boy!

If you love your child, you will want him to have as good a life as possible even though you and his other parent are separated. Your child is as valuable and worthy of being well supported — both financially and emotionally — as he was when you and your ex-spouse lived together.

DECISIONS ABOUT CHILDREN ARE NOT UNALTERABLE

Custody, visitation, support, and other decisions which pertain to the raising of children are NOT cast in stone. They can be changed. It is often impossible to consider all factors in advance. It is equally impossible to predict the future accurately. We must simply be flexible enough to alter arrangements when they no longer fit the needs of the individuals. This is a crucial point to remember. It is easy to slip into the feeling that custody is the absolute right of the parent in charge. This should not be so. Children grow and change, parents change, circumstances change, and even our society as a whole changes. What is valid at one time can be highly invalid later. It is not necessary to be trapped into unbending rigidity. *Those who cannot bend at times may well break.*

REMEMBER

Loving, not owning, is what makes the difference. Although at the moment of divorce, the issue of custody often seems to be of paramount importance, in the longer view it is not that important. What *is* important — whether or not you are the custodial parent — is that your relationship with your children continue. *Not having custody is decidedly not synonymous with losing one's parenthood.* Your obligations, responsibilities, and joys of parenting go on nevertheless.

5

How Children
React to Divorce

Growth, as we are all painfully aware, is not easy. Any mother who has held her breath watching her toddler take his first faltering steps realizes the enormous risks involved in growing. And yet, despite repeated tumbles, crashes with the furniture, bumps and bruises, the child triumphs—he *does* learn to walk! We admire his tenacity and his courage, but most of all we admire his absolute confidence in his eventual success.

Although most of us don't discourage our child from learning to walk (even though his falls and near-falls may pain us), we sometimes unwittingly block our child's quest for emotional growth. Like physical growth, emotional growth also involves ups and downs, triumphs and disasters. For instance, we know that in any given day, a typical twelve-year-old boy or girl can range in emotional age from two to twenty! Two steps forward and one step backward is a common growth pattern for most of us!

Like the toddler who collides with the sofa or trips over an unexpected bump in the sidewalk, divorce represents a number of large stumbling blocks for the child (as well as for his parents). That doesn't mean that your child cannot make the necessary adjustments or that he cannot tackle the problems inherent in the experience of divorce. It does mean, however, that he will need help surmounting the hurdles. Especially during the early months following his parents' separation, your child may exhibit many signs of stress and his emotional growth may become particularly bumpy.

After separation and divorce, we cannot help but worry about our child's development. We watch him struggling with the pain of separation and the disruption of his life and we feel guilty and upset. How often we may reproach ourselves: "Look at the pain I have caused my child." But instead of diving headlong into self-recrimination, we need to keep the following thoughts in mind:

Some Important Points to Think About

1. The tension in our disintegrating marriage was also painful to the child, and in the long run, it was probably more damaging to his development than the crisis of divorce *when it is properly handled.*
2. It is not pain itself which cripples children. *The crippling agent is the inability to confront painful situations and feelings and deal effectively with them.*
3. At every age and at every stage of development, from the cradle to the grave, we face emotional crises and problems. Divorce can temporarily intensify problems, but we must *be careful not to attribute all our child's growing problems to divorce.*
4. We cannot always protect our child from painful and upsetting situations—nor should we; for each time we and our child face up to problems, *each time we explore and develop healthy ways of dealing with crises, we emerge stronger and more whole!*

Your job, as a loving, caring parent, is to help your child find effective ways of facing the crisis of divorce. You will be better equipped to empathize with your child and to offer guidance when you are able to predict some of his reactions to separation and divorce and understand why he is behaving in a particular way. This chapter will help you explore some of the most common responses to divorce found among families we have interviewed.

A Time for Children to Mourn

Donna, herself a child of divorce, was determined to shield six-year-old Johnny from pain. Six months after separating from her husband she reported proudly:

Johnny took the divorce beautifully! He didn't cry or make a scene when his dad left and he's been good as gold all through the last few months. I keep him busy and we do so many fun things together that he just doesn't have time to be sad or mope about the divorce.

After Donna and her ex-husband separated, Donna's feelings of guilt and grief were almost unbearable. Although she cried herself to sleep for months, Donna concealed her anguish and tried to present only a cheerful face to Johnny. She kept him constantly occupied, running from one exciting activity to another.

As time went on, it became increasing clear to Johnny that grief was an emotion that was not acceptable, and so he buried his true feelings. The only external clue to Johnny's inner turmoil was a troublesome rash which developed on his hands and face.

By protecting her son from his real emotions, Donna had hoped to cushion the shock and pain of separation. She loved Johnny and wanted to do the very best for him, but actually she was making the separation even more difficult for him. *When we do not confront the crisis of loss, but instead try to avoid it, we only succeed in prolonging the crisis.* Johnny desperately needed to grieve and mourn the loss of his full-time father and the passing of his two-parent home. Only by being in contact with his feelings could he come to accept the changes in his life.

Dr. Selma Fraiberg, child psychiatrist and author of the book *The Magic Years*, a sensitive and sensibly written guide to understanding and handling childhood problems, defends *the child's right as a human being to experience his emotions fully.* She stresses:

> Mourning is a necessary measure for overcoming the effects of loss. In our efforts to protect children from painful emotions we may deprive them of their own best means of mastering painful experiences. . . . If a child were consistently . . . deprived of the possibility of experiencing grief, he would become an impoverished person, without quality or depth in his emotional life.

For parents, another curious phenomenon frequently occurs. After the crisis of separation, there is often a tendency for us to shield *ourselves* from our children's pain. We don't like to even acknowledge their pain, for their feelings of hurt, anger, and confusion—so akin to our own—threaten to engulf us and make us feel guilty. But unless we can relate to our children's pain honestly and openly, we are powerless to help them.

Separation is a shock to children. They must be allowed and even helped to go through the normal mourning process. A parent who is unable to perceive his child's inner world of feelings and fears needs help. Counseling is advisable for parents and their children, for this gives them a safe place to ventilate and explore the emotions that they are ashamed of and fear.

The Process of Mourning

How do children mourn? Children's thought processes do not match those of adults, for children have their own logic, but their emotions are very similar to adult feelings. Like their parents, children go through the same overlapping stages of shock and disbelief, anger and guilt, and reality testing until they finally come to accept their new situation.

Unlike adults, however, children do not have the ability to think things out in an orderly fashion. Their thought processes are not well developed. They do not fully understand relationships of cause and effect. Instead, they rely on fantasy and play to work out their feelings and conflicts.

The degree and visibility of a child's mourning depend on several primary factors: his personality, the stability of his home life, and his emotional health prior to the separation of his parents. Some children seem to go through the mourning and readjustment period rapidly, without considerable guilt or attendant problems. Others take longer to get used to the new realities confronting them. Some children's feelings lie close to the surface and are readily visible. They laugh easily, cry easily, and fly into tantrums easily. Other children's emotions are more hidden. Often they do not verbalize their concerns, nor in fact do they directly act out their anxieties and fears.

Nevertheless, *all* children are affected by their parents' separation and divorce. Karen, aged thirty, discusses the different ways in which her three children reacted to their father's leaving the home:

After Jim and I split up, four-year-old Susie, our youngest child, became whiny and demanding. Jimmy, on the other hand, acted as if he couldn't care less about what was happening at home. He kept himself constantly busy with the neighborhood gang of kids. And Martha, our oldest, became even more quiet and withdrawn than before. She retreated into the world of books.

I knew what Susie was going through, for her feelings were obvious. She let everyone know that her world had changed and that she did not like it one bit! I could even sense how deeply Martha was affected. At night I sometimes heard her crying. Hers was a private way of expressing sorrow. But I was the most cut off from Jimmy's feelings. In fact, it was a long time before I realized how greatly Jimmy cared. His mask of indifference not only fooled the world—it also fooled me. He was concealing a lot of pain and confusion which finally became evident months after the divorce.

As Karen discovered, children who seem to be in control have just as many feelings about the separation of their parents and the changes in their life-style as do youngsters who publicize their alarm by demanding and clamorous behavior. As parents we must be aware of and sensitive to the differences in our children's reactions.

"WHEN IS DADDY COMING HOME?"

Disbelief may be one of the strongest and most persistent responses youngsters exhibit when their parents split up. They simply do not believe that their parents' separation is real. They often cling to the belief that it is just temporary and that their mother and father will soon be reunited.

Over and over we hear newly separated parents describe their own sense of unreality about their lives. Even when they have helped make the decision to separate, adults have trouble believing that the separation is truly final. Of course, for children the problem is greater. Since the decision of divorce is never theirs, the feeling of disbelief is even more intense.

Jean's experience with her son Randy is fairly typical:

Randy may be no genius, but he certainly is not stupid. He knows that his dad and I are getting a divorce; we've explained it again and again. But this perfectly normal, generally bright child—this child who can rattle off all the names of every dinosaur that ever walked the face of the earth—cannot seem to hold it in his head that his father and I are not going to get back together!

Randy "forgets" because he does not wish to accept the finality of the changes in his life. Actually, even when a child appears to accept the explanation of divorce and to understand its implications, rarely has he made peace with the new realities. He continues to cling to the belief that this arrangement will be temporary; because he loves both his parents and wants them to be together, he believes they *will* be reunited.

The fantasy of parents becoming reunited dies hard. One mother recalled that after she and her ex-husband had been separated for more than six months, her daughter, aged seven, asked, "When is Daddy coming home?" Another mother reports that although her divorce has been final for nearly three months, her six-year-old son still begins many sentences with "When Daddy comes back. . . ." It *is* difficult to let go of the past—even when the past was not totally satisfactory.

"I HATE YOU! YOU MADE MOMMY GO AWAY!"

Just like adults, the child who is confronted with a crisis looks around for someone to blame. Who has pulled the rug out from under his feet? Some children focus their anger on the parent who remains with them—*that* parent caused the other parent to leave. Other children blame the one who left—*that* parent changed his life by abandoning him. Meanwhile other children, as we have mentioned before, blame themselves. Most often, however, a child's anger seesaws (angry at one person and then another) or it is directed at several people at the same time.

During the early months following the separation of their parents, many children become actively hostile. A young father of a four-year-old reported in a baffled tone:

> I don't know what has gotten into Kevin. Everytime I take him over to visit his mother he starts beating on her. He begs to see her, but then when he's with her he becomes terribly angry. Maybe he shouldn't see her at all!

Of course Kevin is angry. And why shouldn't he be? He didn't ask that his parents separate. When life doesn't go as we wish, who doesn't become angry?

Even though Kevin sees his mother weekly, in a real sense he feels abandoned by her. Discontinuing visitation is certainly not the solution, for then Kevin would really feel abandoned. Obviously, he cannot be allowed to hit his mother, but his feelings of anger do need to be acknowledged. She could begin to help him with a simple message, "Kevin, you musn't hit me, but I *do* understand that you are very angry that I am not living with you." This lets Kevin know that his mother understands and cares about his feelings. It may take months, but gradually as Kevin finds out that his mother has not actually abandoned him, that she does care about him, his anger and hostility will decrease.

At the same time that Kevin is focusing his anger on his mother, he may also be harboring angry feelings about his father, wondering if his father caused his mother to leave and if he does not allow his mother to come back. Additionally, Kevin undoubtedly blames himself. Children are extremely egocentric. In a strange way they feel themselves to be very powerful. Kevin may secretly suspect that his mother left him because of something he did or did not do — that in some way he caused her to leave.

It is easy to see why young children whose language is not developed sufficiently to understand explanations become angry with their parents. But older children and teenagers also become hostile. They are reacting not only to the loss of a full-time parent, but also to the changes in their life-style. Children are conservative. They do not like change.

You need to keep in mind that your child will need sufficient time and opportunities to ventilate his anger and guilt before he can begin to come to terms with his feelings of hostility. Gradually, as the months go by, he will begin to accept the changes in his life.

TESTING: ONE, TWO, THREE — TESTING!

All children have a need to test limits. They need to know that their parents care enough to keep them safe by establishing perimeters to their behavior. Strange as it may seem, a child's feelings of security are strengthened by a firm "no" from his parent, even when he objects loudly and vehemently. After separation and divorce the need to test limits is increased. Before your child can accept the performance of the single-parent family, he must test that new reality. Depending upon his age, personality, emotional health, and relationship with you and his other parent, this testing can range from mild to extreme. Betty describes the problems she had with four-year-old Mark:

> At first Mark seemed to adjust easily to our separation. He saw Frank often, and since I had been working for a year before the divorce, he was already accustomed to the day-care center.

But then, about three months after Frank and I separated, Mark really began to act up. He was still fine at the center and he was fine with his father, but at home with me he became a holy terror: crying, babyish, even destructive.

One evening I went into my bedroom and discovered that Mark had smeared my makeup all over the mirror, written on the walls with my lipstick, and had nearly emptied an entire bottle of cologne. I couldn't believe it! Mark had never done anything like this before.

I burst into tears, grabbed Mark, and shook him until he was crying too. Afterwards, when I calmed down, I got Mark to help me clean up the mess. For the first time in weeks he was quiet — and he looked ashamed. I felt terrible. I knew I was failing him.

Then Mark looked up at me and said in a small voice, "Mommy, am I impossible?"

"Yes, Markie," I answered without thinking, "you're pretty impossible!"

"Am I impossible like Daddy? Are you going to have to divorce me too?"

Finally, Betty understood what had been going on in Mark's mind. He had overheard his mother telling a relative that she couldn't continue living with her husband and had indeed used the expression, "Frank is just impossible!" Mark had to find out how bad he would have to get before his mother would also throw him out.

A child — especially a young child — cannot fully distinguish between types of relationships. He is not sure how his relationship with his mother differs from his mother's relationship with his father. He may think: "If Mommy can divorce Daddy because they don't get along, maybe she'll divorce me too if we don't get along." Unable to tolerate the suspense of not knowing the limit, the child seeks to find that limit by his naughty behavior.

Another mother reported a humorous but significant incident of testing limits:

Two weeks after Ken and I separated, Neil, our six-year-old, came into the kitchen and announced with a perfectly straight face, "I think I'll have a chocolate bar for breakfast instead of oatmeal."

Neil's father had been the disciplinarian. With his father gone, who would set the limits? Neil needed to know what would remain the same as in the past and what would be altered in his new situation. Could he really get away with a request as outrageous as a candy bar for breakfast or would his mother provide the necessary boundaries for him?

Testing behavior may range from small incidents of "just checking" like the example above, to provocative behavior such as using obscene language, or even more serious attempts to check limits such as a teenager's refusal to comply with the curfew hour set for him. In all these situations, the common thread is the child's anxiety about his security. Will I be safe in this new situation? Will you care by providing limits for me?

When parents are able to understand their child's concerns, they can be sympathetic and supportive while at the same time providing structure and limits for the child. Understanding the concerns of the child does not mean that you ignore or overlook his out-of-bounds behavior. It does mean that while you continue to enforce limits, you can verbalize your understanding of how your child must be feeling: "I know you must be feeling very angry with me, but you cannot break and destroy my things." As time goes by, the child's testing will diminish — or at least drop to normal levels. Some testing is a vital, necessary, and ongoing process of growing up.

How Will My Child React to Divorce?

Regardless of a child's age, most children experience some fear and anxiety when their parents separate. No two children are identical (not even twins!), and no two children respond to a crisis identically. How your child may react to your divorce depends upon many factors:

1. His prior relationship to his parents
2. His preparation for the changes in his life
3. His own individual personality
4. His emotional stability
5. His age and stage of development

Although, as we have said, all children are affected by divorce, we do not expect a two-year-old to respond exactly the same way as an eighteen-year-old might. Rarely, for instance, do we see an eighteen-year-old start to suck his thumb; often, however, we see someone that age start to smoke. According to Dr. E. H. Klatskin, who has worked with children of divorce, the age and stage of development of the youngster greatly affect his adjustment and reaction to divorce. In the following pages, using much of Dr. Klatskin's findings, we will discuss how a child of each age most commonly reacts to divorce.

INFANCY

According to Dr. Klatskin, the greatest potential hazard for the infant is that his mother, upon whom the baby is dependent, will not be able to adequately meet the physical and emotional needs of her baby. Debbi, twenty years old, is a good example. When Debbi was in her seventh month of pregnancy, Jim suddenly left her. Debbi remembers how she felt.

> After Jim and I split up, the baby didn't mean anything to me. I couldn't eat, I quit my exercise classes, and if I hadn't been so far along, I would have had an abortion. I just didn't care about anything.
>
> During delivery my mother stayed with me. When they brought the baby for me to see for the first time, I didn't even want to look at her. Luckily, my mother was thrilled by her granddaughter. She thought Marla was the most beautiful baby in the world. When I went home it was to my mother's house. Mom took care of Marla while I went to business school. Actually, I had nothing to do with Marla the first few months. I just couldn't bear to be with her. I guess she reminded me too much of Jim and the plans we had made.

Debbi was fortunate to have her mother available to take care of the baby. All of us realize how crucial the early months of life can be. In order to thrive and grow healthily, a baby needs emotional nurturing as well as physical care.

Marla is now almost two years old, and Debbi's life has greatly changed.

> I've got a job now, and a new boyfriend! Things are really looking up! In recent months I've developed real feelings of love for my little girl and I'm looking forward to making a home for her.
>
> Mom has been wonderful to me. She allowed me the extra

time and freedom I needed to grow up and get my head together, and she gave Marla the love, affection, and care that I couldn't give her. Most of all, though, she helped me discover the joy of being Marla's mother.

Unlike Debbi, some single mothers become overly involved with their new baby. Dr. Klatskin warns of the hazards of "smother-mothering." A mother who is raising an infant alone may transfer all the love and attention that she would have given the child's father to the baby. She may overprotect her child and at the same time look to the child for emotional gratification of her own needs. This type of mother who is not able to perceive her baby as a separate human being creates a potentially unhealthy situation for both herself and her baby.

When a mother is overcome by grief and mourning, she needs help to raise her baby and cope with his demands plus the demands of everyday living. It is important that there be others in her life, for the infant may need extra mothering and the mother may need extra support. In addition, a single mother needs to develop interests besides her baby in order to fulfill her own needs. If a woman in this situation does not have her family or close friends to help her, it would be wise for her to seek counseling or a therapy group for support.

VERY YOUNG CHILD

How does the very young child react to the separation of his parents? As the following examples demonstrate, he almost always regresses to an earlier, perhaps more secure, stage of development.

Before our separation, Jamie (eighteen months old) was a fearless adventurer. He'd take on lions and tigers if we'd let him! Now suddenly he won't even go out to the backyard without me. He clings, cries if I leave him, and really prefers to spend all his time on my lap.

If this preverbal child could have talked, he might have explained: "I've already 'mislaid' my daddy (or maybe lost him forever) and nothing seems quite the same now. I'm going to hang on tightly to my mommy!" Seeking the solace of a warm lap and comforting arms during times of stress makes good sense. Whether we are one or fifty, it is what we all would like to do at times.

Another typical reaction to stress is the young child's increased desire for sucking. Martha reports:

> My three-year-old, Jessica, gave up her bottle some months before Don and I separated. Now she's suddenly grabbing her baby brother's bottle. Sometimes she crawls into bed and sucks his bottle; other times she hides the bottle in her closet.

For two-year-old Michael it was the comfort of a juicy, warm thumb which helped reduce stress! His mother reports that recently he sucks so loudly that she can hear him in her bedroom at night. "He only unplugs to eat — and then reluctantly!"

Increased need for sucking at times of stress is perfectly normal for a preschool child (and may even occur in the child of kindergarten age). If parents and relatives are able to relax and accept their child's need for extra oral gratification, the increased sucking will gradually diminish. As most parents realize, it is unwise to attempt to wean a child from bottle, breast, pacifier, or thumb during a period of high stress. Wait until life settles down before asking your little one to take a big step toward maturity.

The same is true about toilet training. If you have not taken the youngster out of diapers, don't try it the week your spouse leaves! If your child has recently been toilet trained, don't be surprised at a sudden increase in accidents. When we realize that something as simple as cutting a tooth or having a cold can make a child more accident-prone, we can imagine the greater stress caused by the separation of his parents and the resultant changes in his daily routine.

The child should not be shamed for his temporary lapses of control. Instead, the parent should continue praising him when he does exhibit control. Putting the child in more absorbent training pants during the day and diapering him at night will save both clothing and the parents' tempers. When parents are already under stress it *is* difficult to see the child lose the control he so recently gained. But if you can pass over accidents lightly and give your child a little extra cuddling and attention, he will soon catch up again.

Sometimes eating problems develop as a reaction to stress. The child may hold food in his mouth, become finicky, or play with his food. If these incidents are not blown out of proportion, they will usually soon disappear.

Often a child's behavior changes. His personality may suddenly seem quite different from what it has been in the past. He may become withdrawn and quiet, noisy and demanding, extremely aggressive, or disturbingly passive. For example:

Brian, who is two, has always been such a happy-go-lucky, hang-loose kid. Now he's cranky and irritable. He whines and cries all the time.

Samantha, who is almost three, is the baby of the family. She's been a cuddly, loving child who seldom got angry. Now she's turned into a cannibal — taking big bites out of her sister and brothers!

Disturbance in regular sleep patterns is also a sign of a small child dealing with increased stress. Most common are the complaints that a child is exhibiting more resistance to bedtime and is having more nightmares. A solution that is *not* generally recommended is to allow the small child to take frequent refuge in the parent's bed. For the child, it is too easy to become dependent upon this arrangement, and he may experience strong feelings of rejection when his parent wishes to stop having the child in her bed. For the parent, the practice raises additional questions: "Am I clinging to my child? Is he replacing my absent spouse? Is this good for me and my child?"

Wiser ways of combating sleep problems might be to try one or more of the following ideas. Sometimes allow your child to sleep on the floor near your bed. You'll both sleep better and the experience will be easier to reverse. An added comfort may be to let your child choose a cheery nightlight to put in his bedroom. Buy a new doll or a cuddly stuffed toy for him to take to bed to give him the extra assurance he needs.

The very young child is at a distinct disadvantage. With his limited verbal ability he can neither comprehend explanations adequately nor ask questions that will bring answers he can readily understand. His life seems out of order — and for no apparent reason! Dr. Klatskin reminds us that the young child is not only responding to the loss of his parent, but also to the break in daily routines which are important to him. However, as new routines are established, the child usually quickly regains his former skills and catches up to his previous stage of development.

PRESCHOOL CHILD

Of all age levels, the preschooler (ages three to five or even six) may have the most difficulty coping with the loss of his parent. During this period, the child ordinarily becomes very attached to and involved with the parent of the opposite sex.

If the child is a boy, he feels somewhat jealous of his father and vies with him for his mother's attention and love. Therefore, if the father suddenly leaves the home, the young boy becomes anxious, worried that his hostility toward his father drove him away. Being that powerful is scary. Furthermore, the boy loves his father and needs him. He certainly doesn't want to lose him.

A girl, on the other hand, harbors a subconscious wish to replace her mother and to become Daddy's one and only love. When her parents separate, she often blames her mother for sending her father away. In addition, she feels rejected by her father. She also has feelings of considerable conflict, for like her brother, she needs and loves the rival parent — in this case, the mother.

Because of their many conflicting feelings, preschool boys and girls often feel particularly responsible for the breakup of their family. They may fantasize that something they did or didn't do caused the parent to leave. For these reasons, the preschooler does not easily accept the finality of the separation. Barbara found that it was a problem every time she had to talk with her ex-husband in the presence of her five-year-old:

> If Ed and I quarrel in front of Kate, she cries for hours. If we are civil to each other, she gets her hopes up again and begs us to get back together. When we explain that it's impossible, she cries and sulks.

The child of three to five years old desperately wants his parents to reunite. Like Kate, it may take repeated incidents of raising hopes and then dashing hopes before the fantasy of reconciliation recedes.

If at all possible, it is wise to establish a visitation pattern immediately after the separation. When the preschool child lived at home with both his parents present, he was better able to control his possessive and destructive fantasies. When one of his parents moves out, however, his anxieties often become magnified. It is important for the child to see his other parent regularly in order to allay the anxiety associated with ideas that this parent is dead or has abandoned him. The preschool child will need frequent reassurance in the months ahead that he has not been abandoned.

After the separation of his parents, the preschooler may react in various ways. Some children regress to an earlier stage of development—thumb sucking, nighttime wetting, daytime wetting, and baby talk. Other children act out their anxiety with demanding, hostile, or loud activity. Some become withdrawn. A common reaction at this age is an increase in nightmares and nightfears. As the child's situation becomes more predictable and stable, these symptoms fade. This is particularly true in situations where both parents continue their relationship with their child. Where the absent parent is not seen frequently, the adjustment will be longer and harder.

SCHOOL-AGED CHILD

Some months after separating from her husband, Marcia was seeking help for herself and Tommy. She complained:

Tommy is such a brat! I just don't know what to do with him. His teacher called me twice this week because he's so disruptive in school. What's more, he's falling behind in his work. He just doesn't seem to be able to concentrate anymore. And because of his fighting at school, he hardly has any friends left!

Marcia's experience with her son is not unusual. When the school-aged child's home life becomes stressful, quite often his schoolwork and his relationship with his peers will suffer first. Like Tommy, the child may have trouble concentrating and paying attention. He may constantly test the teacher, provoking her to set tighter limits. Depending on his specific situation, he may find that school is a safer place than home to act out his conflicts.

Sometimes the school-aged child may resume earlier ways of behaving—bedwetting, fussy food habits, and infantile demands. Or he may act out anger by becoming physically aggressive (bullying, fighting) or verbally hostile (obscene language or an attitude of defiance). Like the younger child, the school-aged child may also be plagued with nightmares.

Stealing is not uncommon at this point, sometimes combined with an exaggerated possessiveness of "his" things. Clearly, the child is clinging to objects he can count on; they won't walk off and leave him. At this stage his stealing cannot be regarded as a moral lapse; his acts are symptoms of his sense of abandonment. Obviously, he cannot be permitted to continue stealing. The parent must explain to him the difference between what is his and what is not his. The very fact of his parent's doing this—because it sets the limits he so badly needs—may make him feel better. Needless to say, if such potentially destructive behavior persists, counseling is definitely indicated.

The school-aged child has one advantage over his younger brothers and sisters. He is capable of verbalizing his feelings and problems. Often a counselor, a friend or relative, or his parents—someone who has a strong relationship with him—can help enormously by listening to him and helping him confront his feelings. With some help, the child can better understand the events in his life as well as his own reactions to those events. When his world makes sense again and his life becomes more predictable, the child will feel increasingly in control. Like the younger child, the school-aged child will soon catch up, mastering his schoolwork and working out his peer relationships.

ADOLESCENTS

Many parents assume that because the teenager is older and is able to understand his parents' reasons for separating, he will have an easy time adjusting. Unfortunately, this is rarely true. The teenager often resents as keenly as the younger child any changes in his life.

We have to look at the teenager himself to understand why this is so. The adolescent—and particularly the younger adolescent—is already confronted with numerous changes. His body is changing, his emotions are in flux (almost hourly they soar and crash), and the demands of his family and society are also changing. No longer does he fit comfortably in the niche of childhood; now he swings precariously between adulthood and childhood. When his family life also changes, it may add almost unbearable stress to an already stressed human being. This is particularly true if the divorce involves moving and having to leave his familiar school and friends.

The adolescent is at the stage of development in which he must successfully negotiate separation from his parents in order to establish himself as an adult. Because his own life and future seem so indefinite and unsure, the teenager craves stability in his home life. He needs something he can count on. Bobby stated the problem succinctly when he remarked:

The way I see it is like this: It's okay for kids to leave their parents—that's the way it's supposed to be—but it's not okay for parents to leave their kids. If anyone does the splitting around here, it ought to be me!

The teenager needs something to pull away from. If his home life is in flux, it leaves him nothing solid to separate from. This causes the teenager to panic.

How a teenager copes with the problems of divorce depends greatly upon his emotional health and maturity prior to the divorce. Problems which have not been resolved adequately will flare up again, often with greater intensity than in the past. When his home life has been fraught with conflict and tension over the years, the teenager will have problems which need to be worked through before he is really ready to live his own life.

Like his younger siblings, the teenager may react in a number of ways. He may act out his problems by becoming hostile or aggressive or antisocial. He may dramatize his conflict by running away. Or he may withdraw, become depressed, or fail in school. He may become dependent on drugs, alcohol, or seek refuge in food. A girl may become promiscuous and eventually find herself pregnant or stricken with venereal disease.

Because the adolescent *seems* mature much of the time, it is often tempting to confide in him all the problems of divorce and to lean heavily on him. The mother or father may make demands on this child to fill the role of the ex-spouse. These responsibilities are too great a burden for most teenagers.

The older teenager often worries that, because his parents were not able to make a successful marriage, he also will fail. He may vow never to marry and may even shun the opposite sex for awhile. On the other hand, the teenager may feel keenly the vacuum created by the breakup of his family and attempt to create a new family—his own. He may rush into an early marriage, seeking the comfort of unity with another person. Counseling (often group counseling) at this stage is very helpful, for the teenager needs a chance to "rap" with others about his problems, to examine his reactions, and to set goals for himself.

Adjustment Pain

In the preceding pages we have explored the ways in which children may react to the divorce of their parents. As parents, we must be sensitive to our children's needs and problems so that we can support them whenever possible. To look at each emotional upset of the child and blame ourselves for it, however, is ridiculous! Remember that *all growing up is painful and upsetting at times.* After divorce we can expect that our children will be upset, angry, and confused. But if we try to deal openly and honestly with them, in most cases problems will begin to smooth out within a few months as the new realities of their lives begin to feel commonplace. While you are dealing with the specific day-to-day problems of your child's adjustment to separation and divorce, bear in mind these larger realities:

1. In most cases the child's inherent need to grow will push him back into a state of equilibrium again.
2. All growing involves some pain and disequilibrium, even when there are no visible crises like divorce.
3. Divorce often presents the family with the motivation to seek help to solve problems which existed prior to divorce.

WHEN A CHILD NEEDS PROFESSIONAL HELP

Some children do not come through the storm of separation and divorce as well as we would wish. These children may mourn too deeply or not mourn at all (denying the very existence of the crisis). They may act out their conflicts over a prolonged period of time, developing symptoms which are clearly worrisome.

Marian, for instance, became concerned about her five-year-old because, although the divorce had become final many months in the past, Jennifer was becoming increasingly withdrawn, retreating into her fantasy world.

Jennifer's always been a very sensitive child, so at first I wasn't alarmed by her growing attachment to me. But as the time went by, she refused to leave the house and would cry pitifully if I insisted.

It sounds crazy, but while she was clinging to me, day by day she seemed to drift farther and farther from me. Her stuffed animals became more real than the people in her life. And then there were the nightmares. She would wake night after night, drenched in sweat and shrieking at the top of her lungs. She was always being chased by something horribly ferocious which she couldn't quite describe.

Obviously Jennifer was in a great deal of pain. She needed help—professional help. A child guidance clinic which Marian contacted not only helped Jennifer play and talk out her problems, but also offered support and guidance for Marian herself.

Antonio is another parent who became concerned about his child:

> Tony, who's seven, had become a compulsive liar following our divorce. Even when telling the truth was far simpler, he devised complicated tales. Nothing I said or did could make him stop.
>
> Then one day when I was picking him up from school, his teacher stopped me and asked whether Anita and I were reconciled and living together. I assured Mrs. Willis this wasn't true. It seems that Tony was constantly spinning tales about his mother and father and sisters and brothers all living together. And as Mrs. Willis knew, Tony has no brothers and sisters! That afternoon I took the first step toward getting help. I knew I was in over my head.

Antonio was wise. If you as a parent feel concerned about your child for any reason, you should seek counseling. If your child's behavior is fairly normal (considering the amount of stress he is experiencing), the therapist or counselor can reassure you and help you find ways to live through the months ahead. In fact, if there are severe problems, you will be advised, and both you and your child can get help to solve them.

If you are having difficulty deciding whether your child needs help or not, the following guidelines may be useful. *Seek professional help for your child when:*

1. The child's symptoms become severe or when they are interfering with his daily functioning.
2. The child's symptoms persist for long periods of time.
3. The child's condition seems to be worsening rather than improving.
4. You, the parent, feel that you cannot cope with the child by yourself, but need support and guidance from a trained professional.

THERE IS NOTHING SHAMEFUL ABOUT ASKING FOR HELP!

Parents often avoid seeking help for their children even when they are very concerned about some aspect of their child's functioning.

There are many reasons for not seeking help: lack of knowledge of where to turn, money worries, shame in not being able to handle all problems, and fear of being blamed for the child's problems. None of these excuses should stand in our way if we really want to help the child. We cannot state too strongly: *If you think help is needed, by all means get it!* It is the mark of an intelligent person to know what he can handle and what he cannot handle by himself. It is sad to see concerned parents wringing their hands, knowing their child has problems and needs extra help, and yet putting off professional counseling. Don't let problems fester and grow! Check out at least a couple of sources of help and choose the one which seems best for your child. Your child deserves the best chance you can give him to grow into a healthy, strong, loving human being.

REMEMBER

Don't blame all your child's problems of growing up on the divorce. At the same time, however, be sensitive to the special problems your child is having. He needs to mourn, grieve, and feel angry about the changes in his life. More than ever he needs your love and assurance that you care enough to keep him safe during this time of uncertainty. While you continue to set limits for him, he needs to hear you say that you understand how he is feeling. If you are very worried about your child's behavior, be sure to get help. In most cases, as the new reality becomes more secure and the routines of his life are reestablished, a child will adapt and regain his balance.

6

Parenting Under Stress: The Early Months

For all of us, there are times when merely coping with the ordinary problems of day-to-day living stresses us almost to the breaking point. The kids squabble, the car doesn't start, dinner scorches, the washing machine breaks down, the paycheck doesn't stretch far enough, two-year-old Jodi has just soaked her sixth pair of training pants—and it's only noon! Sometimes life seems to be an endless march of schedules and demands to be met.

It's hard enough raising children and making a living when two parents are united to meet the demands. But what happens when one parent must cope alone? Problems then can seem truly enormous. Not only does the single parent have to manage all the tasks she handled in the past, but she must also take on many of the tasks which her husband previously assumed. In addition, she may have to find a job (or continue working) in order to support herself and help support her children.

Worst of all, the custodial parent must manage all this at a time when she is upset, confused, angry, and depressed. No wonder the first few months after separation can seem grim and sometimes even terrifying!

"I Can't Cope!"

Sharon, twenty-five, is a mother who is overwhelmed by her feelings of failure and loss. Her reactions are not uncommon. In an almost inaudible voice, often choked with tears, Sharon poured out the story of her recent separation from her husband:

Greg and I were married as soon as I graduated from high school. Because Greg is six years older than I am, I always relied on him. I worked in an office for a couple of months after we were married, but I quit when I got pregnant. Todd was born that first year, then fifteen months later we had Billy, and two years after that, Lisa.

In all that time I seldom left the house. Greg did most of the shopping and made most of the decisions. My whole life revolved around my babies—diaper rash, teething, colic, and potty training. By evening, I had little time or energy left over for Greg.

At first I hardly noticed that Greg was having so many evening meetings at the office. By the time I woke up, it was too late. He had fallen in love with a woman who worked in his office. Six weeks ago he moved out, leaving me with the children.

Sharon buried her head in her hands and sobbed softly. After some moments she regained control of herself and continued:

Without Greg my life isn't worth anything. I just don't know how I can manage. If I were one of those working wives already coping with job, kids, and the house, it would be different. It's easier for them to adjust to divorce, but I've never managed all that.

When the toilet overflowed last week, I ran out the door. The bank statement came yesterday, and I tried for a solid hour to balance the checkbook. Finally I gave up, threw myself on the bed, and bawled. The laundry is piling up and the house is filthy, and I know I should be thinking about getting a job. But I don't have the energy to do anything!

And, worst of all, I can't even handle the kids! They fuss and cry from morning till night. Todd is constantly picking a fight, and Billy looks like a big, overgrown baby with his thumb in his mouth, dragging that ratty blanket wherever he goes. Lisa screams if I put her down. She just wants to be held all the time.

I can't cope with anything. Greg's gone, and I can't stop crying!

The bottom of Sharon's world has fallen out, and she and the children feel panicky. She cannot seek comfort by returning to her familiar world of marriage since that world no longer exists; nor can she immediately step into her new world of the single-parent family (since that reality is still too painful). So Sharon and her family teeter precariously between two realities.

"WHAT'S THE USE OF TRYING?"

For Sharon all the problems and trauma of divorce are greatly compounded by her inexperience with the role of the single woman. As Sharon said bitterly, "What do I know about being single? I flew directly from my parents' nest to my husband's nest!" But does the working mother really have as easy an adjustment as Sharon fantasizes? Barbara would not agree. Like Sharon, she is also overwhelmed as she singlehandedly juggles the demands of children, home, and job.

Every morning I've got to pry Jeremy and Nina out of bed and coax them to eat breakfast and get dressed. They dawdle and dawdle, and all the time I've got my eye on the clock, and I'm getting frantic. I want to be calm, but inevitably I find myself shrieking at the kids.

I drop them at the day-care center, fight traffic, and get to the office late and feeling guilty. The next eight hours I'm cooped up in my tiny, stuffy office pounding a stupid typewriter for an idiot boss.

Then it's rush, rush, rush to pick up the kids, fight traffic again, wash dishes, fix dinner, bathe the kids, and get them to bed. Even then the evening's not mine — I've got laundry to wash and fold, the house to clean, bills to pay. I never get caught up!

On Saturdays when Jim comes for the kids, they run out of here as if they're escaping from Alcatraz. What's the use of all the work and worry? Sure, the kids prefer to be with their father. He has time to play with them all day. I wish I had it that easy!

Barbara's anger is not unusual. She *is* overloaded. The stress of divorce alone would be enough to make her upset, but she is coping with much more. A mother who becomes a full-time parent often feels heavily overburdened by her duties and responsibilities. Like Sharon and Barbara, mothers who love their children and want to live with them are often unprepared for the energy it takes to manage singlehandedly. Angry and depressed, they cannot find viable alternatives.

Although nine out of ten mothers get custody of their children, fathers get custody twice as often as they did ten years ago. As our society begins to shake itself loose from stifling stereotypes, we increasingly find that fathers *can* "mother." Males as well as females can provide nurturing love for their children.

But just like the single mother, the single father also has enormous adjustments to make. Managing alone is not simple. When Mike and his wife separated three months ago, Mike's three oldest children came to live with him. The past months have not been easy for him. Like Sharon and Barbara, Mike is also overwhelmed by the demands of parenting alone. He reports:

I thought being a bachelor father would be kind of fun . . . you know, like some of the stories you see on TV. But the fun isn't so funny. When the kids switched homes, they had to change schools. Because they're all under a lot of pressure to get along in their new school and make friends, they're not as easygoing as they used to be. In fact, they spend most of their time fighting and arguing with each other.

They can't agree how chores should be done or who should do what, and they resent everything I say. I can't stand all the arguing—it puts my nerves on edge—so I end up yelling at them, and that just makes things worse.

Meanwhile the house is filthy, our meals are terrible, and the laundry is piling up to the ceiling. I've gotten so I can hardly concentrate at work because I'm worrying all the time about the kids and everything. I don't want to rush out and get married again, but I've got to admit, I really envy men who have a wife and a clean house to go home to!

Because more women are custodial parents than men, this chapter is slanted toward the single mother. If you are a custodial father, however, you are encountering some of the same problems as the custodial mother, and many of the techniques we suggest for survival will also apply to you.

A TIME TO MOURN

The death of any relationship always leaves the participants temporarily unbalanced. This is especially true when marriages end suddenly like Sharon's; but it is also true when marriages die slowly. Just like the death of a loved one, the death of a marriage plunges us into a period of paralysis and disorientation — a period of mourning and bereavement.

We cannot avoid this mourning period; it is a necessary and vital step toward personal growth and freedom. If we cannot mourn, we cannot come to terms with the changes in our lives. We cannot accept our loss, and thus we remain trapped in the past, condemned to live with our hostilities, guilt, and anxieties.

Most of us embarking upon divorce realize there will be some tough months of adjustment. We expect to feel uncomfortable and upset at first. But the *intensity* and *duration* of our feelings surprise us. We are *not* really prepared for the tidal waves of violent and conflicting emotions we feel.

Mel Krantzler, a divorce therapist and author of the book *Creative Divorce*, discusses the reactions of individuals faced with what he terms *separation shock*. He stresses that the longer and more involved the relationship has been, the more severe will be the reaction to separation. He writes:

> When we have invested a major portion of our time and energies in a relationship, its ending can radiate waves of depression, hostility, self-pity, guilt, remorse, anxiety, and fear too conflicting to comprehend and too powerful to cope with immediately.

Mel Krantzler emphasizes that we are free to rebuild our lives *only* after truly facing our conflicting feelings about our lost marriage and our ex-spouse. This takes time; it cannot be accomplished overnight. For the first few months following separation, it is difficult to cope with the bare necessities of living. Just getting through each day is challenging enough.

When We Need Help

When do you need help? When is it no longer wise for a parent to try to put the pieces of her life together by herself? Sharon confesses, "I knew I was in trouble when after six weeks I still couldn't stop crying. I didn't even have the energy to get out of bed to change the baby's diaper." Barbara sought help after taking an overdose of sleeping pills — not enough to kill her, but enough to shock her.

Mourning the end of a marriage is necessary. For parents and for their children, the act of separation is a severe shock; it will take time before the pain subsides to a dull ache. During these early weeks and months our sense of identity is imperiled and our emotions constantly threaten to overwhelm and paralyze us. Like Sharon, Barbara, and Mike, our lives appear unreal and out of control. We swing dizzily from side to side trying desperately to find a new balancing point.

But we must remember that we are still parents. We don't have only ourselves to worry about. Our children need us. They, too, are upset and shocked by the changes in their lives. Just when our coping powers *are most needed, they are the most depleted!* Our children cannot wait too long for us to put ourselves back together. Their need for comfort and reassurance — as well as stability — is acute.

There comes a point, however, when mourning ceases to be therapeutic and becomes self-destructive. If your reactions are increasingly out of bounds, you need help. There are danger signals. Ask yourself whether any of the following points describe you. If so, you need help *immediately.*

Danger Signals

1. *When the necessities of life are not being met.* The sink is overflowing with dirty dishes, the trash has taken over the kitchen floor, there's only one jar of mustard and a piece of moldy cheese left in the refrigerator, and no one in the family has a clean pair of underpants.

2. *When you're turning night into day.* You are spending the nights pacing the floor, watching the late, late, late show, emptying one cup of coffee after another, filling the ashtray with cigarette butts, and finally tossing and turning in bed until the ringing alarm shrilly announces the new day.

3. *When you're constantly preoccupied with thoughts of death and violence.* You find yourself staring at a display of handguns in a pawn shop window. You reach for one sleeping pill, and you're afraid you'll take twenty. Or you start to swat your youngster's bottom and find yourself terrified that you may lose control and beat him severely.

4. *When alcohol, drugs, or excessive eating are becoming habitual means of escape.* Your usual one drink before dinner has turned into four drinks and to hell with dinner. Or three

meals daily have become one long meal — an uninterrupted eating binge from morning till night. You find yourself relying on pills to sleep, pills to wake up, and pills to cope with the day.

5. *When you isolate yourself, withdrawing from contact with other people.* Day after day you shun friends and acquaintances. You hide in your bedroom, finding innumerable reasons why you cannot see a show, have dinner with a friend, take your kids to the school carnival, or even go to the grocery store.

6. *When you drown your woes in the frantic pursuit of "good times."* You run desperately from one activity to another: lunches, cocktails, dinners, shows, shopping sprees, movies, sex, more shopping, more movies, more sex. The contacts are superficial; the activities, meaningless.

7. *When you're spending excessive energy and time in recriminations and accusations.* You waste your energy, endlessly blaming everyone and everything for your present situation: your ex-mate, your parents, your children, your job, your childhood, your figure, your grey hairs, and so on.

8. *When you're so preoccupied with your own problems that you are cut off from your children and their problems.* Your six-year-old lies in bed clutching his blanket and sucking his thumb; your eight-year-old is beating up kids half his size; your twelve-year-old has turned into a compulsive housecleaner (she's scrubbed the toilet four times this week!); the school has just called to say your fourteen-year-old hasn't shown up at school for three days (and come to think of it, he hasn't been home either!).

An occasional indulgence in such behavior may not be serious. *But when any of these danger signals turns into a frequent pattern, you need help!* A parent who is chronically depressed and isolated (perhaps even suicidal) or always angry and hostile, anxious and tense, is not only *self*-destructive; she or he is *child*-destructive as well.

But there is no need to wait until the signs of trouble become grave. There is nothing shameful about needing advice and support. You are going through some difficult times. Just like your children, you need extra nurturing and support. By seeking help for yourself, you also help your children. You can shorten the time it takes to get back on your feet. And you can find ways to decrease your children's anxiety as well as your own. *By getting help for yourself you are getting help for the whole family.*

HOW CAN YOU THINK WHEN YOU FEEL SO BAD?

Barbara's eyes flashed and her voice rose angrily:

Everyone keeps telling me I've got to pull myself together, stop living in the past, and rebuild my life. That's easy to say, but when you can't think straight and you feel rotten, who's got the energy to plan and build? Not me! I'm lucky if I can just make it to supper time in one piece.

Barbara is right. When you face a crisis as traumatizing as divorce — something that shakes the foundation upon which your life has been built — you can't think straight. You've been knocked off your feet, and you are no longer sure what is right or wrong or what is best for you and your children. You need time to catch your breath. You'll start tackling your problems soon, but you first need some coping techniques to help you get through one day at a time. These techniques won't *solve* problems — problems are not solved until they are faced — but they will buy you a little time. As a parent, you need this time to regain your strength, build confidence in yourself, and continue parenting.

Simply stated, these are first-aid techniques which will help you cope. "Coping," say George and Nena O'Neill, authors of *Shifting Gears*, "is a middle way, lying somewhere between advancing and retreating." In other words, coping is treading water so you won't sink!

FIRST AID FOR SINGLE PARENTS

1. *Find someone to talk to.* It is amazing how large problems seem when we feel alone. All of us need at least one person (and preferably more) who cares and who will listen to us and accept our feelings. The O'Neills remind us that "friends are not merely for comfort and support; they are the threads keeping you connected to the world, the threads that lead you into growth." Especially after divorce, when we have become disconnected from someone with whom we had bonds of a shared past, we need people with whom we have some feelings of continuity.

The kind of friend you need now is one who comforts and reassures you, who gives you her honest opinion when you ask for it, and who helps *you* discover solutions and alternatives. The O'Neills call this type of friend *feedback friends.* They are not mentors; they do not always have answers to your problems, but they are people who "give you honest feedback — they can explore a problem with you and are able to see you with clarity and objectivity." In times of crisis this is especially important.

A few warnings:
Don't wear out your friends with endless rehashes and dissections of your marriage. Even the most interested and concerned friend will eventually become glassy-eyed.

Don't spend long periods of time with people who support your negative thinking. There is a big difference between a person who accepts your angry feelings and one who encourages you to act them out. A friend who recently left her husband made a shocking discovery. Every time she was with her "best friend," she came away feeling more angry than before.

I would complain about my ex-husband and Sally would say, "If I were you, I'd take that guy for everything he's worth." Or she'd say, "If he were my ex-husband, I'd never let him see the kids again!" Finally I realized that instead of helping me find rational solutions to problems, Sally was encouraging my vengeful, irrational side. And that needed no encouraging! So I don't see Sally much anymore.

Don't accept pat answers. The person who so easily tells you what she would do if she were in your shoes is tendering worthless advice. Weigh advice carefully, and act on it only if it really fits *your* situation.

Who are your friends? Make a list of the people in your life who care for you (and you for them) — people whom you respect and whose opinions you value. Don't forget relatives. Sometimes your closest friend may be your sister or brother, your mother or father, your aunt or cousin. "I know it sounds wild," Sharon confessed, "but the person who helped me the most after divorce was Greg's mother — my ex-mother-in-law!"

In times of crisis, friends are your lifeline. Just knowing that people care makes you realize that you are not alone. The love and concern of friends can strengthen you so that you can successfully find your way through the maze of heartache and problems.

2. *Get some relief from parenting.* You need a break from parenting (going to work each day cannot be considered a break). You should not feel ashamed or guilty for needing to get away from the children at times. In fact, by having time to yourself regularly, you are doing yourself and your children a favor. The woman who stays tied to her children, becoming day by day more stressed and strained, cannot be a good mother. Every parent knows that edgy feeling—"If one more kid says 'Mommy' one more time I'm going to explode!" Nobody can be an effective, loving parent when she is so overloaded. You must find time for yourself! Even a couple of hours away can give you a fresh outlook on life. You'll like yourself and your children much better when you return.

Sharon discovered that getting away from her children was not only good for her, it was good for her children as well.

When my therapist strongly recommended that I get a babysitter and get out of the house twice a week for a few hours, I thought she was crazy. What about the children? They became panicky if I went outside to hang out a load of clothes. They'd scream if I left them. My therapist assured me that they needed some time away from me as much as I needed time away from them.

Sure enough, Billy and Lisa cried and clung to me when I left. But the babysitter held one of them in each arm and motioned for me to go. I could hardly sit through the movie, yet I was almost afraid to go home. When I returned Jean had the kids asleep. She admitted that the first half hour had been rough, but after that the children had been great. And the next morning the kids couldn't stop talking about the fun they'd had with Jean.

Sharon's children cried for several weeks whenever she went out, but gradually the crying lessened. "Last week," reports Sharon, "the children couldn't wait to get rid of me!" Just having their mother leave and then return—just as she promised she would— reestablishes trust. Furthermore, it is good for children to be with other adults and young people who are not overloaded with problems and conflict. As Billy, Todd, and Lisa discovered, being away from Mommy can feel good.

Tips on how to get away from your children:

Babysitters: Neighborhood teenagers are often available, usually enjoy playing with children, and need pocket money. If you don't know any teenagers personally, you might get a referral through a neighborhood church, community center, or local high school. Look for older women or a young mother who is home.

Preschools: Check with churches (the preschool programs are usually non-denominational), community centers, and private schools. Programs vary widely in philosophy, tuition, age, hours, and approach. Visit a few before deciding which fits your needs.

Libraries: Often libraries offer a weekly half-hour or hour story time for preschoolers. These programs are usually free on a drop-in basis. It is not a long break for a mother, but it does mean you can run a quick errand or browse in the library shelves without a child tugging on you.

Co-ops or exchanges: In some neighborhoods, mothers have organized an exchange babysitting club. Some mothers like to trade babysitting with a nearby friend—("I'll watch yours on Thursdays; you watch mine on Mondays"). If you don't feel that you can cope with caring for another child, see if you can trade another type of service (ironing?) for babysitting.

Naps and rest times: Don't forget naps and rest times. Even if they are only for half an hour, they give you a chance to take a deep breath, put up your feet, have a cup of coffee, and leaf through a magazine. If your child no longer naps, encourage him to crawl into bed with some toys or books at a regular time each day.

After-school or Saturday activities: The YMCA or YWCA and other community organizations often have programs for school-aged children at nominal cost. Investigate the possibilities in your community. The children will enjoy these activities and you can spend some hours away from them. It is especially important for a working mother or father to have a few hours weekly to themselves.

Visitation: If your ex-spouse lives nearby and visitation is set up on a regular basis, this time can provide you with real relief from parenting. You need to plan the time to use for yourself, so when the children return home, you will feel genuinely refreshed and ready to resume your responsibilities. For working parents whose time is limited, visitation can be especially important. Don't resent the time your children spend with their other parent. They need this time with him and you need the time for yourself.

A note of caution — don't spend your free time on housework or other demanding chores. These free periods should be *recuperative* — read a book, see a movie, chat with friends, or go bowling — do whatever rests and relaxes you best.

Often mothers say, "Getting away from the kids for awhile sounds great, but I just can't afford it!" After divorce, finances are usually tight. But how much would it cost if you became physically or emotionally ill and were unable to care for your children? Being overloaded and tense contributes greatly to poor health. Ulcers, backaches, headaches, and other stress-related ailments are costly, and they in turn add more stress to your life. A little preventive medicine — the few hours a week to yourself — is well worth the price!

With some ingenuity and planning you can carve out some time for yourself. *Remember: a break from coping is not only good for you, it is also good for your children!*

3. *Simplify your life.* When you are in a state of chaos, you need to simplify your life and your routines. Obviously, some things must be done: shopping, making meals, doing laundry, washing dishes, and maintaining the house, going to work. But you don't have to iron frilly pinafores and blouses for your daughter. She and the family can get along just as well with easy-care clothing. Nor do you need to prepare elaborate menus. You know the children will be just as happy eating hamburgers several times a week as they would be eating fancy food with a French name!

When the chairperson of the March of Dimes calls, asking you to be a block worker, say firmly, "No, not this year." There will be other years when you can help out. The same is true of being room mother, serving as president of the P.T.A., or being treasurer for the office coffee fund. Say no! Don't feel defensive or ashamed. You are coping with enough; don't add any extra pressures at this moment. Right now you need all your energy to stay on top; later you will need extra energy to rebuild your life.

Also avoid tackling jobs which breed problems and require decisions. This is not the time to clean out the basement, sort through your dresser drawers, or go through the mess in the hall closet. All these jobs require decision-making: "Shall I keep it or throw it out?" "And if I keep it, where do I store it?" Even minor decisions cause stress; and, to repeat, *you don't need any extra stress in your life.* If the urge to clean the house develops, wash windows or scrub the kitchen floor. Those tasks use nervous energy but do not involve decision-making!

Sit down with the children and make a list of chores which must be done in order to keep the house and the family running smoothly. Try to find shortcuts or ways that you can simplify the household chores. Ask the children to choose from the list a few chores for which they can assume responsibility. Let them know how important their contribution is.

Simplifying your routines has a double benefit. It not only makes your life less stressful, but it also puts you in control — on top of life. And that feeling contributes greatly to your sense of well-being.

4. *Move your body.* Being under stress is like being inside a pressure cooker. If some steam is not let off, the pot explodes! Anger and frustration, confusion and depression all work together, moving you closer to the point of explosion. Like Barbara, you begin to find every part of your life appearing to work against you. And, the worse things become, the angrier and more upset you are.

How can you safely release steam? One of the best ways is to channel the angry feelings into physical activity. It doesn't matter whether you run around the block three times, do pushups, swim, bowl, play tennis, or scrub the kitchen floor. The important thing is to use energy constructively. It is far better to release hostility by slamming a ball across a court than by beating your child, yelling at your boss, or converting your anger into a pounding headache. Again, by choosing your activity, you are establishing control in your life.

One woman who found herself constantly irritated after her divorce set up a morning exercise program. It had an unexpected bonus. Her teenage daughter who was worried about her figure joined her. Sylvia was delighted, for this was the daughter with whom she was having so many problems. Exercising together in the morning (and sharing coffee afterward) helped to narrow the gap between them.

Ask yourself what form of physical activity is best for you. Is it something to do alone (like situps or swimming), with someone else (jogging, tennis), with a team (bowling), or with the children (bicycling, racing in the park, or even jumping rope)? Try to make it part of your regular routine — not something you do when you are nervous. You will be surprised at how much better you will soon feel.

5. *Change a few routines.* You feel lousy—swinging between depression and hostility. There is a huge vacuum. You are still in mourning—still in shock over separation. You and your children all feel the emptiness.

What can you do? One thing you can do immediately is change a few routines. What time have you been eating supper? Was that time established because of the hour your husband came home from work? What time would you like to eat? Would 4:30 suit you and the children better? Or would snacking after school and a late dinner be easier? Did you always eat in the dining room? What about setting the kitchen table and eating more informally? Or what about a little party tonight in the living room? You could take your dinner on trays and sit around the coffee table. Or how about eating early and then popping corn while you and the children watch a favorite television show?

When was the last time you lay on the rug and played cards or Parcheesi? Silly? Maybe, but fun! Or what about sharing a book you used to love when you were a child? Gather everyone together and read aloud for half an hour before bedtime. Your children will appreciate your closeness and you will catch a little of their liveliness, which you need.

In other words, shake the old, stale, useless routines. Even though you don't feel like trying something new, try it anyway. *Putting a little fun where the hurt was is good medicine.* And it is amazing how quickly your mood will change. You and your children will feel more positive about life. As a bonus, you will also find the children moving further toward adjustment.

None of this need be elaborate or require much planning. Just do something spontaneously to get you out of the old rut!

6. *Talk to your children.* When you feel overwhelmed, you need the children's cooperation. But at this time they also feel stress and tend to act out their conflicts. Their problems add to your problems, and this situation can quickly become cyclic. How can you break out of this dilemma?

One way is to be open with your children. As much as possible, answer their questions. If you don't know the answers, tell them truthfully that you are still thinking about things and that as soon as you make definite plans you will tell them. In fact, the more you can include them in the planning, the better.

You don't have to play the stiff-upper-lip role with your children.

It doesn't work anyway. They see through you, and it only makes them more anxious when you pretend that everything is coming up roses when there isn't a flower to be seen for miles! One child, aged ten, said about her mother, "She keeps telling us about how we're going to have a super good life without dad, but I can hear her crying at night."

That doesn't mean you should subject your children to crying jags or hysterics. But it does mean that you can say to them, "Look, I really don't feel too great right now. I know the divorce is best for us all, but it's going to take me some time to pull myself together. Sometimes I'm going to be uptight and cross, and I may scold you when it really isn't your fault. If I do, tell me and we'll try to work things out. Meanwhile, let's all of us try to hang on. And remember, even if I'm not the greatest to live with right this minute, I do love you and I am going to get our lives in order." In one family when the mother was very upset, she pinned a big purple button on her clothing. It said: "Out to lunch." The children knew that they should be careful then. You'll be surprised how much understanding and sympathy children have when they are talked to as human beings!

7. *Treat yourself!* Finally, one of the most important things to remember when you are overloaded and anxious is that you need a reward. Remember how you felt when your teacher pasted a gold star above your first smudgy handwritten paper? Even then, although you knew your line of A's was wobbly and sometimes barely legible, your teacher rewarded you because it was your best effort. Now you are grown up and have no teacher; you have to reward yourself! You deserve this reward, for even if your life is not going smoothly, you are putting a great deal of effort into living.

What can you do to treat yourself? Obviously, for each person it is something different. For one mother it is sleeping until noon on the day her ex-husband has the children. For another it is getting her hair done weekly. Some people have a special hobby or interest on which they like to spend time. For others it is going out to eat with a friend.

What you do is not as important as what it means to you. Hiking in the woods alone may seem grim to one person while spending money on a manicure may seem frivolous to another.

What do *you* like to do? Make a list of some things which are treats for you and, at least once a week, make sure you include them in your life. The early months after separation are difficult and demand a great deal of fortitude from you. You certainly are worthy of rewards and treats. One word of caution, however. Don't reward yourself with things which are immoral, illicit, addictive, or fattening! You'll only create more problems for yourself.

These seven techniques for coping will not solve your problems, but they will keep you on your feet until you can begin facing your realities as a single parent.

REMEMBER

Raising children and managing a home are challenging tasks for two parents. For the newly separated single parent, the undertaking is almost impossible. Your children need your help now! They cannot wait for you to pull yourself together from the trauma of separation and divorce. You will need help to get through the coming weeks and months. Seek the counsel of friends, relatives, or if indicated, professionals. You need to feel support and assurance in order to help your children. Review the first-aid tips for coping. They will help direct you in positive ways of coping and parenting.

7

Creating the Single-Parent Family

You've been separated from your husband for some weeks now. His car doesn't come up the driveway at 5:20; and you do not hear his usual call, "Honey, I'm home!" He no longer sits at his place for dinner, no longer lounges on the couch by the television set watching football games, and no longer bellows from the shower, "Bring me a towel!" He no longer shares your bed, takes out the garbage, mows the lawn, or helps put the kids to bed.

He's gone, and you are left struggling with feelings of relief and loneliness. There's no more fighting, but now, despite the piping of children's voices, the house often seems unbearably quiet.

But *you're* not the only one to notice the quiet. The children notice it too. Remember the first night at dinner when no one sat in Daddy's chair? It remained empty — almost as if he were late, expected at any moment. Now every evening at six, the children still tend to tiptoe through the living room, for this was the time for Daddy's television news. When it's bedtime and there's only Mommy to kiss them good-night, Daddy's *non*-presence is keenly felt.

THE SHADOW FATHER

Daddy is gone, and yet the children and you seem more aware of him than when he was home each night. The house doesn't feel the same. His shadow hovers, influencing the behavior of all members of the family. In some families, missing Daddy is not discussed, and the children quickly sense that talk of their father is definitely taboo. In other families, the children remark wistfully, "I wish Daddy

would come back." Or angrily, "If Daddy was here . . ." In all families, whether the children perceived their father negatively, positively, or a combination of both, Father (or, of course, Mother, if she
is the one who left) may be invisible in the home, but a ghost is
clearly present.

Virginia Satir, the well-known family therapist, explains in her
book *Peoplemaking* how such ghosts affect the people who remain
in the home:

> I believe that anyone who has ever been part of a family leaves
> a definite impact. A departed person is often very much alive in
> the memories of those left behind. Frequently, too, these mem-
> ories play an important role in what is going on in the present,
> and much of the time a negative one. . . . If the departure has
> not been accepted, for whatever reason, the ghost is very much
> still around and often can "bug up" the current scene.

In contrast to the death of a parent, divorce leaves the members of
the family coping not only with *memories*, but also with the *living
reality* of the departed person. It is not only a matter of the absent
father's intangible presence in your home. Except in cases of outright
abandonment, you and your children have an ongoing relationship
with him. This inescapable relationship is what Paul Bohannan in his
book *Divorce and After* calls the "coparental divorce." He reminds
us that although the parents have severed their marital relationship,
the child has not severed his relationship to either of his parents.
Accordingly, the parents must work out a new relationship with
each other based on the needs of their child.

It is no use (nor is it healthy) to deny the reality of the other parent.
Neither is it possible to live as if your husband has just left for a
business trip, leaving you coping temporarily.

The Crippled Two-Parent Family?

Our society is set up for the two-parent family, and although in
1976 nearly 12 percent of families in the United States were headed
by single parents, we continue to view the single-parent family as a
deviant or even pathological model — a crippled two-parent home —
which is incapable of functioning adequately.

Because the single-parent family often views itself as a unit with a
large chunk missing, it frequently does not operate effectively. In
many respects, the single parent attempts to go on as before, but

with one-half of the parenting couple missing, life obviously cannot continue as it did in the past. Mary explains:

> When Tom left, there was a big hole in our lives. I don't just mean emotionally—though that was true, too. I mean the things that Tom used to do—mowing the grass, fixing broken things, keeping the kids in hand, settling fights—after divorce either didn't get done or didn't get done well. It didn't really occur to me to change basic patterns of my life. I didn't think about what would make things easier for the kids and me. I just tried to do the best I could without Tom. And as long as I didn't make any basic changes, the hole that he left continued to fray around the edges, getting bigger all the time.

Mary did not perceive that the single-parent family is a special entity with its own advantages, disadvantages, and unique life-styles. She acted on the premise that her home was an inadequate, crippled structure and it became just that.

As E. Le Masters notes in his book *Parents in Modern America*, research increasingly challenges society's assumption that children must be raised in a two-parent family to be psychologically healthy. As you contemplate making a new life for yourself and your children, keep in mind that children can grow healthily in many kinds of situations providing the following conditions are met:

1. Children must have some basic needs met—love and physical care, understanding, discipline, safety.
2. Children need a sense of belonging—"This is my *own* family where I am an important and unique being."
3. Children need a variety of adults of both sexes involved in their lives so they know what it is to grow up male and female.

CREATING A NEW STRUCTURE

Like Mary, many newly separated or divorced women are overwhelmed by the vacuum left by their ex-husbands. A social worker we know gives this advice: "Stop thinking about the *hole* and start thinking of the *whole!*" There is no way to fill the place someone leaves. We are unique beings who function and relate to others in unique ways. After someone leaves we must restructure our lives to fit the new realities.

It's a little like remodeling a house which doesn't entirely serve our current needs. We can't tear down walls helter-skelter, for if we do the whole structure may collapse. Instead, we must approach our task logically and with care. First we must analyze our needs and then decide what the deficits are. One of the most frustrating aspects of remodeling is that you can't do everything at once. Change has to be made in small, methodical steps. We must organize our priorities. What is most important to change? In what order is change feasible? (Obviously, you don't change the plumbing after you've sealed up the wall!)

How do we remodel our lives after divorce? How do we create the effective single-parent family? *The trick is to begin where you are, working mostly with whatever you already have, moving toward what you want.* Like remodeling a home, there are a few basic steps to restructuring our lives which we shall examine:

1. Take inventory
2. Dream a dream
3. Check reality
4. Set goals and priorities
5. Work your plan
6. Reassess frequently

ASSESSING THE PRESENT

Before trying to change something, you must first know what requires changing. In taking inventory don't delude yourself. Look at your present life without distorting lenses which make everything look either perfect and wonderful or rotten and miserable. Have the courage and objectivity to look at your life and your children's lives and truly assess the reality. Often because we are too close to our own lives we can't see clearly. In that case help may be needed. Karen tells how a trusted friend helped her determine what changes were needed to help her family stop limping along and start living a more positive and satisfying life:

I found myself constantly running yet never catching up. In the past I'd been able to manage my job and still have enough left over for the kids, but with all the stress of divorce, and with the kids reacting to Peter's being gone, things just got out of hand. It seemed all we were doing was fighting with each other.

One evening a friend (who is also divorced) and I decided we would each make a list of all the problems we were having—from the really serious things all the way down to the minor ones that were just "bugging" us. To this day I'm not sure why we started those lists. Maybe we were feeling sorry for ourselves and trying to play "can you top this?" Anyway, we were really surprised at how many of the same problems were on both lists! And we found that often each of us was able to help the other define a problem more clearly than either could alone. The main thing is that just identifying the problems on paper started us getting our lives to working more smoothly again.

Although he didn't plan it that way, Mike's assessment involved his children. He recalls (with some humor, now) that the straw that broke his back was actually a pair of socks—his own—which he saw walking out the door on the feet of his son:

It seems like such a small thing now, but at that moment, those brown socks suddenly became a symbol of all my frustration at trying to get my kids to work together and assume some responsibility for the household. Ben had run out of socks because no one was doing laundry except me and I had finally sworn I wouldn't do anyone else's laundry. After all, those kids were fifteen, sixteen, and eighteen—old enough to do their own laundry. So when Ben ran out of socks and borrowed mine, well, my explosion must have made a record on the Richter scale.

No one went to school that day, and I didn't go to work. We four sat down and for three solid hours we talked about the problems we each saw. It was the best thing we ever did because after we got the problems out on the table, we were finally able to begin planning steps to solve them. It didn't happen overnight, of course, but little by little we did get things straightened out.

Since it is often difficult to assess, pinpoint, and evaluate our problems, we have assembled an inventory to help *you*. Some of the questions may not apply to your situation—others most definitely will. Perhaps there are other questions you need to ask yourself. Feel free to expand the questionnaire to fit your own present life.

TAKING INVENTORY

1. Is your monthly income sufficient to meet your budget (including savings and a few treats)?
2. Do you receive regular, adequate child support?
3. Do you feel secure in your ability to manage your financial affairs (sticking to a budget, predicting and planning for needs, shopping wisely, etc.)?
4. Do you have savings or other resources (credit, relatives who can help, extra money-making skills, etc.) in case of emergency?
5. Is your job satisfactory (room for growth, recognition, adequate salary, good relationships with boss and co-workers)?
6. Do you need to find a job, train for a job, or go back to school for a higher degree?
7. Do you have good child-care arrangements? What about child care for illness, school holidays, and before and after school?
8. Are your home and community right for your family (space, location, recreation, cost, safety)?
9. What about transportation? Do you have a reliable car or can you manage by using public transportation — subways, buses, taxis?
10. Do you have adequate medical and dental care for yourself and your children?
11. Are you free from frequent or severe signs of stress (chronically fatigued, overwhelmed, overweight, underweight, martyred, helpless, bitter and angry, dependent on drugs or alcohol)?
12. Are your children happy in their school setting? Are they making friends, performing adequately, controlling their behavior, and relating positively to most adult figures?
13. Can you take care of your children — managing their behavior, meeting their emotional and physical needs?
14. Are you formulating some new rules and structures to meet current needs (chores, responsibilities, household routines, good times, etc.)?
15. Do you and your children have a variety of interests, ac-

tivities, recreational outlets, hobbies? Are you planning
and creating some good times?

16. Are you increasingly able to accept yourself as "single" – a
    separate, independently functioning human being? Are
    your children able to accept your changed role?

17. Are you and your children increasingly comfortable and
    accepting of divorce, including current living and visita-
    tion arrangements?

18. Do you have a support system helping you raise your
    children (children's father, relatives, church, school, com-
    munity organizations, friends)?

19. Are you and your children able to accept your feelings and
    express them in constructive ways?

20. Do you and your children have reasonable positive self-
    esteem? Are you able to give and receive love?

Look over your answers. Do the problems form a pattern? Are the
problems especially linked to job dissatisfaction? Behavioral or emotional problems? Being overwhelmed with new roles? Does your
relationship with your ex-spouse give you the most trouble? Are
money worries the most pressing concern? (The lack of sufficient
money to maintain the standard of living to which they had been
accustomed is a major problem reported by single mothers.) Try to
make priorities for solving problems. Which problems are causing
the most discomfort? Which have the easiest solutions? Try to be
open and creative in exploring solutions to your problems.

DREAM A DREAM

You've examined your present situation. You've assessed deficiencies and strengths in your life. You're searching for solutions to your
problems. Before drawing up a master plan for putting your life in
order, stop a moment. Close your eyes and take one more step –
dream a little! What would you really like in your life? Furs? A cruise
to Bermuda? A fancy sports car? Do you really wish you were a
lawyer, a doctor, a firefighter, an officer in the marines? Is your
secret fantasy going on a safari, deep sea diving, or becoming a
Masters and Johnson sex therapist?

Don't be hemmed in at this point by the realities in your life. For
the moment, forget that you have only $3.78 in your bank account
and your penny collection has diminished to a record low of seven-

teen cents! Forget that you have three screeching children clamoring for dinner and that the cat just had another litter of seven kittens. Just let your mind soar above the clutter in your life. Erase the ceaseless demands and ask yourself:

> What do I really want?
> If I had my life to live over, where would I want to be?
> If I had three wishes, what would I want?
> How would I like my life to be tomorrow?
> A year from now?
> Two years from now?
> Five years from now?

Write down your dreams. In a day or two, look at the list again. Subtract from or add to it.

Incidentally, your children might also enjoy this game. Ask them to list three wishes. What would they ask for? (Don't be surprised or discouraged to find one of their wishes is that their parents be reunited. As we've mentioned before, that dream persists for some time.) If they feel secure with you and one another, they may wish to share their lists. Don't force them. Children have a right to privacy. You may wish to share your list with them (although you would probably be wise to edit your list if it includes a wish that you had never had any children).

When your wishes seem unattainable, why encourage this exercise of fantasy? Because, as many people realize when they try it, your list of wishes may not be entirely unattainable. Although you may not be able to implement any one of your dreams in its entirety, often you will find that you can make parts of those dreams come true. Sylvia tells how this technique changed her life:

> The life I was living was based on dull routine. I typed reports for an insurance agency from nine to five. Every day was pretty much the same as every other day, and I could hardly bear the prospect of another Monday going to work. When I examined my dream list, it was filled with dreams of adventure. I realized that realistically, with three kids to raise, I probably would never become a tour guide to the Middle East, but I could change my job to something less predictable — a bit more exciting!

I loved houses, enjoyed people, had a head for numbers, and had always been interested in real estate. So I began an evening class in real estate sales. I started as a part-time realtor and, after a few months, took the risk and quit my secretarial job. I've never regretted it! I'm making more money (though not in predictable amounts) than I've ever made, and I'm constantly challenged and excited by my job. In fact, I'm studying now to get my broker's license. I'm ready to go into business for myself!

By studying the underlying feelings or tone of her dreams, Sylvia was able to bring her routinized life more into accord with her secret desire for adventure and challenge. Study your dream list in the same way. Are there any themes running through it? Do you pine for adventure like Sylvia? Or is predictability and stability your strongest desire? Do you dream of a life more orderly than the one you are now living? More financially secure? Do your dreams involve you with more or fewer people than your present life? Do your dreams indicate a need for a bit more spotlight and recognition? You may find ways to incorporate pieces of your dreams as you plan the remodeling of your life.

REMODELING — THE BALANCING ACT

The next step in creating the effective single-parent home is a series of delicate balancing acts — not an easy task, but well worth the effort. Think of a teeter-totter: on one side, what *is* — on the other, what you would *like*. On one side balance your experiences, skills, and needs (the realities of your life) — on the other side, place your dreams. On one side are your own needs and desires — on the other, those of your children. On one side the predictable knowns — on the other, the unpredictable uncertainties.

Balancing involves a series of trade-offs. For instance, as Sylvia said, "When I went into real estate, I had to balance the risk of failure with the risk of losing my mind if I had to spend another year typing those reports. Spending time in a mental institution didn't seem like that much fun!"

What do you have to balance? Look at your questionnaire of present problems; look at your list of dreams. See whether any of your dreams can be modified to help with the problems. For example, foremost on Karen's problem list were financial worries. On her wish list Karen indicated her desire to raise pedigreed Shelties.

I never took that wish seriously, mainly because Peter, my ex-husband, hated dogs. After divorce, it didn't occur to me that I was free to do as I pleased. I had long ago put the idea of raising dogs out of my mind, and until I did the "dream-a-dream" exercise, it lay buried. The funny thing is that my oldest son put raising dogs on his list, too. Only he wanted to raise Labrador retrievers!

Karen and her sons did decide to raise dogs. Not only did the enterprise make their family more cohesive (extra bonus!), but eventually they were able to add extra money to their income from this activity.

Obviously, solutions like this don't always fall into place so easily, but often if we remain open and flexible, we can see alternatives we didn't think of before. Getting help is another way to see alternatives — after all, "two heads are better than one" — especially when the heads are on two separate shoulders!

IF YOU FAIL TO PLAN, YOU'RE PLANNING TO FAIL

In order to make changes in your life, you must plan, make goals, and take concrete steps toward those goals. Be realistic. Setting an unrealistic goal will greatly increase the chances of failure.

When thinking about major goals, make priorities. Remember when we were talking about remodeling the house? You can't do everything at once. What part of your life most needs *immediate* change? What small something can you do *now* to make your life and your children's lives less stressful and more rewarding? Make a list of the steps that will help you reach your final goal — some objectives to follow on the way.

Make the steps so small they sound easy. If you don't break up the major goal into concrete steps, you can easily become overwhelmed. Think of Barbara whom we discussed in the last chapter. She couldn't manage her two preschool children, she hated her job, she was financially pinched, and she felt constantly overworked and tired. With some help from her therapist, Barbara identified two major problems on which to begin focusing:

1. Managing the children better
2. Finding a more satisfying and better paying job

At first both of these problems seemed insurmountable because each involved many intermediate goals and steps. Barbara tells us how she got started:

My first goal was just to get control of mornings. I realized I was so rushed that if Nina spilled her milk or Jeremy dawdled, I'd fly into a rage. And then the kids would start crying and I'd feel guilty and awful. By the time we'd leave the house, the day was well on its way to being rotten.

Barbara decided to try three new techniques the first week:

1. Wake the kids fifteen minutes earlier
2. Help the kids to choose their clothes each night and lay them out for the next morning
3. Set the table and decide on the breakfast menu the night before

"It was amazing," Barbara reports, "how three simple things could make so much difference." Barbara found that her three techniques for getting control of the morning involved a little planning the night before. "That was part of the unexpected bonus! Instead of leaving the dinner dishes on the table at night, I had to get them cleared away in order to set the table for breakfast. It made me feel better to get those dishes done."

Another unexpected bonus was that when Jeremy and Nina chose their clothes (with a little help from Mom), they were much more enthusiastic about getting dressed in the morning. "Often they'd be dressed before I was out of the shower and they felt so proud of themselves!" The next week Barbara added something new:

I told the kids that if they were all dressed and finished with breakfast by 7:55, we'd have five minutes left for me to read a book to them. Only one morning did they miss, and the next day they were ready ten minutes earlier! It's something fun that even I look forward to.

From managing mornings better it was a small step (or actually steps) to finding ways to make evenings go more smoothly.

Finding a better job also involved a process of steps. Barbara again made a list of what it would take to get a better paying secretarial job:

1. Brush up on shorthand
2. Increase typing speed
3. Write a resumé
4. Send out resumé

5. Get a new hairdo
6. Get more stylish clothing

None of these goals could be accomplished overnight. Barbara made a schedule.

I thought it would take me about six weeks to brush up on my shorthand and increase my typing to seventy words per minute. I knew I couldn't afford to run out and buy all new clothes, but I could start sewing a wardrobe and shopping sales for shoes and accessories.

Barbara made a specific time commitment for each of the steps on her list and promised herself that in three months she would have a new job. "I couldn't believe it. It turned out just as I had planned," says Barbara with a broad smile. Each goal that Barbara accomplished made her feel more in control. Her self-esteem rose and as she felt increasingly better about herself and her capabilities; she enjoyed life more. The angry, harried Barbara has been replaced by a more attractive, happier woman who is better able to attend to her own needs as well as her children's needs.

Remember the adage, Plan your work and work your plan. As you can see, planning *is* important! It is the vital first step to change. But to reach a goal, it is not enough to plan: you must also *work your plan!*

ATTACKING THE PROBLEMS

The single-parent home cannot work the same way the two-parent home did. To be effective, the single parent has to be flexible, trying new methods, looking at options and alternatives, and seeking help from others. Over the years, we have met and talked with many successful single parents — both men and women. Are they superhuman? Definitely not! Most of them have struggled with the same problems you are now facing. In general, we found that although the problems are similar, their solutions vary greatly. Each person and each family is unique. Life-styles which are effective evolve slowly and often need to be changed and modified.

ORGANIZING THE FAMILY

One of the first problems the single parent must attack is organizing the family for effective functioning. Many of the rules and regulations that governed the two-parent home do not fit the new structure. Planning how the new family unit will accomplish the daily tasks that face every home may not be the most creative challenge facing the new single parent, but it is a very important first step in creating a successful single-parent home.

RULES, ROUTINES, AND REORGANIZATION

Are there rules in your family? Who made them? Does everyone know the rules? Who enforces them? Can rules be changed? What happens when someone breaks the rules?

What about schedules and routines? Who takes out the garbage and trash, washes the dishes? When is dinner time? When is homework done? How much television can be watched? When? Who chooses? Who establishes bedtime? Curfews? When do teens use the car? Who pays for the gas? Who feeds the dog, waters the plants, mows the grass, does the shopping, pays the bills, fixes the leaking faucet? Who provides the treats and plans the fun times? How and when and by whom do all the jobs in the family get done?

In most families these tasks usually do get done, but some families manage more efficiently and pleasantly than others. We all know families which are ruled by disorganization, constant crises, and endless bickering. Without some order and structure, we are indeed thrown into chaos — an exhausting condition!

Families, like all organizations, adopt ways of getting things done. Virginia Satir calls this process "family engineering." She points out:

> It isn't too different from engineering anywhere else in that a family, like a business, has time, space, equipment, and people to get its work done. With any kind of engineering, you find out what you have, match it with what you need, and figure out the best way to use it. You also find out what you don't have and figure out a way to get it.

Family engineering is a vital part of restructuring the single-parent home, since when a family member leaves, for whatever reason, the resources of the family are temporarily diminished. The family needs to reassess and reorganize. For example, if Father always took out the garbage, the kitchen is going to reek if no one takes over the job.

The needs of the family may also change when a member leaves. What point is there in having dinner at 6:15 (the time Dad used to get home) if all members of the family are now home and hungry at 5:30? The rules too may need to be altered. If a child was used to telling his mother that he was leaving the house and now his mother has a job, he can't call her every few minutes to tell her where he's going and what he's doing. New rules will have to be worked out.

Satir suggests that before making new rules, we first need to check whether we all know what the current rules are. Often, she says, children don't really know the rules well enough to comply. Next, we need to evaluate each rule and see whether it now applies.

Try to decide exactly what it is you wish to accomplish with rules. For instance, it is important to know where your children are at all times. If they can't ask your permission to go somewhere after school, what can they do? Leave a note? Check with a neighbor? Ask you before they leave for school in the morning? What will be the new rule? Remember, for a new rule to work it must be enforced consistently. When rules are not consistently used, children tend to test their limits and their behavior becomes increasingly difficult to manage.

Who makes the rules? Who establishes the routines? You can run your family democratically — one person, one vote — or autocratically — *you* make all the decisions. The best way is a combination approach. Sometimes you need to take the reins and make decisions. Often, however, you can get the children together and all of you can try to work out solutions. When a child suggests an alternative and it is adopted, he has a vested interest in making his suggestion work.

Keeping the children involved in family engineering is wise, for in the coming years you're going to need all the help and positive group spirit you can get to make things work. It's also good practice for the children in becoming adults. As much as possible, try to strike a balance. Don't always dictate how things will be done, but don't be afraid to put your foot down at times. Sometimes children need the limits of your firmness.

A LIST OF SUGGESTIONS

Following is a list of suggestions for family engineering. Use some ideas and think of others.

1. Divide up chores. If someone especially loves to clean the toilet, by all means let him do it! Otherwise, rotate chores.
2. Make a weekly chore chart and post it on the bulletin board.

3. Sometimes make something pleasant (like dinner) contingent upon a chore being finished.
4. Make contracts with your children for special jobs. Reward with money, treats, or favors. Remember to use liberal amounts of praise and recognition!
5. Decide how television viewing will be handled. Is it a privilege or a right? Is voting on shows possible? (How many hours your children watch is *your* responsibility.)
6. Family councils are excellent as a format for decision-making. Find a time which is convenient for everyone and try not to allow anything to interfere. Elect a child secretary each week or rotate the job. Keep notes and date them. They become a fascinating diary! Establish an agenda each week so problems can be aired. Be sure to put *positive* items on the agenda, too.
7. If mornings are chaotic (and they often are), try to organize them better. Have clothing ready the night before. Simplify breakfast menus. Set homework, books, or other items which have to be taken to school or work in a spot by the door so they won't be forgotten. Plan the use of the bathroom during rush hours!
8. If dinnertime is the problem, know your menu before you leave for work. Defrost something in the morning. Have the children responsible for setting the table, helping you in the kitchen, or even starting the dinner before you get home.
9. Cook ahead on weekends and freeze dinners for the week. If you make spaghetti or macaroni and cheese one night, make a double portion and freeze the remaining half so you can use it on a busy evening the following week.
10. Don't underestimate how much responsibility your child can handle — even the little ones. A ten-year-old can be trained to sort laundry and set dials. An eight-year-old can run the vacuum (not as well as you, perhaps, but not badly either)! A four-year-old can make sure the dog is fed and his bowl of water freshened. How good children feel when they know their contributions are valuable!

Remember that although you may be tempted to believe that organizing the family takes too much time, routines actually save time and reduce conflict. A final word of caution: *be flexible. We*

advocate rules and routines, but not rigidity and regimentation.
Nothing stifles growth and pleasure faster than becoming a slave to
routine. As always, strive for a middle ground.

MANAGING THE FIX-ITS

"Mommy, Mommy!" Billy wailed as he ran into the house. "The
chain just came off my bike and I can't put it back on! I've tried and
tried. I need Daddy to help me fix it!"

Part of reorganizing is finding ways to manage the jobs the absent
parent used to do. In many homes, "fixing it" is Father's role. After he
leaves, you can't let everything fall into ruin. Somehow jobs like
fixing Billy's bike, putting a new washer on the dripping faucet,
painting the house trim, and servicing the car must still be done.
There are really only two alternatives: either you must find *someone
else* to do those jobs or *you* must take over.

FINDING OTHERS TO HELP

Some women are not comfortable in the fix-it role. Others work
and don't have time to repair the house. Betty, thirty-four, with
three school-aged children is very frank:

> I think it's great to be a handywoman, but it's just not my bag. I
> grew up in a household of boys and neither Mom nor I ever so
> much as picked up a screwdriver. When I got married, Frank
> repaired everything. Now it's hard for me to shed old attitudes.
> I just can't imagine myself lying under a sink with a wrench in
> my hand—and besides, I'm all thumbs.

Betty was fortunate to have her brother living nearby. A few times a
year and in emergencies, he does repair work around the house.

Carol, a mother of four young children, had a different approach.
As a pathologist working long hours in a hospital, Carol had little
time, energy, or desire to tackle repairs or maintenance jobs.

> Our large, old house was rapidly falling apart. The kids were
> forever bringing me pieces—doorknobs, hinges, screws, and
> chunks of plaster which had mysteriously fallen out of the wall
> just as a child walked by! I was getting desperate. Then one
> night I had this crazy idea. The next morning I placed an ad in
> the neighborhood paper for a retired handyman who liked
> children. I received a surprising number of calls!

Carol chose a gentleman who lived a few blocks away. "Pops," as the children call him, had been recently widowed, lived far from his grandchildren, and was very lonely. He enjoyed spending time at Carol's house doing odd jobs and was willing to help out for nominal compensation. And the children loved "helping" him. Carol's idea paid off in rich dividends for everyone. The children's lives were enriched by their new "grandfather," Carol felt reassured that the house was not going to collapse, and an elderly man found himself important and needed again.

When thinking about help for chores, don't forget neighborhood teenagers who need extra money. Or find an older teen or college student who can do the necessary repair jobs. Check with the high school or college near you.

Sometimes, however, a solution which initially seemed ideal becomes untenable. Joan and Jim's divorce was the highly civilized type that other divorced people envy (and distrust). It seemed perfectly reasonable for Jim to come over periodically and take care of the house, lawn, and car. But soon Joan discovered that the day after Jim came over, the children were excessively irritable and demanding. The problem was soon brought more sharply into focus. Joan reports:

One day I heard the kids arguing with a neighbor child. Debbie, who was then five, was screaming, "My daddy does too live here. You'll see him tomorrow!" It suddenly dawned on me that even though we'd been divorced for over a year, it really wasn't very clear to Debbie. In fact, I realized Jim and I didn't really accept the divorce as final either.

Especially for younger children, this kind of situation is very confusing. When the children see their father back in his accustomed role, their hopes for reconciliation rise. Then when he leaves, all the old pain engulfs them anew. In this case, Joan and Jim needed counseling to help them define their situation and deal with their own feelings.

MANAGING THE FIX-ITS YOURSELF

Some single mothers are perfectly comfortable and capable of assuming the role of handywoman. They like the hammering and fixing and enjoy being responsible for these jobs. We know a woman who took a course in car maintenance and now regularly gives her car tune-ups. In fact, she also cares for her neighbor's car in exchange for babysitting before and after school. Learning new skills is both challenging and a boost to your ego. The more capable you are, the more confident you become. Your self-esteem cannot help but rise as your ability to care for yourself and your children increases.

However, be prepared for criticism as you take on fix-it chores. Your children, used to Daddy's ways, may give you unsolicited advice or make gloomy predictions. "That nail is *not* going to hold up that painting. Daddy would use a bigger one," or "If you want to know, Daddy always kicks the dryer to make it start again." (You don't want to know, but sure enough, you kick it and it starts again!) The refrain, "That's not the way Daddy does it!" repeated often enough can send the most placid woman into a rage. Karen, after hearing this for the umpteenth time while she was changing a light bulb, lost her temper and shouted back, "It may not be the way Daddy does it, but it *is* the way Mommy does it!" Her outburst was a good assertive statement, but as Karen admits, "It would have been a bit more effective if I hadn't at that moment stepped back and fallen off the stool!"

If your children (especially teenagers) are prone to give advice, include them in the adventure of making repairs. You may be surprised how much they already know—especially if they've tagged their father, "assisting" him with household chores and repairs.

HOW TO ACQUIRE NEW FIX-IT SKILLS

1. Check the local library for simply written and diagrammed how-to books. Also check with utility and appliance companies. They often publish easily followed manuals and guides.
2. Check into mini-courses at adult or community education centers. They offer a wide variety of courses at a nominal fee.
3. Get a handy friend to teach you a few basic survival skills like replacing an electric plug, changing a tire, and handling a few simple tools.

Becoming a "fixer" only requires instruction and practice. Turn to outside resources for the know-how, and with children in the house you'll have plenty of opportunities to practice!

SOLVING MONEY PROBLEMS

"I have no problems *with* money," a young mother corrected us, "My problems are all *without* money!" Lack of money ranks high on most single parents' lists of concerns. Few women today request or receive alimony, and child support payments rarely cover the children's total needs. Most mothers are soon pressed to find ways to make ends meet. Basically, there are only two ways: (1) increase your income or (2) decrease your expenditures. Of course, the most effective plan combines the two approaches: decreasing your expenses while increasing your income.

TIPS FOR INCREASING YOUR INCOME

Increasing your income may be difficult, at least initially. Generally it involves finding a job or finding a better paying job. Either task will take time and must be approached systematically for best results. Here are a few tips to keep in mind:

1. Start with a skill inventory. What can you do? How marketable are your present skills? What new skills could you acquire in a reasonable length of time? (Remember your hobbies and avocations. What skills do they involve?)
2. Set realistic goals. Determine the steps which will be needed to reach each goal.
3. Check with job counselors for availability of jobs. Get description of skills needed. Watch for trends. Check the help wanted ads in the newspaper. Check government listings of jobs available. Talk to personnel at trade schools, colleges, or universities.
4. Write a good, legible, and well-organized resumé. You can get professional help or look in the library for a book which shows you the format. Be sure to include volunteer work which emphasizes your skills.
5. Ask people for letters of recommendation which specifically mention the qualities you feel are your strengths.
6. If skipped or partial child support payments become a problem, consult your lawyer or district attorney. Increasingly, states are working cooperatively to help enforce child support stipulations. It's better to seek counsel than to involve your children in games of withholding visitation or asking your child to inquire about missed payments.

TIPS FOR DECREASING YOUR EXPENSES

The second approach to financial solvency involves a considerable amount of ingenuity and thought but it can provide some immediate relief. If you can manage to cut $25 a month on your food bill, $10 on clothing, $5 a month on your utilities, and $3 a month on gasoline, you will have $43 more each month. "But," you say, "I don't know where to cut anymore!" Perhaps one or two of the following tips may help you think of new ideas for saving money.

Buy day-old bread from the bakery or from the day-old shelf at the supermarket. (Our kids call it "used" bread!)

Check the shelf at the supermarket in which slightly limp or overripe produce is stocked. (Overripe tomatoes, for example, are wonderful when cooked.)

Use powdered milk to stretch whole milk. When it's chilled the children won't even notice.

Clip low cost recipe ideas from magazines and post them on the bulletin board where you'll be reminded to use them.

Put one of the children in charge of clipping and saving coupons. Make sure you take the coupons (and the responsible child) to the store with you and plan your menus around the bargains.

Use house brands instead of national brands when possible.

Check in your paper for weekly or monthly leader items at special prices and for seasonal best buys.

Use leftovers wisely. Freeze bits of this and that to make your own TV dinners or soups. Let each child assemble his own TV dinner.

Include a meatless night in the week. Exchange a beef night for a bean night!

Cut back on junk foods. They are expensive, fattening, and non-nutritious. When the TV munchies occur, substitute home-made popcorn for a bag of potato chips.

Cut back on desserts and drinks low in nutrition. You'll save money on food and dental bills.

Avoid convenience foods which are more expensive. If you're working you will, of course, have to balance the need to conserve money with the need to conserve time and energy.

Let older children plan and shop for a week at a time. Reward the ones who provide tasty, nutritious, and economical meals!

Sometimes cook in the evening for the following night. This enables you to use cheaper cuts of meat which require slow cooking, permits you to bake beans, or make soup—all the time-consuming but delicious meals which you don't have time to do when you get home from work. A crock pot that cooks while you work can also be used for these dishes.

Never shop for dinner on the way home. When you're hungry and harried, it's almost impossible to resist impulse buying— and that always increases the food bill!

Check the thrift stores for clothing and other goods. Remember that your attitude greatly affects your children's acceptance of used items. If you convey a sense of martyrdom, anger, or embarrassment, they won't want to wear anything from Goodwill. If, however, you convey enthusiasm and a sense of adventure, they'll also get caught up in the bargain hunting.

If you must buy a car, check with a mechanic or a trusted and mechanically inclined friend. A used car may appear to be a bargain (and indeed it may be), but if it devours gas and oil and suffers from an odd assortment of aches and pains which will keep it in the repair shop, it may be no bargain.

Consider the pros and cons of keeping your present home. You will especially need to balance the financial savings against the psychological discomfort of uprooting the family.

If you own a home with equity, check with a financial advisor in your bank about the pros and cons of borrowing against the equity.

Consider taking in a college student or older person as a roomer.

Become aware of family services in your community. Do you qualify for low-income benefits such as food stamps, free or low cost medical and dental care? Are counseling and therapy services available free or at nominal cost?

Ask about scholarship possibilities for your children. Many preschools, camps, community centers, and so on, offer full or partial scholarships for families in need.

Consider whether your children qualify for free or reduced fee lunches at school.

Consider inexpensive recreational possibilities such as the zoo, museums, community swimming pools, Little League baseball games, picnics with friends, overnight camping trips (sometimes in your own backyard), the library, free concerts, etc. Check your newspaper for free or inexpensive events and activities and include them in your schedule.

Cutting down financially doesn't have to be as grim as it first appears. Many families find they spend more time together and feel closer because they had to pull together to find solutions to financial problems. In a school essay simply entitled, "Money," a ten-year-old girl wrote, "Since the divorce, Daddy and Mommy are poorer now and we get to do a lot more fun things than movies. Like we have bicycle races in the park and we eat hot dogs and baked beans more often and we wrap our birthday presents in the comics instead of wrapping paper." This child sees few drawbacks in a bit of well-planned poverty!

EXTENDING THE FAMILY

When we view visitation with the other parent not as something to be tolerated at best and to be dreaded at worst, but as a positive, enriching experience akin to the extended family, we free our children to develop an open guilt-free relationship with their other parent.

Elizabeth, divorced three years ago, is a single mother of two children. Asked to share her feelings about visitation, she answered thoughtfully:

You know, it's funny, but in a way my ex-husband is my best friend. Oh, not in that we can confide in each other, but as a support and backup person with the kids. For example, it's wonderful knowing that I can leave town for a few days with-

out worrying about babysitters or whether the kids are missing
me. I know they're happy and safe with Joel.

Elizabeth and Joel's children are fortunate, for their parents have
been able to dissolve their marital union without dissolving their
parental partnership. Elizabeth explains:

> I think of Joel like my mother used to think of her mother-in-
> law — my grandmother. After an hour with Grandma, Mom
> would start to climb the walls. But we kids loved Grandma and
> Mom used to let us visit on weekends and in the summer. Just
> because Mom couldn't stand Grandma didn't mean *we* couldn't
> love her. That's the way it is with Joel. He drives me wild, but
> the kids adore him and he's crazy about them. Why shouldn't
> they love each other and spend time together? Besides, just
> being practical, I gain from the arrangement. Every other
> weekend I get a break from the demands of "Mommy,
> Mommy!"

Elizabeth's attitude is remarkably healthy. Obviously, she does
not always see eye to eye with Joel (after all, they are divorced), nor
does she pretend to. But she supports the relationship between the
children and their father. She recognizes Joel's importance to the
children and appreciates the second home he provides for them. She
knows he loves and cares for Heather and Justin as much as she does,
and he wants to help them grow into healthy, happy adults.

A LIST OF VISITATION HINTS

Making visitation work takes two basic ingredients: sensitivity
and practicality. Here are some hints which combine both.

Don't view sending your child to your ex-spouse as sending
him to the enemy camp. Keep the extended family model in
mind.

Don't allow clothing and packing to become a problem. If your
children are over eight years old, they are capable of deciding
what to pack, and of packing it. Don't nag. If they take wrong
clothing or insufficient amounts, it's up to their father to make
his expectations clear.

The older the children, the more they should handle visitation
arrangements. You don't always need to insert yourself. Al-

though you and your ex-husband will probably have some general guidelines in mind, older children should increasingly assume the responsibility of communicating with their father and letting you know what the arrangements will be.

If your child has the sniffles or even the chicken pox, don't immediately cancel visitation. His father helped care for him before the divorce when he was sick; he still can. Of course, be sensitive, but caring for sick children is a part of parenting.

Be home when your children return from visitation. It's lonely to come home to an empty house. If an emergency makes it impossible, notify a neighbor to be on the lookout or provide a babysitter. Remember, however, there are no substitutes for Mother's welcoming arms.

Don't "pump" your children for details about their father's life, but do show some interest when they talk about their visitation periods. Again strive for the middle ground.

Finally, be sure you find satisfying activities for *you* to do on visitation days so you won't resent your children's good times away from you. The more full and vital your life is, the more you can allow your children to enjoy theirs.

GETTING HELP FROM OTHERS

What if your ex-husband is far away and sees the children infrequently or not at all? More than ever you need to find ways to extend the family — for your children's sake as well as for your own. You simply cannot be in charge day and night without a break and still be an effective parent. Other people who love your children need to be involved with your family. Look at your resources. Do you have family living close by — grandparents, brothers, sisters, cousins? Or do you have a close friend (perhaps another "single") who might be willing to take your children one weekend in exchange for your taking hers another time? What about someone in your church group or in a group of single parents? Forming close ties to other people is an essential part of learning to trust and care.

MAKING GOOD TIMES

Sung lustily and a bit off key, our family's theme song is "Look for the Silver Lining." Of course it's corny! We always laugh as we sing it. But we love it, for among the corn are gems of truth. Somehow singing about hearts full of joy and gladness, and looking on the sunny side of dark times, does indeed give us a shot of optimism.

Nobody can live well on a constant diet of work and worry. Remember how harried, martyred, and angry Barbara felt? Of course her children could not wait to escape from her. You've got to find or make rays of sunlight to illuminate your life.

The good times do not have to involve major planning or large expenditures. Think back to your own childhood. What did you especially enjoy? Sledding down the steepest hill in town? Picking crab apples off the tree in the backyard (or the neighbor's backyard)? Catching lightning bugs? Walking with Mom or Dad on a warm summer night to the nearest ice cream parlor for a double-dip cone? Shopping with Mom for new shoes without any of the other children along? And maybe stopping for hot cocoa afterward?

Sure, the Disneyland trips are exciting, but the little moments of happiness linger and bring back warm memories of childhood. Be creative and spontaneous. Get the children to contribute fun ideas which are not expensive. It is often an idea thought of on the spur of the moment that adds zip to life. For instance, one weary mother who came home after work to a messy house agreed to race the children. If they could pick up and vacuum the living room before she was ready to serve dinner, they would eat their dinner Roman fashion, reclining on pillows around the coffee table. The children loved it! Barbara had a similar idea:

Last week we were driving home after a long, hot day. The kids were arguing and picking at each other. I felt my stomach knot and knew it was going to be a bad evening. When we got home the apartment was unbearably warm. Nina was already in tears and Jeremy was running around like a monkey. In the past I would have fed them a can of soup for dinner, and afterward cried myself to sleep. But suddenly, I remembered my therapist's words: "Put some fun where the pain is."

I quickly spread peanut butter on bread, scraped a few carrots, gathered up some oranges, found the graham crackers, a flashlight, our library books, and an old bedspread, and off we went to the park for a picnic! While the kids played on the swings, I finished my novel — a reward to me — and later, as it grew dark, they joined me on the spread to hear their books read by flashlight. Nina fell asleep and had to be carried to the car. The kids enjoyed it so much that night picnics are now a summer tradition!

Barbara's night picnic cost nothing extra, but she and Nina and Jeremy will long remember the special warm glow of that evening.

IDEAS FOR CREATING SPECIAL TIMES

Plan frequent trips to the zoo, museum, library, or whatever other facilities your town or city offers.

Set aside entertainment money. If you have to cut your food budget to do it, take that money and put it in a jar so the kids can see that money saved benefits them. Let them help decide what should be cut and where the saved money should be spent.

Give each child a chance to plan a day or part of a day. He can make a meal or direct the family on an excursion. The older children can check the newspaper regularly for listings of free or inexpensive community events.

Provide the children with materials for a special make-up-your-face day. The children will love the freedom to experiment with trying to look like clowns, animals, and so on.

Plan bicycle excursions, races in the parks.

Plan a treasure hunt. One of our children's fondest memories is a treasure hunt around the block as part of a birthday party one year when we had little money for fancier entertainment.

Plan a time for sitting down with albums of family photos — either of the children or of your family when you were a child. Share some stories of your childhood.

Encourage the children to act out their favorite stories. Collect "costumes" from Goodwill. They may also wish to make up their own stories to act out.

Make mealtimes more fun. Play guessing games, or tell round-robin stories. Ask each to share the best part of his day. Vary what you eat, with whom you eat, and where you eat.

Have special times for "rapping" or telling ghost stories. This is another good time for sharing stories from your childhood. Children love to hear about you!

Tramp through the woods, gathering fall leaves or beautiful stones. Make a bonfire and toast marshmallows.

Try to create an atmosphere of celebrating life. Create new traditions around already celebrated holidays such as birthdays, New Year's Day, and Thanksgiving as well as previously uncelebrated holidays like Friday the 13th, Good Report Card Day, Compliment-from-My-Boss Day, and First-Lost-Tooth-of-the-Month Day. Also keep in mind occasions which arise spontaneously like the day Neil put his hand into the sock box and pulled out matching socks on the first try. An obvious good omen like that deserves celebration!

REMEMBER

As a single parent, you must discover or invent new patterns of living to replace the old ones that no longer fit. Don't be blinded by tunnel vision, for too often we limit ourselves by narrowly perceiving life and its possibilities. Feel free to imagine ideal ways of working out problems—you will undoubtedly give birth to innovative solutions. With imagination, often seemingly impractical or highly unorthodox ideas can be adjusted to make them practical and realistic. Be open and unafraid to try out and adopt life-styles and roles which uniquely fit your family's needs.

8

Part-Time
Bachelor Parent

As we have seen, the recently divorced mother has tremendous adjustments to make, and the first few months of being single can be frighteningly demanding. But what about her ex-husband? Are his adjustments to bachelor part-time father easy?

Don, a tall man with dark, curly hair, is the father of a six-year-old boy. Nine months ago his marriage ended. He reports:

I thought it would be a cinch to pick up where I left off before I was married. Somehow, the word "bachelor" recalled memories of parties, chasing women (and being chased), and a free, swinging life. And even though I knew all that was nearly ten years ago, still I took for granted that becoming single again would be fairly simple. You go out one morning, find an apartment, move in a few things, stock the refrigerator with beer, put your name on the mailbox and, snap, you're a bachelor again!

But I was totally wrong. These past nine months have been an eternity. I had no idea how lonely I'd feel and how much I'd miss my son. It hit me the first night. I came home from work, unlocked the door to my little, bare apartment, and suddenly I was overcome with grief. Troy wasn't hanging on me, trying to get my attention. Carole wasn't making her usual sarcastic remarks. My apartment was just as tidy as I had left it that morning. I was free—and all alone. I sat down on the couch and cried.

THE SWINGING BACHELOR?

Many women suspect that once their ex-husband is free of the daily responsibilities of being a husband and father, his life becomes simple and carefree. Barbara said bitterly, "My ex-husband is probably dining by candlelight at some swanky restaurant gazing into the eyes of a beautiful chick and here I am stuck with a date with the dirty-laundry basket!"

But returning to bachelorhood is not as simple or as pleasant as Barbara fantasizes. While his ex-wife is overwhelmed by too many demands on her time and energy, the ex-husband is equally overwhelmed by too much emptiness in his life. The apartment is unbearably quiet, the evenings stretch out interminably, and women do not always pursue him. Without the children to force him into coping, he may go bar-hopping to fill the empty hours or spend his time brooding and feeling sorry for himself.

It will take many months of pain and disorientation before the bachelor father is able to remake his life. Because he is the one who leaves the children and usually the one who leaves his home, his life seems particularly strange and disconnected from the past. He feels uprooted, lonely, and isolated—a stranger even to himself. In a sense, he has lost even more than the custodial parent has—he has lost the sense of belonging to a family.

In addition, because he is the one who most often moves out of the home, he often carries a tremendous sense of guilt. Although he knows that it is untrue, he feels that he has abandoned his children. In past years, our society has pointed the finger of blame at the parent who leaves, almost regardless of the circumstances. Although this attitude is slowly changing, its effects continue to linger.

Don discusses how he felt during those first months after separation:

> All I could think about was my son. I felt like such a rotten father for leaving him. In fact, I felt like a traitor. If I couldn't stand living with Carole, how could I walk out and leave Troy with her?
>
> I'd remember how Troy looked—tears running down his grimy face—as I kissed him goodbye. At that moment (and for weeks afterwards) I felt I was abandoning him totally— jumping ship and leaving him behind.

Moving out and leaving your children behind does seem like a terribly final step. You know that you'll see them again, but for the moment it does seem as if you are closing the door on your relationship.

MOTHER AS PART-TIME PARENT

Until recently, it was rare for a mother to choose to become the non-custodial parent, and our society certainly did not support her in that choice. Her friends, acquaintances, and even her family inevitably suspected her of being unfit to parent in some way (alcoholic, promiscuous, or perhaps a child-beater). The guilt she feels is often greater than that of the non-custodial father.

Although the number of non-custodial mothers has increased in recent years, our society still does not accept the non-custodial mother as fully as the non-custodial father. This is particularly true when daughters are involved. As a society, we are more apt to accept a man raising his sons (especially teenagers) than a father raising his daughters.

As we discussed in Chapter IV, there are many reasons why a woman might decide to become the non-custodial parent. It is the mark of a very mature and wise woman to be able to perceive the needs of her children with clarity and dispassion. Sometimes the decision to be the part-time parent is a temporary arrangement; sometimes it is permanent. In some cases the mother may have custody of some of the children, while the father has custody of the others (so that each parent is both a part-time parent and a custodial parent). The trend toward flexibility in custody decisions is healthy — particularly when the needs and desires of the children, as well as those of the parents, are taken into consideration.

For June, aged thirty-four, the decision to become the non-custodial parent was agonizing. When June and her husband split up, their only child, eleven-year-old Sheila, stayed with June. Soon after the divorce, June remarried and moved across the state to join her new husband. June reports:

> For Sheila, moving was awful. She not only was away from her father, she was also away from my parents who had always been close to her. Some months after I remarried, Sheila's dad also got married again. He married a woman with three kids. When Sheila went back to visit over the summer, she found she now had a large family — and she loved it! Her grandparents

were close by, she had new sisters (one her own age), and a brother. By the end of the summer she'd also grown close to her stepmother.

In the fall, Sheila came back to me, but she didn't do well in school. She kept to herself and was sad a great deal. Although Sheila couldn't tell me, I knew what was wrong with her. But she's my only child! I couldn't bear the thought of not having her live with me. I had missed her so much through the summer.

After a lot of thought (and a lot of tears), I called Sheila's dad and discussed the whole thing with him. We agreed he should have custody of Sheila.

So I became a part-time mother. Frankly, it's hard sometimes. I do miss her! I see her every couple of months, talk to her on the phone every Sunday, and we spend part of vacations together.

Although June's decision to relinquish custody was terribly difficult and painful, it was possible because of her love for her daughter. As June discovered, a part-time mother who loves her children, is interested in their development, and provides emotional support can still be an important part of her children's lives.

Because the non-custodial parent is more often a father than a mother, we have used many male references and examples in this chapter. If, however, you are a part-time mother, most of the techniques for part-time parenting apply to you. Simply change the "he" to "she"!

FEARS AND CONCERNS

If you are a parent who has been close to your child, you cannot help worrying about your relationship to him after divorce. How can you continue to be a good parent when you are not with your child every day? Undoubtedly, some of your deepest concerns are listed below.

1. *My child may forget me.* Obviously, your child is not going to forget about you, but because separation is painful, sometimes a child may act as if he doesn't care about the parent who is no longer with him on a daily basis. This is the child's way of protecting himself from his pain and acute feelings of loss. As you continue to be involved with your child, he will become increasingly assured of

your love and concern. His pretense of forgetting you or of not caring about you will gradually be dropped.

2. *My child may hate me for leaving.* Children often do initially blame the parent who leaves for the divorce. In Peggy Mann's sensitively written children's book, *My Dad Lives in a Downtown Hotel,* a young boy's feelings of anger, guilt, and sorrow following the separation of his parents are eloquently captured. We are deeply moved by Joey's attempts to deal with his initial reaction of loss and to work out his relationship to his father who left. Like Joey, children have very mixed emotions about separation. They blame each parent and they blame themselves. However, as they begin to see that they have not really lost their parent, they are able to accept the new realities in their lives and make peace with themselves and both their parents.

3. *My child may need me and I won't be there to help him.* After separation and divorce, life is not the same as it was for any member of the family. There *is* some initial heartbreak for both child and parent as each must accept the separation. No longer can you be on hand to give comfort and advice each time your child is hurt. On a daily basis, his mother who lives with him must now be the primary giver of comfort. But you can still help your child. He needs you as well as his mother. You will, however, have to learn new ways of keeping communication open. Later in this chapter and in the next chapter we will discuss various methods of strengthening the noncustodial parent's relationship with his child.

4. *My ex-wife may use her influence to turn my child against me.* Hurt, angry, and confused, your child's mother may indeed try to use the children to bolster her ego. She may blame you either directly or indirectly for the divorce; tell the children that they have been abandoned; complain that you do not send adequate money for their support; or make derogatory remarks about your personality and character. And because she is with them more than you are, initially she may be successful. The children are confused, and they are very willing to have someone to blame for the changes in their lives.

But this is a tactic which generally boomerangs. A child does not want to believe negative things about either of his parents — after all, he is a product of both of them. If you continue steadfastly to be a loving, caring father, after a few months the children will begin to weigh the evidence. If their mother has not been telling the truth about you (and children have a nose for truth), her word may seem increasingly unreliable. Getting into arguments with your child about which parent is right or wrong is never as effective for refuting lies as constant, weekly proof of your love, interest, and concern for your child.

5. *My ex-wife may not be able to handle the children and they will become wild and unruly.* After separation, the intricate system of checks and balances which existed within a family is disrupted. The single custodial parent has to learn to parent alone, and as we have seen, this is not easy. Before separation, you had a voice in the type and amount of limits which were set for your child. Now that you are no longer in the home, the child will need to test his new situation. Will Mommy set limits and keep him safe? Will you as his now part-time father also care enough about him to set limits? In the months ahead your child will be involved in increased testing behavior.

Furthermore, in reaction to the stress of changing life patterns, your child's behavior may become more extreme than it had been. For instance, an acting-out child may become a little demon; a withdrawn child may now appear closed off. It is easy to fall into a pattern of blaming your ex-wife for the children's behavior (particularly when it is worrisome or out of bounds), but as time goes by and new ways of relating are developed, the child will again find his balance.

BEGINNING VISITATION CAN BE AN ORDEAL

How can you lessen your own worries and at the same time smooth the way for your children? What is your role now that you are not the custodial parent? How can you be a part-time parent? The *key* to answering these questions *is the contact you maintain with your children;* for only by staying in contact can you continue to be an integral part of your children's lives.

"Visitation," remarked an insightful six-year-old, "is a long word that just means being with Daddy all day on Saturday instead of a little bit all through the week." Whether it is once a week on Saturdays, every other weekend, or after school on a weekday, visitation does simply mean getting together with the non-custodial parent. But because visitation was not part of the past, it takes a while for father and children to know how that time will feel and how it will be spent.

GOING "HOME" TO PICK UP THE KIDS

Because the pattern of being together is so altered from the past, the first few visitation times feel awkward and strange. What is more, for the father who must pick up his children, just the going "home" aspect of visitation can be a real strain. All the words in court and all the legally signed documents do not convey so poignant a feeling of finality as to stand in front of the door to your own home (and you do still think of it as yours) and no longer be free to walk in.

Hank, forty, remembers that first Saturday he went home to pick up his children for visitation.

Saturday was one of those beautiful, crisp October mornings. Automatically, the car drove me home. Before I knew it, I was parked in my usual spot in the driveway. I hadn't meant to park there—the street seemed more appropriate—but now I couldn't back out. That would have really looked ridiculous.

The kids weren't on the porch waiting for me as I had hoped they would be. Instead, I had to go to the door. Getting out of the car, I walked through the fallen leaves to the front door. I suddenly felt angry with Pauline. Wasn't she ever going to rake up all those leaves? A lump grew in my throat as I remembered the fun the kids and I used to have raking up the leaves into a big pile. The kids would take turns jumping from the porch stoop into the leaves.

At the door, my hand involuntarily reached out to turn the doorknob. Then I remembered. It wasn't my house anymore. I rang the doorbell and stood waiting. I couldn't help looking over my shoulder to see if the neighbors were staring at me. I felt so conspicuous just standing there waiting.

To everyone—the children, the parents, and even the neighbors—the father's standing on the doorstep ringing the doorbell symbolizes the change in the family structure. How strange and painful it is to have to wait until the door is opened, for this house and yard still feel so much like home. Everywhere you are confronted with familiarity: the rosebush you recently pruned, the hedge which demanded your attention every two weeks, the screen door you had intended to paint. Your newly rented apartment certainly doesn't have this homey feeling.

Finally, after a seemingly interminable wait, the door is opened, and again, the awkwardness of the situation confronts you. Hank recalls the dilemma:

> Tommy threw open the door and the kids descended upon me. Barbara hadn't finished her breakfast, one of them informed me, and Johnny was pulling on my arm, begging me to come see his new turtle. I stood rooted in the doorway. I didn't know what to do. Stay out or go in? Just then Pauline came downstairs and invited me in. We were very polite and kind of stiff, not really wanting to look at each other. The kids were all watching our faces closely.
>
> At last Barbara was finished eating. I quickly double checked with Pauline about returning time, and the kids and I left. As I got into the car, I realized that I was still clutching Johnny's prize turtle! Facing Pauline and picking up the children had been more of an ordeal than I had been prepared for.

Those first meetings of parents and children are an ordeal, for after separation we do not know exactly how to relate to our ex-mate. We want to be cool, controlled, and proper, but our emotions constantly threaten to take charge. The formal, stiff attitude we adopt to protect ourselves (and our children) from our real feelings of turmoil is unnatural and awkward. The children do watch to see how their parents relate to each other. Always hopeful there may be a reconciliation, they are attuned to all the nuances of the moment.

The only comfort we can offer is that, as the months go by, pickups will gradually become more routine and easier to handle. The pain of separation will no longer be so acute.

A MONTH OF SATURDAYS

Initially, each member of the family greets the beginning of the pattern of visitation with worry. The child worries that his father may forget and not come for him; the mother worries about her reaction to seeing her ex-husband; and the father worries about facing his ex-wife as well as facing his children.

One father remarked that after he separated from his wife, each month suddenly seemed full of Saturdays.

> A month of Saturdays! I looked forward to those Saturdays and I dreaded them. What would I do with the kids? Would they want to be with me? I kept telling myself to relax—after

all, they were my own kids. Still, I used to feel nervous and strange.

If there has been a period of absence, the discomfort is more acute. Parents and children who have not seen each other for some time may feel a little like old lovers who meet unexpectedly after several years' absence. Each knows the other achingly well, but neither can think of appropriate words to bridge the gap of absence and hurt. It is very important to each of them to make a good impression.

A father reported a bit sheepishly, "You know, the first time I picked up my son and daughter, I was more nervous than twenty years ago when I picked up my first date!" And children also feel the changes. Twelve-year-old Jason remarks, "It's really weird. When Dad lived at home, I could go out and get a hamburger with him and I didn't have to change out of my blue jeans. Now Mom makes me wear my good slacks."

Linda's father was shocked when he met his fifteen-year-old at the door.

> I hadn't wanted to embarrass my teenage daughter by taking her out looking like a "square." So I bought some jeans and sneakers and changed out of my business suit before I picked her up. The door opened and here was Linda all dolled up with a dress, hose, high heels, and even her long hair tied back! We looked at each other in amazement and then doubled up laughing!

Linda's father discovered a truth encountered by most newly separated non-custodial parents: it is difficult to figure out the new expectations!

TREATS TOPPING TREATS!

Many newly divorced fathers are initially caught off balance by the idea of visitation — a time when parent and child are suddenly required to spend a whole day or an entire weekend locked into "togetherness." No wonder a father panics! He feels that he is expected to entertain his child, that he must provide "good times" for that child, and that he certainly must not allow him to become bored or unhappy.

Typically, a father or non-custodial mother picks up the child in the morning and then feels obliged to fill the hours with "fun." That means restaurants, movies, circuses, shows, bowling, football games, more restaurants, the zoo, museums, more movies, and shopping sprees. Each week's visitation begins to seem more burdensome than the week before. After all, how many ice cream cones and monkeys swinging from a bar does it take before the novelty wears thin? And yet it is so easy to fall into this carnival attitude. One has to do something with the day.

In the long run, a steady diet of ice cream and cake never nurtures. It is far better for everyone when the part-time parent provides a balance of a few exciting times and many more ordinary but fulfilling ones.

CONTINUING THE PARENT-CHILD RELATIONSHIP

How can you make the time you spend with your child meaningful and satisfying? How can you bridge the awkwardness to find ways of relating which are comfortable again? Probably the most important factor which determines how comfortable you and your children will be together is the degree to which you both feel *continuity* in your relationship. Let us examine some of the ways the noncustodial parent can provide an ongoing relationship with his child.

"VISITOR" OR SON AND DAUGHTER?

When you lived full-time with your child, that child was definitely your *son* or your *daughter*. Now he or she no longer lives with you. In legal terms, the time your child spends with you is called "visitation." This is an unfortunate choice of words, for the word, *visit*, carries a formal and transitory feeling. The person who visits is a *visitor—a guest.*

But children don't want to be placed in the guest category—someone who comes to visit for awhile, interacts politely with you, and then leaves, not to return for some time. Your child wants to be more than that to you. Linda said heatedly, "I don't want to *visit* Dad. That sounds like going to see Aunt Amelia. I just want to *be* with him." Linda's relationship with her father is far too important to her to carry the label of "visit."

If your child is visiting you, he may interpret this to mean that he is "on vacation." He may feel that the time spent with you is not part of his *real* life, for real life, as we all know, involves responsibility and routine as well as an occasional exciting treat. *Vacation*, on the other hand, is a period of "non-reality" — time removed from the context of daily life.

All of us have heard of tourists who go on vacation to Mexico or another country and behave in ways they would never dream of in their own hometown. The same is true of your child. If he is "on vacation" at your house, he too is tempted to behave in ways which are out of bounds. It is important for your child (as well as for yourself) to make the time he spends with you part of his *real* life.

A HOME AWAY FROM HOME

How can you go about making your time with your child more real? First, let's look at where you live. What does your new home mean to your child? Is it a place where he *belongs*? Does your house or apartment give evidence that you are still a father or mother? Does it contain parts of your child?

"But my child already has a home," you might reply. Of course he does. He lives primarily with his custodial parent. That is his first home and there should be no confusion in the child's mind (or yours) that that is his main home. But does that mean that your place cannot be home also?

Years ago, when parents lived in the same community as their parents, the home of the grandparents often served as an important second home for all members of the family. A child might spend weekends or even several weeks of summer vacation at his grandparents' home. And certainly at Christmas or Thanksgiving it was expected that family members would "go home" to Grandma and Grandpa.

There was no confusion as to where a child belonged. In some ways he belonged in both homes. His first home was with his parents and his second home was with his grandparents. The child of divorce has a similar situation. He has two places where he belongs. You and your child must accept the fact that the child will spend more of his time (and usually have his strongest roots) at his custodial parent's home. But it is important that you, the weekend parent, provide a second home for your child — an additional home where your child has some of his roots and where he belongs.

THESE ARE MY POLKA-DOT DADDY'S HOUSE PAJAMAS!

One of the most rewarding tasks of the weekend parent is creating that second home for his or her child. How can this be done? What makes a home a home? Obviously, it is not merely the amount of time one spends in it. Some houses never feel like home!

Probably it is a lot of little things which create a feeling of warmth and belonging. For five-year-old Susie, home means having a place in the bathroom for her toothbrush, a glass on the sink marked "Susie," and her bathrobe hanging behind the door. Eight-year-old Kathy leaves her polka-dot pajamas hanging in the closet at her dad's home. Seven-year-old John's stuffed monkey, one of his footballs, and his game of Monopoly remain at his mother's house ready for use on the weekend. It is immensely reassuring to Susie and Kathy and John to find all their things in the same place where they left them when they return.

Leaving something behind says, "Even though I am not here through the week, something of me *is* here. *I belong!*" It also says, "I will be back again." And most importantly it says, "I know you won't forget me while I am not here." These are all significant messages, and the sensitive parent will try to create an environment which reassures the child that indeed, *he does belong.*

Of course, it is easy to fix a special place for a child when the parent has sufficient space. In fact, the child or children may even be able to have a bedroom of their own. But what about the parent who lives in a small apartment? Bob, for instance, had to use a great deal of ingenuity to make a place for his two young boys. His apartment consisted only of a living room, a small bedroom, and a kitchen-dinette.

> I wanted the boys to know they belonged here as well as at their mother's, but my cramped quarters almost defeated me. I decided to start with a bulletin board in the kitchen. That was a big hit! The boys hung up some of the paintings they had done at school. Then we added a bunch of snapshots — not only of the kids and me, but also of their grandparents, Mopsy-the-Mutt, some of their friends, and even a snap of their mother. Now they've got their whole family represented here. When we have friends over, this bulletin board is the first thing the boys take them to see.

Having pictures of their family made the boys feel less cut off when they were with their father. In a way, it brought their two homes a little closer together — closing the gap. Bob's problems weren't all solved, however.

The worst problem I had was trying to figure out some sleeping arrangements. In this little place there just isn't any room for extra beds. At first I tried having the kids sleep with me—they slept fine, but I spent the night pushing elbows and knees out of my stomach and back!

Then I tried putting them on the couch, but I resented having to go to bed at the same time they did. Finally, the boys solved the problem. Sleeping bags! They love to camp out and "camping in" is the next best thing! So now they spread out their sleeping bags at night either in my room if I'm entertaining or don't want to turn in early, or in the living room. I can even move them once they're asleep and they hardly wake up at all. In the morning we just roll up the bags and stash them back in the closet. It's great!

By the time Bob added some low shelves in the living room for the boys' books and games, his house really did begin to look as if it were also inhabited by two active young boys.

One creative weekend mother went to the Salvation Army and found a small foot locker. She painted it to match the "mod" decor of her living room. During the week it is an end table—with a lamp, magazines, and an ashtray on top of it. On weekends, she clears it off. Inside the trunk are all her kids' toys and games that they keep at her place!

By using either existing furnishings or finding a few inexpensive pieces of furniture, there are many possibilities for creating nooks and crannies for storage and for display of the children's art work, possessions, and treasures. *The main goal is to make your home a place where your child belongs!*

Quantity Versus Quality of Time Together

When you and your wife lived at home with your child, you may have spent a whole weekend in the same house, but rarely did you spend an entire day (not to mention a weekend) interacting solely with your child. Obviously, you spent some of your time with your son or daughter—often mealtimes or television time—but then each person pursued his own interests. You generally had projects of your own—puttering around the house, watching a football game, reading, catching up on office work, cleaning the garage or yard. And your child had his own interests. He rode his bike (or took it apart for the umpteenth time), played with neighborhood kids, did his homework, listened to records in his room, read, took part in or attended athletic events; or (if a teenager) spent endless time chattering to his friends on the telephone.

Sure, you and your child may have shared some activities together, but only for a limited amount of time at a stretch (rarely more than a couple of hours!). No one expects children and parents to spend an entire Saturday or weekend involved together in the same activities.

After divorce, the non-custodial parent and his child do not have the same amount of time available as they did in the past, but it must be kept in mind that *it is not necessarily the amount of time spent together that counts; rather, it is the quality of that time which is important.* For example, a father can sit behind his newspaper muttering an occasional "uh-huh" to his child's questions, but that minimal involvement hardly qualifies as time spent together. A few minutes spent focused on your child is worth hours spent together (but apart) in a room.

Visitation Worries

Visitation can get out of hand. One father, for example, felt terribly overwhelmed and depressed. The time he spent with his son was increasingly unsatisfying to both of them. During a counseling session, he made a list of some of his most pressing concerns about visitation.

1. What are we going to do all day?
2. What are we going to talk about?
3. How many Saturdays can we go to the zoo?
4. What if Tommy doesn't enjoy himself?
5. What if the weather turns bad and we're stuck in this crummy little apartment all weekend?
6. What if Tommy gets bored and wants to go home to his mother?
7. What if Tommy never wants to come back again?
8. How can I go on spending so much money entertaining him?
9. What if Tommy finds me "square" or "straight" or whatever a non-swinging father is called these days?
10. What if I can't sit through one more Saturday kiddie matinee?

Tommy was also asked to make a list of his worries about visitation. In many ways, Tommy's list paralleled his father's!

1. What if Dad forgets and doesn't pick me up?
2. What are we going to do all day?
3. What if I do something wrong or bad? Will Dad want to come get me again?
4. What if I can't think of anything to say to Dad?
5. What if I say something about Mom, and Dad gets mad?
6. What if Dad doesn't have enough money to keep taking me out?
7. What if Dad finds out he'd really rather play golf with his friends on Saturdays?

Thus, we see that both the child and the non-custodial parent are worried. Underneath, however, the child and his parent are really concerned about one central issue: "What will I be to you and what will you be to me now that we don't live under the same roof all the time? Will we continue to love and be important to each other?" The parent-child relationship certainly can continue (and even grow stronger if it was weak in the past), but you will have to use wisely the time you and your child have together to insure that your relationship will develop and grow.

ROLE OF THE PART-TIME PARENT

We talked about how your child doesn't want to be merely a visitor in your home. In the same way, he does not want you to treat him like an occasional visitor who must be "shown the town." Instead he wants, and more importantly *needs*, evidence that you still love him as a *parent*—love him enough to set limits for him when necessary, to play with him, to counsel and support him, to help him with projects or homework, to give him the freedom of unplanned time, and to allow him (even encourage him) to help you with your chores.

In other words, the same relationship which existed before divorce should be continued after divorce. The ways and means may have to change, but that special sense of parent-child togetherness must continue. Your child may have other adult male figures in his life, he may have friends, he has his mother, and he may eventually have a stepfather. But as long as you keep in mind that your primary re-

sponsibility to your child is the same as in the past — to be Father —
your relationship to your child will remain unique.

If you love and care about your child and if you make that love
and care known to him, your place in his heart is assured. No one can
completely replace you! Your child gains by having his father (or
mother if she is the non-custodial parent); you gain by having your
son or daughter.

How to Plan Meaningful Time

It is easy enough to say that it is important to continue being a
parent after divorce. But how is it done? The child no longer lives
with you, and you no longer have final say in most of the decisions
regarding his well-being. What do you do with a child whom you see
only once a week or every other weekend? After divorce can you
create or even strengthen your relationship with your son or daughter? The answer is yes, but it will require effort and thoughtful
planning by you to insure that the limited time you have together is
meaningful.

Robert, forty-three, divorced for five years and the father of four
children, sums up the problem:

> Successful part-time parenting involves walking a delicate line
> between creating an unrealistic atmosphere of hoopdedoo and
> boring the pants off your kids!

Robert is absolutely right. An atmosphere of "It's always
Christmas and Fourth-of-July around here" is unrealistic and even
unhealthy, but an atmosphere of "What a drag to be at Dad's" certainly won't build a strong parent-child relationship either! The best
approach to part-time parenting is to include some fun activities in
combination with ordinary realistic activities of family living. Robert discusses how his attitude toward visitation changed:

> When I was first divorced, I was sure that after six weeks the
> kids would refuse to come with me. So I tried to bribe them
> with movies, sodas, new clothes, and games, and the general
> attitude of "at-all-costs-keep-them-happy." I was really
> brought up short one day when I told the kids I had purchased
> tickets to a big football game. My oldest son looked actually
> pained and said, "We did that last week. Do we have to go?" I
> knew right then that something was seriously wrong!

So we had a big pow-wow and each of us made a list of the things we wanted to do on weekends. I was really surprised. The kids wanted to stay home—my home, that is. They wanted to wash the car, read the comics, ride bikes, cook, and stuff like that. Don't get me wrong. They didn't want to discard the especially good times, but they wanted something more solid from me.

What is a typical weekend now at Robert's house? Robert picks up the children, who range in age from eight to sixteen, every other Saturday morning. They return home Sunday night.

Not all the kids come over at the same time. The big ones have lessons and football games and other teenage interests. They catch up with the rest of us later in the day. We've had to develop some flexibility in scheduling over the past couple of years. And sometimes we have an extra kid. I encourage the children to invite a friend occasionally.

On the way to Robert's house, the children usually accompany him to the grocery store where they plan and shop for the meals they will be eating and preparing together. A lively reporting session ensues during which everyone catches up on the events of the past two weeks. Then weekend plans are decided upon.

Usually we choose one activity like going to a ball game or restaurant, or a trip to the nearby mountains—something we can all look forward to. Then we plan the rest of the weekend around that activity.

For Robert and his children the rest of the time is spent in the usual family activities: preparing meals, watching television, visiting friends, riding bikes, a trip to the library, and, of course, reading the comics on Sunday morning!

Lisa, sixteen, the oldest of Robert's children, talks about her feelings regarding visitation:

I always look forward to going over to Dad's place. It's a break from being at Mom's, and we have a good time. We especially like cooking dinner. We laugh and make mistakes and sometimes our cakes don't come out looking like Mom's—but we eat them just the same! And we like to just sit around in the evening and rap with Dad. Dad bought us some old secondhand bikes that we leave in the basement of his apartment, so each weekend we always plan a bicycle expedition. It's really not so much the special things we do as the little things I like. Just being with Dad is fun.

Robert's approach to visitation is very sane. He tries to provide real experiences for his children — experiences which help the children perceive their father in a variety of roles. They see him shopping and preparing meals, doing the laundry, lounging, visiting with friends, helping them with projects, planning and enjoying excursions, and in general being himself. He is no longer trying to impress his children or bribe them with treats, but instead Robert and his children have a chance to enjoy each other without pretense.

When your children see you against the backdrop of your real life, they relate to you as a real person. They cannot indulge in fantasies for long. They will quickly discover that you are neither a wonderful superperson nor a malevolent figure who has abandoned them. You remain their parent — the same parent they had before divorce.

TWENTY TIPS FOR SUCCESSFUL VISITATION

It takes time to get used to new patterns of relating and it takes effort and real desire to make the new patterns work. Here are some points to remember:

1. *Be on time.* No one likes to wait and wonder! If you must be late, phone. Being consistently late or unpredictable tells your children that they are not important to you.

2. *Make sure pickup time is not a time of hassles.* This is not the time to iron out problems with your ex-spouse. This is the beginning of your children's time with *you.*

3. *Follow visitation agreements.* Establish confidence and trust by adhering to the visitation schedule agreed upon. Your children need to be able to count on you.

4. *Don't make appropriate clothing an issue.* If your children always arrive inappropriately dressed for the activities planned, buy them a couple of outfits and leave them at your house. This is a small price to pay for peace.

5. *Involve your children in planning visitation time.* When your children help plan an activity, they will work harder to make that activity a success. Sometimes letting a child invite a friend makes the day more fun.

6. *Plan some special activities as well as some ordinary ones.* If everything is special, "special" quickly becomes ordinary and mundane! A dessert topping a dinner of meat and vegetables makes a more satisfying menu than an exclusive diet of ice cream and cake! Don't forget quiet times together; they are just as important as "hoopdedoo" times.

7. *Establish new rituals and traditions.* Enrich and enliven your life and your children's lives by creating new ways and times to celebrate life. If a child is not at your place when his or her birthday comes, celebrate it later.

8. *Plan activities with your children's needs, ages, and interests in mind.* You don't need to entertain children every moment; neither do you have to bore them by dragging them to places and activities which do not hold their interest. If you have several children of varying ages, you need to plan diverse activities. Don't forget to include some activities which can be carried on each week. Tennis matches, continued checker or chess games, collecting coins, or reading chapters from a book, for example, are looked forward to and add a sense of continuity to visitation.

9. *Make your home a second home for your children.* Your children are not visitors — they are your own children. Include their things among your own. Make a place for them.

10. *Remember birthdays and other important days.* Let your children know (in time!) that your heart is with them on those special days in their lives. If it is possible for you to attend a recital or school play or other event which is important to them — be there. Otherwise a phone call in the morning wishing good luck is a thoughtful way of expressing concern and love.

11. *Don't involve your children too much in your dating life.* As we shall be discussing in Chapter 11, your children have ambivalent feelings about your dating — particularly soon after divorce. Wait until there is someone special in your life, and even then, go slowly.

12. *Don't start something with your children that their mother will have to finish.* For instance, don't sign a child up for lessons which require mother for transportation. She will resent the infringement upon her life and it puts your children in an awkward spot.

13. *Don't constantly criticize the children's other parent.* Your children need to respect both parents. Avoid name-calling and "put-

downs." Communication about each other is tricky business. We will discuss this more fully in Chapter 10.

14. *Reexamine and evaluate the visitation schedule and pattern from time to time.* Needs and desires change over the years. Visitation should not be a static institution. Rather, it should reflect the needs of the people involved. Especially as children get older and their social lives becomes more active, adjustments may be necessary.

15. *Recognize your child's mixed feelings about visitation and divorce in general.* It is easy to forget how long a child continues to mourn and be angry about the separation of his parents. Accepting new patterns and realities takes time.

16. *End visitation on an up-beat.* Plan a final activity each visitation period which leaves you and your children feeling good. Don't make packing bags the last thing you do. Pack early and then, before your children leave, take a ride, go for an ice cream cone (oral treats are particularly comforting!), or go bowling.

17. *Plan a little for next time.* It is reassuring to know ahead of time what the next time together will include.

18. *Remember that going back home is often painful.* Each time your children return to their mother, they realize anew that they can't have both parents together. Often they react with tears or anger or become withdrawn. Understand these feelings and reassure them that you love and miss them.

19. *Return the children on time.* Don't get involved in the "game" of worrying your ex-spouse. Being late makes life harder for your children, for they become pawns in the conflict between you and your ex-spouse.

20. *Continue to parent.* These are your children; you are their parents. They need you. Within the framework of the new realities — continue parenting.

Remember

After divorce, the non-custodial parent does not automatically "lose" his children. Unless *you* sever your ties with your children (or allow them to wither gradually away), your relationship with your children can remain vital and highly satisfactory. The relationship will undergo some changes, but it definitely can continue to be an important part of your life and of your children's lives.

9

Long-Distance Parent

No matter how much we wish it were not true, *distance does alter parent-child relationships.* When you live far away from your child, seeing him only once or twice a year, you cannot maintain the same relationship you had when you were close by, actively involved in your child's growing up. That is not to say that if you are a long-distance parent you cannot build a strong, meaningful relationship with your child. You *can*, but it takes considerable concern, thought, effort, and money in order to remain involved as a part of your child's life. Even then, your relationship with him will still change; it cannot be exactly as it was before.

After spending several weeks during two consecutive summers with his father, Chris, eleven, summed up the difference:

> In some ways, Dad still feels like my dad. But in most ways he really feels like my favorite uncle. Most of the time I live with my mom, so she's the one who's really raising me. But I'm glad I still have my dad because I love him and I like spending part of the summer with him. But it *is* different from when he used to live in town. Then I used to see him just about every week.

Even though the relationship with his father now feels different from the past, it still continues to be a very important relationship to Chris — in fact, it is central to his being.

How Do Children Feel When Their Parent Moves Away?

No matter how well a child understands the reasons why one of his parents moves away, he cannot help but feel rejected, angry, and —

to some degree — abandoned. When you tell a child you are moving
far away, he immediately feels that this is the end of his relationship
with you. You'll go away and you'll forget about him and he'll never
see you again.

Most children cannot project that it is possible for a relationship
(and especially a parent-child relationship) to remain intact and vital
across a great span of miles and months. Without a great deal of
evidence to the contrary, the child suspects that he will be "out of
sight, out of mind." He fears that even if you don't completely forget
him, he will be relegated to a much lesser place in your heart and
mind.

All children want to be a central part of their parents' lives — they
need to be important. When one of their parents moves away, they
take the move personally. If they have been emotionally close to that
parent, they will feel keenly the loss of frequent contact. If their
relationship has not been close, they experience the move as confirmation of suspected rejection: "See, Dad really didn't care enough
about me to stay nearby."

CHANGED REALITIES

In some cases, one parent moves away from the other right after
the separation or divorce. In fact, it is part of the new reality with
which the child is presented. Separation anxiety for this child is often
considerably more acute than for the child whose non-custodial
parent continues to be close geographically. A child with a long-
distance parent cannot as easily check that his parent is alive and still
loves him.

In other cases, the move may occur several months or years after
divorce. The custodial parent may move, taking the child with her,
or the non-custodial parent may leave. Either way, the child's contact with his non-custodial parent is sharply decreased, and he is
plunged into a new period of mourning as he tries to accustom
himself to the changes in his life and his renewed feelings of loss.

Indeed, unless the move involves a very small distance, the realities for the child and his parents are considerably altered by the
move. The child's contact with his other parent will be much more
limited and infrequent, and no matter how satisfactory vacation
visits are, they are not the same as when the child was with his parent
regularly and frequently.

In addition, the relationship between the child and his *custodial* parent also changes, for even more than in the past, this parent becomes the major nurturing and rearing person in his life. In most ways, this parent is actually raising the child singlehandedly and must assume greater responsibilities for parenting. Both children and parents will have to explore the new situation and find ways to adapt to these new realities.

WHY PARENTS MOVE AWAY

After divorce, parents often relocate in a different town or city. In a highly mobile society like ours, moving is a way of life. After divorce, parents develop new interests, new life-styles, and new social and business contacts which may lead them geographically (as well as philosophically) away from the other. There are many possible reasons for moving. Let us look briefly at some of the most common causes and examine how some parents evaluated the consequences of each.

BATTLING PARENTS

Just because you and your ex-spouse are legally and physically separated, it doesn't necessarily mean that you are emotionally divorced. Of course, in the early months you are definitely *not* emotionally separated. It take months to disentangle your lives and to establish yourselves as single people. Often professional help is needed to achieve autonomy.

In some cases, where parents find it very difficult to separate emotionally from their ex-spouses, their children may become the focal point of their parents' conflicts. Mike and Betty are good examples of parents who were unable to part and rebuild their lives effectively. After three years of divorce they were still warring with each other. Their children (as well as themselves) were worn out from the battles. Finally, after several months of counseling, Betty decided to move away.

> I hated to leave all my friends, my job, the house, and everything familiar, but fighting with Mike was taking every bit of energy I had. Of course, the children were upset about leaving their school and friends, and Mike was furious about the decision, but I took the plunge and sold the house.
> During the summer while the kids were with their father, I accepted a teaching position in a town 150 miles from where we

had been living. By the time the summer was almost over, I had found a house there. I felt somewhat settled and was ready to help the kids get accustomed to their new surroundings.

It was rough at first. They were all pretty homesick and angry about the changes. But now, after two years, they are settled and happy with their new life here. We're close enough that their father is able to see them regularly, but far enough away that we avoid the almost daily battles of the past.

For Betty, Mike, and their children the move was a good solution. Because they were only separated by 150 miles, the children were not cut off from their father. However, the distance was enough to provide an opportunity for the parents to disentangle themselves emotionally. The children were then freer to work out a satisfactory relationship with each parent without guilt and anxiety about loyalties to the other.

A FRESH START

Another common reason for moving, especially in the early months of divorce, is the desire to make a clean break and begin a new life. When the parents' social circle is small or when both parents have been employed by the same firm, it may be difficult to establish a new life in the same geographic area, for no matter where you go, you keep bumping into each other. Moving away seems to be the answer.

Sometimes, however, a desire to move is motivated by feelings of failure. Nothing seems to be going right, you are disoriented and uprooted; you don't feel you are important to anyone. Or, like Mike and Betty, you just cannot seem to make peace with the divorce, and post-divorce conflict is making life miserable for everyone.

What parent has not at some time considered "getting away from it all," cutting his remaining ties and setting off for new horizons? This is especially true of the non-custodial parent. It is easy to become discouraged and to convince ourselves that our child would be better off without us and that his other parent could then raise him without interference. This argument may seem especially valid if the child's parent has remarried, providing him with a stepparent. "What does my child need me for?" you might ask yourself. "He's got a new stepparent now." But *you cannot be replaced* by a "new parent" anymore than one child in a family can replace another. Your child wants *you*—his own father or mother. He has continuing need for both his parents—whether or not there is a stepparent.

Although a fresh start may be very appealing to you, be sure you weigh the price of becoming a long-distance parent. If it is at all possible for you to find a way to put down new roots and feelings of belonging within the same community or in a nearby community, it is preferable to moving.

JOB ADVANCEMENT

Sometimes job pressures cause parents to move away. For instance, for one reason or another, a parent may lose his job and find it impossible to obtain employment in the same locale. Or his company may offer him a promotion which entails relocating. Some firms (and of course the military) may simply transfer him. Or a man or woman may wish to pursue a new line of work which involves moving to a different part of the country.

No matter which reason applies to you, the outcome is the same. You must very carefully weigh the pros and cons of such a move, realizing that moving involves monetary as well as emotional expenses. You will lose the frequent contact with your child, and your relationship with him will undoubtedly be altered. On the other hand, you must consider your own welfare. Jake discusses the problem:

> I was offered a terrific opportunity for advancement with a substantial raise, but the catch was I'd have to move to the West Coast. I had one week to make the decision. I wavered back and forth for days. Of course I wanted to go. It was challenging and exciting (not to mention flattering), but I hated to leave my kids. On the other hand, I knew I'd be miserable if I said no and I was afraid I'd end up blaming and resenting the kids for spoiling my chance.

After weighing the pros and cons, Jake decided to take the job, promising himself and his children that a large portion of his raise would be spent in flying his kids from Cincinnati to California. In contrast, David chose to forgo advancement:

> I had a chance to buy a well-established business at a really good price, but it was in a city far from here. At any other time in my life, I'd have jumped at the chance. But now with the

divorce, things are changed. I'd only get to see my kids for a
few weeks in the summers. I didn't want to be that far from
them. It just wouldn't have been worth the extra money I'd
make. They need me — and frankly, I need them!

Usually, it is not wise to sacrifice your personal fulfillment and
growth for your child, for such a sacrifice will undoubtedly be communicated to him. Your child, quick to blame himself, doesn't want
to think of himself as the cause of your unhappiness and lack of
fulfillment. Will you feel like a martyr if you stay in a job and a
community "for the sake of the children"? In later years, will you
resent passing up this opportunity if you never get another chance
like this one? Will you feel that you've let your children down by
moving away? Will you later feel bad that you missed so much of
their growing up? Before you accept or reject a job offer, you must
evaluate your situation and your feelings honestly.

REMARRIAGE

A large percentage of divorced parents remarry. Remarriage always involves change, and one change may be moving. Again, this
is something which must be evaluated in the light of your own
personal circumstances. If possible, it is usually desirable to stay
fairly close to your children so that contact can be maintained. After
their parents' remarriages children worry greatly that they will be
forgotten or gradually cut out of the lives of their parents. They need
concrete assurance that this will not happen.

Mary faced hard decisions about the custody of her children,
remarriage, and moving:

When Tom and I agreed to split up the children, a lot of people
thought we were crazy. The three oldest lived with him and the
two younger ones lived with me so every weekend they were
together. It really worked out great — until I fell in love with
Lance.

Lance and I had dated a lot in college years ago. His sister
and I have been close friends for all these years and when Lance
got a divorce, she took it upon herself to do a bit of matchmak-
ing. The next time he flew in from Chicago, she fixed us up with
a date. Well, we really hit it off and you'd be surprised how
many "business" trips Lance had to make to Denver that year. I

really felt great until Lance asked me to marry him and move to Chicago.

Tom was furious when I told him I was marrying Lance and taking Anne and Holly to Chicago with me. But I had decided that I just couldn't pass up the chance of a life with Lance and he wasn't about to leave his job in Chicago—he was vice-president of his company! I knew I'd miss seeing Jonathan, Pam, and Joe, but I just had to go; so I did.

Well, about six months later we were all pretty distressed. Both Anne and Holly hated their new school and really missed their brothers and sister, and I did too—more than I ever dreamed possible. I cried a lot. Jonathan was so involved in his senior year in high school I don't think he had much time to miss the little ones too much, but Pam and Joe used to do a lot with their sisters and were very upset with the new arrangement.

Things were so bad I was beginning to worry that Lance would like to get rid of all of us. Lance and I finally sat down one evening and talked until 3:00 A.M. We finally agreed to ask Tom if he would take Anne and Holly to raise with their brothers and sister. I agreed that I would find a job and that most of my money would be spent keeping in contact with my kids—trips to Denver, lots of phone calls, plane tickets for them to come to Chicago. You know, it's been more expensive than I ever thought it would be, but it's really worked out great. I see the kids at least every other month and we call all the time. I still miss them sometimes, but everyone seems to be pretty satisfied with this arrangement.

Mary's decision to remarry and move away caused considerable pain for herself and her children. Eventually she worked out a compromise that was costly, both financially and emotionally—she paid a price for what she wanted and needed. Fortunately, her solution was supported by the others involved in her life.

Examine the Consequences

As we have seen, there are sometimes valid reasons for leaving, and in a few cases, the distancing can actually be beneficial. More often, however, both the child and the long-distance parent suffer, for their contact tends to decrease year by year until each is only a peripheral part of the other's life. It doesn't have to be like this, but unless you work at keeping contact, the relationship will wither.

A basic question that can be asked is how much you care about your child. If you care deeply, you must consider your relationship to him and weigh how moving will affect that relationship. Ask yourself:

1. Am I willing to accept the changes in relationship with my child which will result from the move?
2. How do I intend to maintain contact?
3. Am I willing to pay the price for keeping contact? (Phone calls, plane fares, etc., are costly!)

It is easy to assume that infrequent contact is hardly worth the effort and money — that it cannot be very productive or important to the child. Our experience with children of divorce tells us that infrequent contact can be very meaningful and important. Often it is difficult to gauge the true worth of keeping contact (especially when we are close to the problem). The expense of a short visit may seem too costly for the amount of time spent. But the message of self-worth and personal value that your child receives is incalculable. It cannot be measured in dollars and cents! And the satisfaction the visit brings *you* is also immeasurable!

When Your Child Moves Far Away

What can you do when your ex-spouse decides to move far away, taking your child with her? Unfortunately, your options are few. Even if the original custody decree contains a provision blocking the removal of the children from your state of residence without your consent, enforcement is difficult and expensive. Of course, that is not sufficient reason to omit such a provision. It *is* worth including such a statement in a court settlement, for most of us prefer not to be in contempt of a court agreement even when the threat of enforcement is weak. However, once the child and his parent move away, you are usually forced to adapt to the changes implicit in being a long-distance parent. We know of one case where the father followed his ex-wife across the country in order to be close to his children and felt it was worth the price. Generally, however, it is not advisable since this can rapidly become a game of chase, and the emotional and financial costs become too great.

Tips for Staying in Contact with Your Child

There are many ways to stay in touch with your child. Some cost a good deal of money; others are relatively inexpensive or even cheap. Probably the two ends of the spectrum can be represented by airplane tickets and postcards. Each is important, and in its own way each is valuable. Although more exciting, a plane ticket does not replace your weekly letter or card saying, "Today I thought about *you!*"

The following is a list of ways of staying in contact with your child. Of course, no parent could possibly do every one of these things. This is merely a list of suggestions and possibilities which may give you ideas. In reading over this list, try to think of ways of applying some of these suggestions to your individual situation.

LETTERS, POSTCARDS, AND GREETING CARDS

One of the most important and inexpensive ways to stay in contact is by writing. Unfortunately, this is time-consuming and many people tend to put it off, convincing themselves that they will write at greater length when they have a little more time. But good intentions are not enough.

A letter to your child does not have to be a chore; he is not a critical audience. He doesn't care if the letter is perfectly written. As representatives of the greeting card industry have been telling us for years: "It's the thought that counts!" Your child wants desperately to know that you think about him often.

How can you make correspondence easy for you and still give your child the joy and reassurance of hearing from you regularly?

1. Buy an assortment of small note cards—the kind which have cute or funny pictures on them. You will not be so intimidated by writing if the space in which to write is not too large!
2. Buy picture postcards. Children, especially young children, love the glossy photos. Buy several at a time and then address and stamp them. Once a week, you can write a message and drop it in the mailbox on your way to work.
3. Buy a supply of greeting cards. Have birthday cards, get-well cards, and thinking-of-you cards on hand. For young children, there are cards with soft little bunnies and cherubs on them; for older children, there are joke-type cards; and

for even older children, there are sophisticated, humorous cards. There are all types of cards for every occasion and every mood. If your card shop does not have cards made for inserting money, your bank does. An occasional dollar is always a welcome treat.

4. Include clippings from newspapers or magazines which might interest your child. Look for something which is appropriate to his age and interests. Remember that very young children (who pose the most problems with written communication) love colorful pictures of anything that is part of their world—animals, children, flowers, trees, food, people, babies, etc.

5. Illustrate your notes and letters with your own drawings. Your children don't care if you are an accomplished artist or not—they'll love your attempts. Little stick figures illustrating your recent activities are especially delightful (even to the older child who may groan and tease you about your artistic abilities).

6. Buy manila envelopes into which you can tuck larger magazine clippings, children's magazines such as *Jack and Jill, Seventeen, Mechanics Illustrated,* or even comic books. Coloring books and a flat box of colored pencils or crayons can be sent to smaller youngsters.

7. Keep on hand a few "flat treats" that can be inserted into any letter: a balloon, a stick of gum, or a certificate for a treat at McDonald's.

The trick is to set up your communication center so that you do not have to disrupt your daily activities to send your child something *regularly.* Buy many cards and envelopes at a time. Stamp and address them immediately. Make it a point to send something each week on a certain day. Your child will love being able to predict the arrival of his mail.

If he does not answer your letter, don't get discouraged. Remember that you're older and more mature; he's a child. Encourage him to write, but don't threaten that you will discontinue writing. Some of these hints may nudge him into responding:

1. Send him a package of funny note cards. Write your name on the envelopes and stamp them.

2. In your letters, ask him concrete, direct questions (or a checklist) that he can answer easily.
3. Send him a postcard of questions with multiple-choice answers that he can check and send back to you. They can be silly and lots of fun!
4. Or write the beginning of a short, ridiculous story for him and ask him to write the ending — or a few paragraphs. The story can grow week by week.

Use your imagination (or somebody else's)! Remember: *it is the contact that is important.*

TAPES

In this age of technology, tapes are a wonderful way to stay in touch. For a birthday or Christmas gift (or for no special occasion) consider giving your child a tape recorder. And, of course, also give yourself one. Hearing your voice is reassuring and thrilling to your child. It makes you seem very close. And you will enjoy receiving tapes from your child (or children).

It is usually wise to think ahead (and even jot down) some things you want to say. If you have several children, make sure to address something personal to each one. Children enjoy taped letters and are usually eager to respond by tape.

One father, Tom, sent each of his children a tape of a book that was appropriate to his age and interest. The children were delighted with their personal storytelling tapes, and the youngest child insisted on taking the tape recorder and tape to bed with him every night so that "Daddy can read me my bedtime story."

Taping stories was so popular with his children that he has recorded many, many books and stories over the years. In fact, at present the whole neighborhood of children is breathlessly following the episodes of *Treasure Island!* Tom says, with a smile of satisfaction, "When the kids grow up and are tired of listening to the tapes, they can donate them to the library for the blind!"

PHONE CALLS

Regular telephone contact is one of the best ways to close the distance between you and your child. Children really look forward to the time set aside for talking long distance with you. A few pointers:

1. Try to set up a time that is convenient for both you and your child — a time that is free from interruptions.
2. If you promise to call at a given time, *call!* Don't break your promise.
3. Jot down ahead of time a list of items you want to remember to bring up. Knowing what you want to say keeps the call from degenerating into a series of aimless questions like, "Well, son, what's new?" Such questions tend to be dead ends.
4. Remember the questions a good reporter asks: Who? What? Where? When? Why? These queries will elicit more than a flat *yes* or *no* answer. Questions such as, "Did you have a good time at the Fourth-of-July picnic?" too often will be met with an answer of "Uh-huh." It will be more helpful to ask instead, "What was the best thing about the picnic?" and "What was the part you liked the least?"
5. If you have more than one child make sure each gets to talk an equal amount of time. Alternate who is the first to talk and who is the last. Remember that children are very worried about equality. One father sent his children an egg timer to keep close to the phone so they could easily time each child's talking.

Talking with your child by telephone is a good time to try to hear more than just his words. Listen for indications of how he is feeling in response to events in his life. This is not an easy task, but it is well worth the effort. It's easy to flood a child with words and really not hear what is going on in his life.

GIFTS

Gifts are also another way of saying, "I am thinking about you and I love you." They need not be extravagant or expensive. In fact, small, inexpensive gifts sent frequently are a more effective way of keeping in touch than a large, expensive gift sent once a year. This is especially true of young children who highly value getting a package in the mail.

Some parents fear that giving a gift — unless it is for a special occasion — will spoil their child. Others worry that giving gifts may mean they are trying to buy their child's affections. It is wise to look at the intent of giving. If you were living nearby would you buy your child an ice cream cone? Would you take him to a movie, a baseball game, or the circus? Would you occasionally buy him a model airplane, a doll, or a record? Of course you would! Then there is no reason why you shouldn't continue to give your child an occasional treat, even though you no longer live with him. If you give a gift because you care, or because the item is perfect for your child, you are not "buying" him. What should you give your child? Here are some guidelines:

1. *Age and interests.* First, keep in mind his age and interests. If he is six years old, an expensive, complicated science kit is inappropriate — even if you hope he will be a scientist when he grows up!

2. *Gifts that involve others.* Don't buy things that the child's mother or another adult will have to spend time, energy, or money putting together or caring for. For example, an adorable puppy may be just what your child wants, but you'd better check with his mother first. In the end, she will be responsible — no matter how much your child assures you that he'll take total care of the dog.

3. *List of needs and wants.* Ask your ex-spouse for a list of things your child needs or particularly wants. You don't have to limit yourself to that list, but it can serve as a guideline.

4. *Clothing.* Keep files on the current sizes and measurements of your child or children. Sending the wrong size is disappointing to the child and is difficult for the parent who must make exchanges.

5. *Individual versus group gifts.* If you have several children, you might alternate giving a group gift with sending something to each child. Usually individual gifts are more successful, but sometimes a group gift works beautifully. For instance, one father made a hit by sending a popcorn maker to all of his children.

6. *Books.* Don't forget to check with your local librarian before you buy books. She can help you make good choices. Scan the book before you send it so that you and your child can discuss it later. You can share experiences through books.

7. *Inexpensive gifts.* Don't think that because a gift costs little or is free, it is too trivial to send. A father from the West Coast sent his children who lived in Kansas a box of seashells. The children were fascinated. One child even went to the library to find a book to identify the shells. He was then able to share his collection with his science teacher and classmates.

8. *Collections.* Adding to a collection is a wonderful way of showing an interest in your child. Collections and hobbies give both the parent and child a sense of continuity over the years.

9. *Magazine subscriptions.* Another gift that represents continuous giving is a magazine subscription. Be sure that you choose a magazine that is geared to your child's age and, if possible, his special interests. Again, your librarian can advise you.

Buying, packaging, and sending gifts is time-consuming and often a nuisance, but the process can be made easier by following some of these hints.

Stock up on gifts. Accumulate gifts slowly, as you find them, instead of waiting for a special occasion and then rushing out frantically to buy something. As you do your normal shopping, watch for appropriate gifts — a pair of fancy socks, a comical stuffed animal, bubble bath in a fancy package, a paperback book, a special pair of extra warm gloves, a model car or plane. As you find articles, store them on a shelf in your closet until you are ready to send them.

Stock up on packaging supplies. Have plenty of boxes of various sizes on hand so that you don't have to search for one that fits. Remember that your local post office sells special mailers, both large and small. Buy a few to keep on hand. Also purchase a supply of tissue paper, wrapping paper, strapping tape, string, and brown paper. When everything is readily available, there's a higher chance you'll get the job done!

VISITATION

For the long-distance parent and his child, visitation is particularly important. Because your time of physical contact with your child is so limited, you must make the time that you are together count. Before making plans, however, you need to be aware of the special problems that the long-distance parent and his child usually face.

If you have not seen your child for many months, there will be an initial period of strangeness. Twelve-year-old Jeffrey, who lives in California with his mother, discusses the strangeness he feels when he visits his father in Chicago:

I hate that moment when I get off the plane. I'm always scared that maybe I won't even recognize my dad. And then after we pick up my suitcase and we're in the car, I get this awful feeling in my stomach. Dad and I both start talking real fast, and then we don't know what to say and there's this long silence, and Dad keeps saying, "Well, Jeff, you certainly have grown!" I guess he feels funny too and can't think of anything to say. Every summer we have to get used to each other all over again.

And indeed, if the absence has lasted many months, you *do* have to get used to each other all over again. Children grow quickly and the ten-year-old you were with last summer is not quite the same boy or girl at eleven. So much happens in the course of a year!

Not only does your child feel strange and somewhat cut off from you initially, he also feels a resurgence of the old anger: Why did you have to go away? Why did his parents have to get a divorce? In the first few days you are together, your child may mask his anger, but as the weeks go by and he feels more secure with you and more familiar with his surroundings, the honeymoon period may end and some of his hostile feelings may surface. He will need to test your love again: Will you keep him safe? Will you help him control his destructive feelings? How much do you love him? Your child wants proof that you still care about him despite the geographic distance between you.

Share your feelings. What can you do to help your child and yourself over the emotional hump of the first couple of weeks? First, remind yourself that your child has a right to all of his feelings. In fact, you probably share many of his fears and concerns. Tell him that. Verbalizing how *you* feel is always a good beginning. It opens the door to sharing. You might say something like this:

You know, I'm always so excited to see you that I can hardly wait for your plane to land. But I'm always surprised at how you've grown and it makes me feel kind of sad and a bit angry that I'm not with you to share all your growing up. In fact, I feel somewhat left out. And when I'm first with you I don't know exactly what to say. I guess we both have to get reacquainted again—but I'm sure looking forward to catching up!

This tells your child that you share some of his feelings and that you genuinely care!

A call to the custodial parent. As soon as you get to your place, a call to his mother is a good idea. If you suggest it, the child doesn't have to worry that wanting to call his mother may upset you. A young child especially feels homesick quickly and may long for the familiar sound of his mother's voice. His longing for his mother may make you feel inadequate, jealous, rejected, and irritated. These are normal feelings, but as you focus on your child's need for comfort and reassurance, you will recognize the importance of regular phone contact with his custodial parent. He needs to know that the other half of his world still exists and that his mother misses him.

Schedules and routines. Remember your child has to make some large adjustments to fit into your household. This involves considerable shifting of gears. He will not only have to get used to different schedules and routines, but also to different expectations. Be sure that you explain the rules of your house. (Only a few major rules initially, please!) This will be particularly important if your home includes stepsiblings or half-siblings. Your child's relationships with others in your household will be discussed in the following chapters.

Be sure you include your child in simple chores and household tasks like helping with meals, making his bed, picking up the living room, etc. Remember, your child wants and needs to belong in your home! And, by the way, the time you and your son or daughter spend washing and drying dishes is excellent for chatting and closing the gap between you. Make chores a fun or sharing time, not a disciplinary measure. The message of "Let's get these chores done and then we'll have time to do something fun that we've planned" is always sound.

Shifting homes is not easy. It requires considerable emotional agility to keep your balance in an unfamiliar situation. Your child cannot help but feel somewhat tense and anxious until he regains his footing.

ESTABLISHING NEW RITUALS

After divorce we must find and create new ways to celebrate and mark special (and not so special) occasions. For the non-custodial parent and for the long-distance parent in particular it may take extra thought and ingenuity to develop new rituals. Here are a few examples:

Birthdays. You may not be present on your child's birthday. Is a card marking the occasion sufficient? Probably not. But a birthday call is a fine way of saying, "The first thing I thought about this morning on this special day was *you,* my birthday child!" This is the beginning of a new ritual—one that the child can look forward to.

One long-distance father of five children had a wonderful idea. Since his children were all born in the fall and winter and he is not with them at that time, he plans a gala "Merry *Un* Birthday Party."

This is the climax of summer visitation. Each child and their father and stepmother draw a name from a hat and must then *make* a gift for that person. There's plenty of homemade ice cream and cake and the children are encouraged to invite any friends they have made over the summer as well as relatives who live nearby. The party, held on the eve of the children's departure, creates a warm and festive end to visitation.

Summer Thanksgiving. Another long-distance parent has summer Thanksgiving with his children since, as he says, "I feel the most thankful for my blessings when I look around the table and see the beauty of my three children's faces!" They have turkey and dressing and all the trimmings in July!

A Night with Dad. "In our family," reports a youngster, "we each have one night in the summer when we go out alone with Dad. We get to choose a movie or bowling or something like that and a place to eat. We draw straws to see who's first, second, and third." Many part-time parents have found this an excellent way to get to know their children better. It is best, however, to save the night for going out to the last part of visitation; otherwise, the strain of making conversation may be too much.

Rituals are important to children. How often we have heard the children say proudly, "At Dad's house (or at Mom's) we *always* do" such and such activity. They look forward to the repetition of a good time — even if the event is as seeming inconsequential as a stroll every Friday evening to an ice cream parlor. Ritual and repetition help make a familiar, secure world.

REMEMBER

In the final analysis, the knowledge that you care will sustain your child through the dark hours (and even children of two-parent homes have dark hours during the painful process of growing up). But because you *are* far away, you must make special and continuing efforts to insure that your child *knows* you care. It isn't easy — but because you *do* care, you can do it!

10

Pitfalls
and Problems

A therapist listened as a distraught mother aired the problems she was having with her daughter, Samira, age fourteen:

Ever since her dad left about six months ago, Samira has been constantly in trouble. She can't get along with her teachers — I've been called in for conferences twice this month because of her behavior — *and* she's been cutting classes too. She used to have quite a few girl friends, but most of them have dropped her. Samira's been so nasty to them! And at *home* — well I hardly know where to begin! She picks one fight after another. We're having terrible battles! And you should hear how she talks back to me. I don't know where she learned such language! If I had ever talked to *my* mother like that, I'd have been thrown out of the house!

Samira and her mother are obviously in severe conflict. As the session progressed, it became evident that Samira's mother deeply resented her daughter's close attachment to her father, and in turn, Samira was extremely angry with her mother for "driving Dad away." In another session, Samira unloaded some of her anger:

Mom hates Dad so much that she can't see how I feel! I love Dad. I don't want to have to start hating him in order to get along with Mom. You know, she won't admit it, but the real truth is — she wants *me* to be just as divorced from Dad as she is!

Samira put her finger on one of the most difficult problems of divorce for parents and children. After separation, you and your child are attempting to pursue two *opposite* goals. While you are striving to *end* your relationship with your spouse, your child is trying (sometimes desperately) to *preserve* his relationship with his other parent. And the hardest part is, if you are a concerned, caring parent, you must *help* your child maintain, and even strengthen, his ties while at the same time work to sever your own ties. This is obviously no easy task — but it is necessary for your well-being and *your child's.*

Because some parents cannot emotionally separate from each other and still allow their child to stay involved with each parent, severe problems can develop. In this chapter we shall explore some of the damaging problems that result when parents divorce and become absorbed in satisfying their own selfish needs, oblivious to the effects their actions have on their children. We shall also look at some of the troublesome behaviors which children sometimes develop when their parents are involved in post-marital battles. Finally we will call attention to some of the problems that occur when parents and children become confused about their respective roles.

We hope that this chapter will help you avoid some of the worst pitfalls. If you find yourself already mired in one or more of the problems cited, try to find ways to extricate yourself before further damage results. Often parents facing these problems need professional help. If you need counseling or therapy, get it. Your child's mental health is priceless.

POST-MARITAL BATTLING

First, let us look at some of the most common problems which grow out of parental conflict and examine briefly why parents and children behave as they do.

RETALIATION

The desire to hurt or "get even" with an ex-spouse is a common emotion after divorce — especially when separation and divorce have been recent and stormy. The danger, of course, is that parents may succumb to the temptation of using the children to hurt each other. Such "games" obviously do great damage to the children involved.

There are many ways in which parents use their children to retaliate against their ex-spouse. Some mothers use their children to send barbed messages to their ex-spouse, such as "Ask your dad when he's going to send the support check." Or they deny visitation with the father until the support check arrives or until all overdue child support payments have been paid. A father, in turn, sometimes withholds support payments in order to "get even" with his ex-wife for some offense. Sometimes the intent is to pressure her into allowing more visitation with the children. Visitation and child support, however, are legally separate issues, and although it is tempting to use one or the other as leverage, it is not wise, for the child is the one who suffers. If there are problems with visitation, see a lawyer. If your support check does not arrive, that also is a legal matter. Don't use your child as a pawn!

Some types of retaliation are more subtle. There are custodial parents who intentionally or unintentionally sabotage visitation with the other parent. One youngster seen in a child guidance clinic reports:

> Every time I get ready to see Dad, Mom starts a fight with me about something else, like cleaning my room or talking about my grades. By the time I leave, I'm in a bad mood and then I take it out on Dad.

Another child reports that his mother makes him feel guilty when he leaves to visit with his dad. "She says, 'Have a good time,' but I know she doesn't mean it; she always seems either sad or mad."

Whether parents use their child for retaliation consciously or unconsciously, the result is the same: pointless suffering of children. Often these parents are not fully aware of a child's conflict and pain. It frequently takes a crisis (usually the child's acting out and calling attention to his acute distress) before these parents are able to face the problems and realize how detrimental their behavior is to their child.

Kenny is a teenager who was used by his parents as a pawn in their battles. He reports bitterly:

> Neither of my parents really gives a damn about me. I'm just their ball to knock around. I'm only important to the one who doesn't have me. What they don't know is that neither of them really has me. I just pretend so I can get all I want.

Although Kenny got much of what he thought he wanted—a motorcycle, television, expensive clothing, hi-fi equipment — he did not get what he really wanted and, more importantly, really needed: his parents' genuine interest and love. For years, Kenny's mother had belittled and downgraded her ex-husband, constantly pointing out his flaws (both real and imaginary). She attempted to break up Kenny's involvement with his father by using flimsy excuses to deny visitation. But Kenny's father was also involved in continuing conflict. He undermined his ex-wife's control, encouraging Kenny to rebel against her. Furthermore, both Kenny's parents tried to buy his love and allegiance by constantly giving him expensive gifts.

Kenny became increasingly hostile and cynical. It is no surprise that at fifteen he ran away from home. When he was located, he refused to return to either of his parents' homes; instead, he was placed in a group home for emotionally disturbed adolescents.

DEMANDING TOTAL ALLEGIANCE

Some parents vie for their children's undivided allegiance. This may be related to attempts to turn the children against the other parent, or it may be rooted in the parents' attempts to bolster their own sagging egos. The underlying motivation makes little difference in how children feel when they find themselves caught in this type of conflict.

Anthony's case is typical. A graduate student of social work reports what she observed and heard as she watched Anthony and his therapist through a one-way mirror:

Anthony sat hunched on the couch in the therapy playroom. His knees, stuck inside his T-shirt, supported his chin. His face had a tight, pinched look, making him seem both older and younger than his eight years. As he talked he pulled his shirt, stretching it out of shape. He said:

"Last year when Mom and Dad got a divorce, they told Mark and me that we were supposed to live with Mom and we were supposed to be with Dad on weekends. But Dad wanted us to live with him, and so he started giving us a whole bunch of presents and taking us out to eat and places. He said that Mom didn't know how to raise boys — especially big boys like Mark.

"Then Mark started fighting with Mom all the time, and he'd run away from Mom's and take the bus to Dad's apartment. Mark wanted me to go with him, and I kind of wanted to because it's more fun at Dad's, but I couldn't leave Mom. She cries when I leave, and she says Mark and Dad have already left her. She says I'm her baby and I'm all she has left in the world. But I don't *want* to be all she has left!"

Anthony paused for a moment. He tugged hard on his T-shirt and his eyes filled with tears.

"I don't know what to do. I'm all stretched! I think I'll run away to the caves in the mountains. Nobody will find me. Even if they call me, 'Tony, Tony, come back!' I won't listen. I'll just close my ears, 'cause I really hate all of them!"

There are many Anthonys, children of divorce who, for one reason or another, feel they must take sides, giving total allegiance to one of their parents and turning their back on the other. Surely, Anthony's parents didn't really want him to suffer. They certainly never sat him down and said, "Tony, you must choose between us!" Yet that is the very message that Anthony received.

Why do so many divorced parents seem to want and even *need* their children's total allegiance to themselves? One answer lies in the divorce experience itself. When parents break up a relationship which had been invested with love and mutual support, their self-esteem becomes shaky. Psychologist Myron Harris notes:

> The disturbances of self-esteem, the shock to each person's sense of interdependability, the fear that one has failed in a meaningful relationship, all lead to an intensification of the struggle to find solace and security for one's self.

In the midst of divorce we all need extra bolstering and support. It is not at all uncommon for parents to turn to their children for confirmation that they are still needed, loved, and important. In fact, some parents need and want their children to parent *them*! Unfortunately, too often a parent's overriding need for support and love includes the demand that the child give his full allegiance to that parent. Of course, as in Anthony's case, the demand for unshared allegiance is usually not stated openly. Rather, the parent communicates his or her needs in more subtle ways. Anthony's mother did not say, "Tony, love only me!" but her crying was a powerful way of fostering guilt and of tying Anthony to her.

The issue of taking sides is a common problem for children of divorce. But when a child must side with one parent against the other, he cannot help but have feelings of guilt and anger. *Either way he chooses, he loses.*

DENIGRATING OR DENYING THE OTHER PARENT

Susie, age eight, has a problem. She knows her father, and she knows that the picture her mother draws of him does not fit *her* picture.

> When Mom starts talking about Dad, I want to cover my ears or run out of the room. She gets so mad and the more she talks about him the madder she gets. She says awful things about him. I think most of what she says isn't true, but I'm not sure and then I get afraid to say anything because she gets mad at me too. I wish she wouldn't say those things.

When Susie's mother starts belittling and degrading her father, Susie becomes less sure of what she thinks she knows. Can her father really be as bad as her mother says? Can Susie trust her own perceptions? Can she trust her mother?

Talking about the child's other parent can be difficult. When we are angry and hurt, we tend to exaggerate the shortcomings of the one with whom we are angry. Judicious honesty is best. If your judgment might be colored by intense feelings—say so. Your ex-spouse must have some positive qualities—acknowledge them. If your child's other parent has some traits that make you see red— share those feelings with your child. Always remember to tell your child that it is his responsibility to assess his parents' qualities—both good and bad. Try to avoid insisting that your views of your ex-spouse should become the views of your child.

While trying to avoid saying all the ugly thoughts you have about your child's other parent, don't overcompensate and slip into another pitfall—glorifying your ex-spouse. If, while talking with your child, you mention only the marvelous and charming qualities of your ex-spouse, the child may rightly wonder how you could possibly put him through the wrenching experience of divorce when you still regard his other parent as wonderful.

Some parents, motivated by extreme anger and the desire to avoid expressing that anger in front of their children, take a different approach which has equally disastrous results. They simply ignore the existence of the other parent. They act as if the other part of their child's world does not exist. Marie, age nine, explains how it feels:

When we come home from a weekend with Dad, Mom acts as if we'd just been outside playing. And if one of us mentions anything about the weekend, she either walks out of the room or starts talking about something else. She doesn't even use the word "dad" or "father" anymore. If she must talk about Dad, she says things like "When is Greg picking you up?" It gives me the weirdest feeling! She wants to pretend that I don't have a father anymore. But I know I do.

Marie is acutely aware of her mother's attempt to deny the existence of her father. Having to separate her life into two totally distinct compartments — Daddy's world and Mommy's world — makes her anxious. Marie knows that her mother's pretended indifference covers a great deal of anger and pain. "I try not to mention Dad," she confesses, " 'cause it makes her *so* mad." Marie must be constantly on her guard, filtering what she says and leaving out anything that relates to her father. That *is* difficult and it leaves Marie in a state of continual anxiety.

It takes time before you can view your former spouse as a human being like any other — a person with good qualities and bad, with strengths and weaknesses. During the early months, when your emotions are inflamed, you will need to be careful not to turn your children against their other parent. Your children must continue to relate to both their parents and at the same time maintain their own identity and integrity. Denying the existence of a child's other world or trying to convince him that his other parent is totally bad will make him feel anxious and angry and will eventually erode the trust and regard your child has for you.

CHILD SNATCHING

Newspapers and magazines frequently feature stories about children who have been "snatched" by the non-custodial parent (and sometimes snatched back by the custodial parent). Child snatching, as this particular type of kidnapping is commonly labeled, is one of the most extreme examples of what can happen when battling parents seek to "win" the war against their ex-spouses without regard to their children's true welfare. "I've never known of a child-snatching case where one parent doesn't say it's a rescue and the other that it's a snatching," notes Jack Sampson, professor of family law at the University of Texas. "Most of the time it's simply marital warfare."

ACCORDING TO THE *National Observer*, each year an estimated 25,000 to 100,000 children are snatched by their parents, and — because of the rise in divorce and the ambiguities of the law — such cases are increasing yearly. The emotional effects on the victims are usually devastating. Arnold Miller, organizer of Children's Rights, Inc. (a clearinghouse for information and guidance and a lobby for legislators), estimates that "ninety percent of all abducted children who are returned to the custodial parent eventually must undergo psychological treatment to repair the psychic damage done during the uprooting."

And some children are never returned to the custodial parent. The parent may spend thousands of dollars on detectives and tracing procedures without success. Years may pass; the children may be grown before the parent sees them again. What can be done about child snatching? At the present time, once it happens, little or nothing. The time to take action is *before* it happens. Remember the old adage: An ounce of prevention is worth a pound of cure!

DEFUSING THE BATTLES: SOME THOUGHTS

Behaving responsibly is not always easy. It is often especially difficult for parents who are coping with the emotions of separation and divorce. As a responsible parent you may have to muster extra strength and resolve in order to behave in ways which will benefit your children. Here are a few reminders which may help. Think about them *before* you make important decisions:

1. *You are not an ugly despot.* Your emotions and murderous impulses are quite normal and understandable. (They may even be very justifiable!) Neither is your former spouse a totally depraved person. You are both trying to cope with powerful emotions and struggling to make a successful transition from one life, which you have known very well, to another which is new and uncertain. Examine what you are feeling and why. Self-awareness is a vital part of good mental health. But monitor your negative impulses! Remember you also have impulses that are positive. Today, for the sake of your child, these must prevail! You cannot control the behavior of your ex-spouse, but you *can* control your *own.*

2. *Your child needs less anxiety — not more.* Throughout the turmoil, the conflicts and battles, and the pain of separation and making new adjustments, your child is constantly trying to lower his tension and distress while maintaining his balance at the same time.

Because he is young, his skills are limited; his insights and understandings are immature; and his need for parenting is greater than ever.

Disentangling yourself from the battles with your former spouse is essential for the well-being of your child as well as for your own. The child who is caught in the middle between battling parents must cope with considerably more stress than if his parents (even though divorced) are united in caring for him. His security is deeply threatened. With no solid ground under his feet, he cannot mature in healthy ways. It takes energy to grow up; this child's energy is being tied up in anxiety.

3. *You are responsible for your own actions.* A friend of ours is fond of quoting the wisdom of her mother who used to admonish, "Remember, what goes around, comes around." Her mother firmly believed that if you behaved in ways that hurt others, the hurt would come back to *you* someday. Whether you subscribe to this universally encountered notion or not, one thing is certain: you must "live with yourself" for many years to come. To be happy, you need to think well of yourself. Try to behave in ways that tell you that you are a good, responsible parent.

4. *Today is just one spot in your life.* It is easy to feel that today is forever — that today's emotions and problems will be just as intense and important to us in the months and years to come as they are today. Be assured — by those who have been there ahead of you — that it just isn't so. The hurt *will* diminish; the games *will* be less frequent and, hopefully, will eventually end; you *will*, undoubtedly, have many years of meaningful contact with your children as they grow up, move away, and perhaps marry and have children. Life *will* go on. Plan to be a responsible parent today, tomorrow, and throughout the years to come.

PROBLEMS OF CHILDREN IN CONFLICT

A child who is in severe conflict is not able to control his impulses as well as a child who is not so stressed; nor can he think, plan, and solve problems as well as the child who is not overwhelmed by anxiety. The youngster caught between warring parents has *more* problems in his life than most children, and yet he has *less* ability to work them out. While trying to lessen his conflict and still maintain his balance, he often impulsively uses behavior which, instead of ameliorating the situation, compounds his problems. He may act out anger and fear by running away, by lying, by stealing, or by adopting other antisocial behavior. Or, he may become overly submissive and compliant, trying desperately to please both his parents.

These are not *bad* children; these are children in pain who are trying to reduce that pain — or at least call attention to it. Children in conflict also do many of the things which ordinary children do in any family: they try to pit their parents against each other; they attempt "blackmail" to get what they want; they tell tales; and they indulge in a variety of other troublesome behaviors. In "normal" families, these manipulative behaviors are generally more quickly identified and dealt with, but in families facing the disruptions of divorce, they are apt to become intensified and go unchecked. Divorced parents need to be particularly sensitive to the ways in which their children may attempt to manipulate them. Let's examine a few of the problem behaviors which may show your child needs help.

BLACKMAIL AND TYRANNY

In situations where parents are warring and each desperately needs and wants the child's allegiance and love, the parents may become afraid of denying anything to the child. Rather than say "no" or risk confrontation, they hand over the keys of control to the child. An insecure child may really exploit his parent's hunger for love and approval. Haim Ginott, in his book *Between Parent and Child*, describes these children as tyrants who rule over anxious servants — their parents. The child seems to say, "If you don't give me what I want, I won't love you." Or even worse, "I'll love Daddy (Mommy) better than you."

In some cases, as soon as a restriction appears in one home, the child threatens to run away to the other parent's house. If his parent capitulates and gives in to his demands, the child is indeed powerful — too powerful! *Too much power makes a child anxious and scared.* He wants the adult to be in charge. Running back and forth between homes is a very dangerous game, for it not only keeps the child too powerful, it also keeps him from facing and solving problems.

Dr. Ginott makes a distinction between "permissiveness" and "overpermissiveness." To accept a child's undesirable thoughts which are expressed symbolically, he believes, is being wisely permissive. For example, a child may say, "I hate you! You don't ever let me do anything. I want to go live with Daddy because he's nicer than you." Accepting your child's anger at you helps him and you deal with that anger without engendering excessive guilt. Try to react to your child's feelings rather than to his specific threats or accusations. "You're really angry with me, aren't you? Let's try to write down all the things you're angry about and see what we can do about them" is a far better response than reacting to the threat of his running away. Letting a child act out his anger in ways which are destructive is "overpermissive" and is never in the best interest of the child. It increases his anxiety by making him less certain that he can control his angry impulses. Instead of acting out, your child would rather divert his angry impulses into words and be helped to solve his problems.

Parents who allow their child to blackmail them with threats or unacceptable behavior are being "overpermissive" with their child. They are encouraging him to develop undesirable habits and attitudes which will greatly hamper his becoming a mature, responsible adult.

SPYING, TELLING, AND PITTING

Some children attempt to pit one parent against the other. To some degree, this is normal and happens in most families where children live with both their parents. For example, Mother says, "It's time for bed now, Johnny." The child runs to Father and begs him to read him a story. Without realizing that bedtime orders have already been given, Father complies. Then Mother walks into the living room, finds Johnny ensconced on Father's lap and crossly says, "Johnny, I told you it's time for bed—*now!*" And if Father and Mother are in accord, Father will back Mother up, and realizing he's been duped, he'll pack the child off to bed with a few stern words.

In a family where parents live together, manipulations like these are usually quickly discovered and can be stopped. But what happens when parents are not living together? Obviously, it becomes more complex! Listen to Marsha describe her problem:

> For a long time David and I didn't realize that Jason was running tales back and forth between us. To me, he would say things like, "At Dad's house I get to watch any TV show I want until eleven or even midnight!" Of course, Jason knows how much I'm against indiscriminate TV watching. He knows I'll get angry with David.

What I didn't know is that Jason was doing the same thing to his dad. He'd tell him that I had bought myself a bunch of clothes and bought him nothing. Or he'd wear his old sneakers and tell his dad he didn't have any others. He'd get David really mad at me.

One day David called me. He was madder than a hornet. "Just try and move Jason out of the state without consulting me! You'll end up in jail!" I didn't even know what he was talking about. When he calmed down, he told me that Jason had told him we were moving away. Well, it wasn't true. David and I began talking and found out that Jason was telling each of us a lot of lies — or at best some truth badly distorted. We agreed that from then on we wouldn't believe half of what he says — especially his wilder tales. It's amazing what's happened. Since Jason can't rile us up anymore, he's quit making trouble. Now he's playing straight with us.

After separation, when it's more difficult for parents to check things out with each other, some children take advantage of their parents.

"I WANT TO LIVE WITH DADDY!"

Sometimes it is difficult to determine what is really going on in a particular situation. Danny's father reports:

I can't stand it when Danny begs me not to take him back to his mother's. Usually this happens when he's been a whole weekend with me. He starts crying and he begs to live with me. He tells me that he doesn't like living with his mom. I just never know what to do and I feel so awful.

What are the possible motivations for Danny's behavior? Before you jump to the conclusion that Danny is obviously dreadfully unhappy and neglected in his mother's home consider some of the other reasons why Danny might cry and cling.

First, the father may be encouraging Danny to want to stay with him. He may subtly (or not so subtly) be giving Danny messages that his mother is not a good person to raise him — that she does not love Danny sufficiently and is not providing a good home for him. In addition, he may be playing the "good-time Charlie" role, never scolding or setting limits, and providing a constant carnival of entertainment for his son.

Another reason Danny may sometimes want to stay at his father's home is that he is comparing his week*end* life with his father with the week*day* life with his mother. As we all know, the two are not comparable. There is bound to be more fun, leisure, and relaxation on Saturday and Sunday than there is on weekdays when life is largely dictated by schedules, demands, and other constraints. No wonder it seems better to live with Daddy!

Danny may also be involved in trying to "stir up" his father against his mother. Keeping his parents emotionally involved with each other keeps alive the hope that they may once again come together and be his parents under one roof. By carrying tales of unhappiness back and forth, he may also be trying to alert his parents to his need for more attention.

More than likely, however, Danny is simply reacting to the end of his visitation time. Over and over each week Danny has to let go of his father and separate from him. For weeks and months after divorce (and sometimes longer), each time children have to separate they experience anew a surge of anger and disappointment, reliving their old pain. They continue wishing their parents were together under one roof so that they won't have to split their time between two adults they love.

If your child begs to stay with you, what should you say? If you are fairly sure that his home life is not really as grim as he paints it (and usually it is not), you need to assure him that you love him dearly, but for the time being at least, you and his mother have decided that it's best for him to live with her. Don't allow him to seduce you into a long discussion or debate. Instead, try to listen to the real messages. Let him know that you do understand how hard it is for him to leave you, particularly when the time spent together has been gratifying and good. Tell him that his mother also loves him and is providing a good home for him. By being supportive of her efforts to raise him, you lessen his anxiety that he can pit you against her. Remember that he really does not enjoy being the person who keeps you and his other parent churned up and angry.

Problems of Abandonment and Neglect

The newspapers frequently report cases of child abuse. Many report situations where severe beatings by a child's parent ended in hospitalization or even death. Others involve reports of severe physical or medical neglect.

Neglect and abuse, however, often do not show up as bodily harm. Not being sufficiently loved and valued by his parents has a profound effect upon the child who depends on his parents' nurture for his own emotional growth. If he is not valued, he cannot value himself. In her book *Peoplemaking*, Virginia Satir makes a strong point: "I am convinced that the crucial factor in what happens inside people and between people is the picture of individual worth that each person carries around with him." When children have low self-esteem, when they do not value themselves highly enough, their ability to give and receive love becomes stunted. Without a doubt, such children will bear scars of psychological deprivation.

NEGLECT BY THE CUSTODIAL PARENT

What if you have good reason to believe that your child is being neglected or abused by his custodial parent? Sometimes after separation and divorce, a parent really is not capable of taking good care of a child. The parent's own problems and needs may eclipse the child's needs, leaving little strength for effective parenting.

Physical Neglect or Abuse. If you think there is actual physical neglect or abuse, you owe it to your child to have the situation investigated. Start by consulting your lawyer who can advise and help you. If your child shows up with unexplainable bruises or lacerations, get help quickly. Young children are especially vulnerable to beatings. Angry, anxious parents who are highly stressed can do great physical as well as emotional harm to their children.

Emotional Neglect or Abuse. Although the scars are just as real, it is difficult to change situations where the neglect is emotional instead of physical. Although judges are increasingly sensitive to the problems of psychological neglect, they recognize that this type of neglect and abuse is more difficult to assess and prove. As a result, custody changes based on psychological abuse or neglect are often not possible.

However, children in these homes do need help. Anne, a young teenager who lives with a disinterested mother, expresses concern for herself as well as for her younger brother, Dale, age four:

Mom is too busy to have time for my little brother and me. Between her work and her dating, there's nothing left over for us. Our life is empty and dull. I like to be at my girl friend's house because there I feel more love and warmth, but I can't leave Dale behind. If I don't stay with him, he's stuck with babysitters. He mostly just sucks his thumb and watches television.

I don't know why Dale and I can't live with Daddy. He really wants us. Dale is so different when he spends vacations with Dad. He becomes more mischievous — like a regular four-year-old. But Mom doesn't want to let go of us. I think she's afraid her friends would think she's a rotten mother if we lived with Dad instead of her.

Anne's father was deeply worried about his children. He knew how unhappy they both were, but he had been advised that gaining custody of a teenage daughter and a preschool son would be very difficult. His lawyer counseled him to wait until his son was a little older before taking the case to court.

Meanwhile, what can Anne's father do to alleviate Anne and Dale's unhappiness? Must he stand by and watch his children become increasingly troubled? To some degree, the answer is yes. Sometimes we don't have the power to make a situation perfect. However, even without custody, Anne's father *can* provide her and her brother with an important — even essential — relationship.

What Can a Non-Custodial Parent Do? When a child's relationship with the custodial parent is weak or flawed, that child especially needs the relationship with the non-custodial parent. If you are the non-custodial parent and you have strong concerns about the quality of care your child is receiving, keep in mind: more than ever, your child needs *you.* In fact, the love and support he receives from you may be his lifeline. A child who suffers from the emotional deprivation of a disinterested or disturbed mother needs a fully satisfying relationship with the other parent.

How can you give your child the extra support needed to cope with a living situation which is far from ideal? Shelly's father tells us how he was able to help his daughter:

After the divorce I became increasingly angry with my ex-wife. I had wanted to raise Shelly myself, but she had insisted on custody. But she was never home with her. She left for work early, leaving Shelly to get breakfast for herself.

As time went by, Shelly began to be tardy to school. Furthermore, her grades slipped and she even was cutting school — in the sixth grade. She used to tell me how miserable she was and I sympathized with her a lot.

One day I was called in to see Shelly's school counselor. When he brought up her tardiness and poor grades, I launched into an attack against her mother, explaining her neglect and disinterest. The counselor listened sympathetically and then said, "Mr. Kelsey, did it ever occur to you that *you* are also contributing to Shelly's irresponsibility? Feeling pity for Shelly and excusing her behavior by blaming her mother isn't helping her. She needs more than your pity. Help your daughter be responsible and feel good about her own accomplishments."

That counsel was valuable, for Shelly's father was able to see more clearly how he was teaching her to make excuses rather than take responsibility for herself. Shelly remembers how the situation improved.

After the school conference, Dad and I had a long talk. He told me we could work together on the problems I was having even though I still wouldn't be living with him. He started phoning me every morning to check if I were out of bed and getting dressed. It got to be kind of a game. I'd try to be up and eating my breakfast before the phone rang. After talking to Dad, I'd feel better. I'd hurry and get to school on time and I went back to studying and doing my homework. Maybe I'll be on the honor roll next six weeks!

Another father we know phones his son and daughter every afternoon at 3:45 just after they get home from school. Their mother does not get home for two hours after they are home. This "checking in" time gives the children a chance to share events of the day. It is an important time for them.

A Warning. Be aware of the messages you are conveying to your children about their mother. You should be honest and help your child understand his custodial parent's shortcomings and problems; but if you constantly downgrade her or encourage your child to turn against her, you will only cause more problems. If your child must live with a disinterested or neglecting parent (for whatever reasons), he needs all the help he can get in order to work out a satisfactory relationship with her. Don't fan each incident of psychological neglect into a roaring fire. That only makes it more difficult for your child to cope effectively.

Visitation. Another way you can help your child is by making the time he spends with you truly satisfactory. Keep in mind that he needs your emotional support and your interest more than most children of divorce do. Don't let visitation time turn into a routine of running from one meaningless activity to another. Make sure there are some "fun" times, of course, but also make sure there are some quiet times just for being together. For younger children especially, it is often quite effective to set aside a special "holding time" in which they sit on your lap enveloped by your arms, just talking and being close to you. The child who does not receive sufficient nurture from his custodial parent needs extra attention from you!

Time Changes Things. Don't forget that situations change as time passes. The disinterested mother who has insisted on custody in the early months of separation may later be able to relinquish custody as she builds a new life for herself. Her needs and desires may change. In addition, social and legal attitudes are gradually changing. Increasingly, fathers are gaining custody of their children when it is in the best interest of the child.

Even if your child is not living in as good a situation as you would like, if the deficiencies are not too great and if his relationship with you continues to be vital and nurturing, your child can grow up strong and healthy.

THE ABANDONING NON-CUSTODIAL PARENT

In almost all cases, after divorce the contact between the child and the non-custodial parent is lessened. Although children initially find the adjustment difficult, most are able to accept a parent's moving out of the home without becoming totally engulfed by feelings of guilt—provided, of course, that visitation arrangements start immediately. But what about the child whose mother or father leaves and does not return? Or the child whose parent leaves suddenly after a quarrel and is not seen for an extended period of time?

Children who have been abandoned by one parent have severe adjustment problems to face. All the feelings of grief, anger, guilt, and fear that children experience following their parents' separation are considerably more acute for the child who actually has been deserted by one of his parents. In fact, such children go through much of the same stages of anger, denial, and mourning as other children do when a parent dies. Knowing that the parent is still alive, however, makes it even more difficult for the child to accept the finality of the loss.

"When Mommy Comes Back" Being abandoned is devastating to children. It is not uncommon for such children to turn to a world of fantasies in order to cope with the intensity of their distress. A grandmother, recruited to help out when her grandchildren were abandoned by her daughter-in-law, reports:

> When Sarah and Tamara's mother left, my son, Matthew, was really stunned. I had tried to tell him for years that she was no good and was running around, but he never would listen. Now he knows! She ran off with another man and has only been heard from once — five months ago — when she sent a postcard from Mexico!
>
> Those two girls have really suffered. They cried and cried at first, but I just kept telling them that they were better off without that mother of theirs. She wasn't any good! You know they don't cry anymore, but they keep telling each other how it's going to be "when Mommy comes back." They often make up stories of how she's so beautiful and how she's going to come back and bring them lots of presents and stuff. It really upsets me.

Although Grandma means well, her own rage with her daughter-in-law combined with her lack of understanding of the girls' feelings stand in the way of her being able to give Sarah and Tamara the nurture and love they desperately need. For her son, Matthew, the task is enormous. Not only must he cope with his own hurt and anguish, his feelings and fantasies, but he must also help his daughters. In addition to needing care and attention, they also need to be comforted and reassured that they were not to blame for their mother's leaving. Having lost one parent, these children worry greatly about losing their father too. Matthew and his family are still in severe crisis; professional counseling is needed to provide support as well as help for them to understand and cope with the problems they face.

Super Parent or Ugly Demon. Most children of abandonment carry a very unrealistic picture of their absent parent, perceiving him as both worse than he really is and better than he really is, for their feelings are very ambivalent. They are angry and hurt by the abandonment, yet they continue to long for reunion. As time passes, the abandoning parent may undergo a metamorphosis in the child's mind. He may become a kind of Super Parent—all loving and powerful, good and beautiful. Or he may be remembered as Super Demon—evil and ugly, though still very powerful. Most often the child swings between those two extremes.

Children who have regular contact with the non-custodial parent are able to check the growth of such fantasies. By seeing their parent regularly and experiencing firsthand that parent's humanness (his strengths and frailties), they are less apt to distort reality. But the abandoned child has only his memories, wishes, and fantasies, plus the messages he receives from his remaining parent and relatives, to help him form a picture of the parent who has left.

Counseling for Support. Most often the remaining parent will find that professional counseling is extremely helpful. It is not easy to face all the feelings that abandonment engenders and the problems that it causes. Just the stress of waiting, hoping that the absent parent will return (or will *not* return), takes a considerable toll from all members of the family. In addition, the fact that the marriage is not actually terminated makes it very difficult for the remaining parent to build a new life.

Counseling is recommended where total abandonment has taken place. Such assistance can help the parent come to grips with the problems in the family as well as provide him or her with a safe place to vent hostile feelings. Coping with his or her own emotions can make a parent better able to help the children work through their emotions.

Waiting for Daddy. There are more ways of abandoning a child than total desertion—there is *emotional* abandonment as well. The child whose parent is undependable and who contacts him only once in a while has also been abandoned to some degree. In some ways this type of desertion is even more cruel, for the child repeatedly builds up his hopes and then is let down time after time. The unkept promises, the forgotten birthdays, and the lack of sincere interest in the child's life cause the child continuing anguish and may seriously impede the child's ability to be trusting.

When fourteen-year-old Tim speaks of his father, his eyes flash angrily. His tall, gangly figure is capped by a mop of orange curls which flop wildly as he emphasizes his points:

My dad is a real jerk. He doesn't care about anyone but himself. Oh yeah, he pretends sometimes. "Tim," he says to me, "how are you doing now that you're in junior high?" I've been in junior high for more than two years already and he acts like I just got there.

When I was a kid I used to believe every word he said. He'd tell me, "I'll be by to pick you up at nine o'clock," and I'd be waiting by seven. Mom would say, "Tim, don't get your hopes up. Remember, your dad isn't that reliable. Think of something else you'd like to do today just in case he doesn't come." But instead of listening to her warning, I'd get mad at her.

Then I'd sit watching out the window, waiting and waiting. Around noon I'd finally realize he wasn't coming. But I still wouldn't act mad at Dad. I'd say, "Dad probably had a flat or maybe he had an appointment he forgot about." And Mom would just look sad and walk away. What a jerk I was! I just couldn't admit my own dad didn't care enough.

But now I'm older and I've finally got the picture. Mom and I don't need him. He can just spend his life driving around in that fancy car showing off to his girl friends. I know one thing. I'm not spending my time waiting anymore. I've got more important things to do with my life!

Tim has a right to feel hurt and angry. For years his father toyed with his feelings. Although he lived in the same town, Tim would not hear from his dad for weeks or more at a time. When Tim would call, his father would make excuses for his absence and would then promise to take Tim out next week on some great excursion. In spite of his past experiences, Tim would build up his hopes again and again. Finally he gave up, but the feelings of hurt and bitterness are still there.

HELPING CHILDREN OF ABANDONMENT AND NEGLECT

How can you help your child accept his other parent's lack of interest in him? First, be as honest as possible. Don't fall into the pitfall of making excuses for the disinterested parent. In the introduction to the excellent children's book *The Boys and Girls Book of Divorce*, child psychiatrist Richard A. Gardner advises parents *not* to tell their child that the absent parent loves him when it is obvious that the parent shows little or no interest in the child. Like Tim, your child will eventually come to know the truth, and if you've lied, his respect and trust in *you* will diminish. How can your child learn the meaning of love if you are claiming that his other parent's disinterest is love?

Second, you need to assure your child that he is a good, lovable human being. The problem belongs to his absent parent; it does not belong to the child. Children often feel they are to blame for their parent's neglect. They believe that if they were better children, their parent would want to be with them more often. They need frequent assurance that their parent's failure to love them does not mean they are unlovable.

One Hundred Loves. A child can be told that his father (mother) loves him as much as he is capable of loving — that love is not always full or complete. Too often it falls short of what the child needs and desires. A father we know explained it this way to his son:

> I know how much it hurts you that your mother doesn't see you very often. You want her to love you and care for you, and when she doesn't see you or call you, you feel hurt and angry.
>
> The problem is that you need and want *and should have* one hundred loves. You'd like Mom to give you that full one hundred, but she can't. She simply does not have that many loves to give you. It's too bad, because you deserve all that love, but wishing isn't going to change the situation. In fact, if you keep hoping to get all one hundred loves from Mommy, you'll always be disappointed and hurt.
>
> But you still need one hundred loves in order to grow up. The best way is to take the ten or twenty loves that Mommy *can* give you and get the rest of your loves from other people in your life who also love you. *I* can give you some of those loves — probably fifty or sixty, and your stepmother can give you some and so can your grandma and your brother. If you gather all the loves that everyone can give you, you may even have more than the one hundred you need, and you will be happier and richer in love than if you keep insisting that Mommy give you more than she can give.

If your child is not receiving the amount of love he needs and wants from his other parent, this explanation can greatly help him understand the problem. As time goes by, he may begin accepting the fact that his other parent cannot love him as fully as he wishes and may increasingly turn to those in his life who can give him the love and reassurance he needs.

Every child has a profound lesson to learn about his parents. He must learn to accept them as they really are — beauty, warts, and all! Over the years your child will decide for himself what he likes and respects about each of his parents. You cannot force your insights on your child, nor should you. Developing his own opinions and insights is part of growing up and becoming a separate, independent adult. Don't be surprised if for some time your child does not wish to accept the truth about the lack of love and interest that his absent parent displays. Often, as Tim's mother learned, the child must experience the hurt of being forsaken and disappointed again and again before he can finally accept the realities.

Through this painful process, your child needs to hear your constant messages of the love and approval *you* have for him. As he finds that other people continue to love him, he will increasingly be able to confront his feelings about the abandoning or neglecting parent. Gradually, he will shed his fantasies and build a more realistic picture of his parent. Eventually, he may even be able to feel honest compassion and pity for the defect in his parent's character which keeps him from fully experiencing the joy of loving his child and being involved in his development and growth.

ROLE PROBLEMS

When parents split up, relationships among all the members of the family cannot help but shift and change. The role the child has in his mother's home may be quite different from his role in his father's home. When parents remarry and stepfamilies are created, role definitions become even more of a problem. In most cases, within a year or so after divorce, members of the family begin to feel fairly comfortable in their redefined roles. Relationships between members of the family become more clarified and individuals are usually able to interact in healthy ways, meeting each other's needs.

Sometimes, however, children and parents have problems getting their needs fulfilled and they use each other in ways which are not so healthy — ways which actually limit their development and cause problems. Let us look briefly at some of these situations.

MOMMY'S BABY

After separation from their husbands, some women feel terribly alone and abandoned. A mother who has "lost" her husband through divorce may stifle her child's growth, unconsciously desiring to keep that child "Mommy's baby." Her needs to possess someone who won't leave her may be so great that she attempts to make the child overly dependent upon her. It is not merely that she buttons his clothes and ties his shoes; she ties him to her apron strings as well. Because she is so afraid of "losing" him, she doesn't allow him to establish himself as an independent, autonomous person. By such behavior, she is retarding his growth and development.

Needless to say, this causes many types of problems for the child. He may become clinging and demanding, fearful and withdrawn, or just plain babyish. This change in behavior will undoubtedly bring other problems—especially as this child relates to peers. He may be ridiculed at school or avoided by the other students. As he is kept in an overly dependent position, he will undoubtedly feel increasingly impotent and angry. Mothers and children who are involved in this type of problem usually need counseling or therapy to help them understand the dynamics of the relationship and find healthy ways of meeting their needs.

MY CHILD—MY PARENT

Some mothers who feel emotionally abandoned relate to their child in a different, but equally disturbing manner. Instead of encouraging the child to depend and lean on her, the mother begins to play a dependent role to the child—forcing the child to assume a parental role. Especially if the child is a girl, she may be expected to manage most of the household tasks as well as care for her younger siblings. She will also be expected to give support to her mother and perhaps even serve as a confidante.

The older child or teenager who becomes entrapped in this kind of situation is usually capable and sensitive, often with a highly developed conscience. She may want desperately to win and keep her mother's high regard (and pleasing her this way may be the only way she receives attention and affection), so she strives hard to manage. But in the process she loses her own childhood. She is forced into carrying responsibilities and burdens which are too great for her. Since she is not an adult, she cannot manage as well as an adult.

As she copes with problems clearly beyond her ability, she becomes anxious and her self-esteem may become shaky. Furthermore, the child who assumes responsibility too early may also find that she doesn't fit into the world of her schoolmates easily, for she is both too old and strangely enough, too young. After all, while playing parent to her mother, she has missed the nurture *she* should have received.

Like the overprotected child, this youngster also feels inadequate and angry and may later have difficulty separating from her mother, establishing herself as an independent adult. Her guilt, anger, and low self-esteem, combined with the entwinement with her mother, greatly hinder her own development.

MY LITTLE MAN — SUBSTITUTE SPOUSE

Another way parents sometimes attempt to get the nurture they need is to relate to the opposite sexed child or teenager as if he or she were the absent spouse. For example, we've all heard of women who talk about their young son as "my little man." These mothers foster a relationship with their son which is clearly inappropriate. Lacking a man in her life, the mother turns to the son and relates to him as if he were her man. In its mildest form this may mean that there are definite sexual overtones to the mother-son relationship; at the most extreme, the mother and son may actually engage in sexual intercourse.

The same may be true about a father and daughter. The father may turn to his daughter for confirmation that he is a man — a sexual being. Again, there may be heavy sexual overtones to the relationship or there can be actual incestuous involvement. In either case, the child or teenager will later have problems with his or her sexual development and maturity. A woman who is now in therapy discusses her involvement with her father:

> Although my parents lived together, my father was the one who always bought my clothes for me — from bras and underwear to coats and boots. He used to comment on my figure and he took pride in my looking good. When I started dating, he was very jealous and always found fault with every guy who came around. He used to brag to his friends that he couldn't tell my voice from my mother's on the telephone and often would say something sexual to me thinking I was Mom.
>
> I've been married three times and have had dozens of affairs and involvements which have not worked out. Not until recently did I finally realize that my relationship with my dad — which I must admit I encouraged — has interfered with my re-

lating sexually and maturely to men. I feel guilty and unfaithful when I look at another man. Furthermore, my relationship with my mom has not been satisfactory. In fact, I'm just now beginning to get to know her and appreciate her.

Of course all mother-son and father-daughter relationships have some sexual feelings. But treating your son or daughter the same as you would your spouse is a dangerous practice. That child's healthy maturation will be seriously impaired.

YOU'RE JUST LIKE YOUR FATHER (MOTHER)

"When my mom says, 'You're just like your father', it's no compliment!" says sixteen-year-old Craig.

"The other day my dad got mad at me and said that the way I talk reminds him of my mom. I know he doesn't like Mom, and I don't think he likes me either," complains a young girl.

The results of an informal survey we took recently confirms this young lady's suspicion. Most often a parent who says to his child, "You're just like . . ." is thinking of a negative quality. Whether the comment is meant to be a compliment or a cutting remark, the child does not generally benefit from such observations. If he is viewed as being "just like" one of his parents, he is being robbed of his uniqueness and cannot take pride in his individuality. Your child is not a replica of you or of his other parent, and to perceive him as such is setting him up for trouble. Even if your child looks exactly like you or his other parent or has many mannerisms which are similar to one of you, remember that *he is himself—a unique human being*!

MOM, THE FOOTBALL COACH

"Every Saturday I play football with my two sons," relates a young mother proudly. "The neighbors think I'm crazy, but I love it! Two years ago when I threw out my 'ex', I told him we didn't need him; that I could raise the boys myself with no help—and I have!"

In this day of unisex and fusion of traditional roles, mothers and fathers are freer to define their parental roles more broadly than in the past. This can sometimes be confusing, but it can also be healthy and liberating, for it offers the opportunity to live a life with less denial and pretense. But the parent who goes the next step and says, "I can be both father and mother to my child—he doesn't need another parent!" is on dangerous ground. This attitude is bound to lead to trouble, for until there is truly no distinguishable difference between a man and a woman, one person cannot be both father and mother to a child. A boy needs a man (even on a part-time basis) to learn what it is to be a man; and a girl needs a woman or women in her life to learn what it is to be a woman. You cannot be both mother and father — nor should you try. If your child is lacking a father, find other men to fill in. Your child can join the Boy Scouts or a boys' club; or there may be a male relative who will take a special interest in him. The same is true if your child is lacking a mother. Find female substitutes who can spend time with your daughter. Meanwhile, there's no need for you to feel guilty for being either a man or a woman. Biological differences are real, interesting, and valuable.

REMEMBER

Helping your children grow and mature in healthy ways in spite of (and perhaps because of) your divorce is possible. Think about your situation. Which problems, if any, cited in this chapter are making trouble in your life? What can you do to make changes? Do you need help? Be careful not to let problems grow until they are unsolvable or even irreversible! Thousands of parents have the insight and compassion to raise their children effectively after divorce *without succumbing* to the problems cited in this chapter — you can too!

11

Dating and
Remarriage

"First comes love; then comes marriage; then comes Mary with a baby carriage!" Remember that old jump-rope ditty? From love to marriage to children — that was the natural order of life. But for the single parent it is different. Before the single parent even meets a likely candidate for love and possibly marriage, the children are already there!

In fact, as Mark, forty, discovered, not only are they there, but they may have also appointed themselves the interviewing committee. Mark remembers vividly the first time he arrived at Judy's house to take her out to dinner:

I was standing in the living room waiting for Judy to finish dressing when six-year-old Justin and eight-year-old Karen appeared. Two pair of dark eyes surveyed me sternly. After some moments Justin asked, "Are you taking Mama out?"

"Yes," I answered almost meekly.

"Where are you taking her?" It was Karen's turn now. I named a fancy restaurant downtown.

"Do they have fried chicken?'" Justin asked. "It's Mama's favorite, you know." I didn't know.

"No," I answered, becoming defensive, "but they *do* have beef wellington, tournedos, and scampi." They were definitely not impressed. Both of them were frowning and signaling their disapproval to each other. Obviously, I had failed this part of the interview. Luckily, before they could continue the inquiry,

Judy sailed into the room, whisked them toward the babysitter and their bedrooms, and hurried us out the door!

A BOYFRIEND FOR MOMMY?

"Mommies can't have boyfriends!" said ten-year-old Jodi indignantly.

"Yeah," chimed in her brother. "Boyfriends are for teenagers like Susie." The two, nodding emphatically, turned to their seventeen-year-old sister for confirmation.

"Well," said Susie with a touch of embarrassment, "it does feel kind of weird to have Mom out on a date while I'm sitting at home on Saturday night."

These youngsters, like your own, are reacting to the changes in what they perceive to be their mother's role. Before the divorce their mother didn't date — at least during the years they knew her! What is she doing going out with a man? In the eyes of the court and within her social circle, she may be considered legally divorced, but to her children, she is still *Mother* (tied in their minds to Father) and *mothers don't date*.

"My kids are more old-fashioned and judgmental than my father ever was," laments a young mother. "If they had had to give their permission the first time, I never would have been married!"

Children *are* conservative. They do not readily approve of change and especially not change in their parents. As we shall see in this chapter, each time you make a change in your role — whether it is dating, living with someone, or marrying — your child will feel uneasy and anxious about his own place in your world. Because the children spend more of their time with their custodial parent and because marriage for this parent means the addition of a new live-in parent for the children, their reactions to their mother's dating may be more intense than their reactions to their father's dating. Therefore, we shall focus more on the implications of a custodial mother's dating and remarriage. However, most of the discussion and suggestions are applicable to the part-time father as well.

HOW CHILDREN REACT TO PARENTAL DATING

When you first begin dating, your child cannot help but feel somewhat emotionally threatened. There are many reasons for this. First, your child has not really given up all his hope and fantasies that his parents someday will be reunited. As long as there are no other potential mates in your life, he continues to feel hopeful. But when you begin to show an interest in someone else, he becomes panicky, realizing that the possibility of reconciliation is increasingly remote.

Second, although you and your former spouse are divorced from each other, it takes a long time for the child to "unhook" you both in his own mind and accept your autonomy. Your child believes deep down that since you and his other parent are both related to him, you are still related to each other. And in a way he is correct, for responsible parents do indeed maintain a parenting relationship of some kind through their child. But of course after divorce you are free to involve yourselves with others. However, your child continues to feel that you and his father are being disloyal to each other when you date others.

Third, your child cannot help but distrust your dates, for he sees each one as a potential stepparent who may try to replace his own father. He doesn't want to like your date; it makes him feel disloyal to his natural parent. Often children try to sabotage their parent's involvement with a man or woman. Asking questions and making comments which are superficially innocent but have an underlying hostile tone is one way that children guard against liking another person and letting him like them. Justin and Karen, as we saw earlier, were very adept at this technique. The child's subconscious hope is that dislike and non-involvement will be mutual and thus the intruder will be scared off!

Finally, your child may react jealously to your interest in another person. This is especially true if you have been single for some time, though even when children live with both their parents they don't like sharing their mother with their father or vice versa. Your child would much prefer to have your undivided attention and affection than to share it with someone else. He particularly doesn't want to share you with an outsider. Your child views the men or women in your life suspiciously, for he is worried that the exclusive relationship he has enjoyed with you may soon be changed.

And yet there is a paradox, for despite his anxieties and fears, your child may really want you to remarry. He is not so totally opposed to your dating as he first leads you to believe—and even as he first believes. Most children do want to live with a father and a mother. Furthermore, many children who are sensitive intuitively understand that their mother or father needs adult love and companion-

ship. As you begin dating and forming relationships with men or
women, your child—and especially your teenager—may come to
realize and appreciate that a parent who feels attractive and worthwhile is far happier than one who becomes buried in work and
raising children. If he is not overwhelmed by feelings of disloyalty
and guilt, he will gradually be able to accept your dating and, despite
his initial resistance, may even come to like some of your friends.

DATING ADVICE

Many of the single parents we interviewed had suggestions and
sound advice for dating parents. Their counsel is valuable and may
help smooth the way as you and your children adapt to the changes
in your role.

1. *Go slowly!* Remember that your child can adjust to many
changes in his life so long as he is not forced to adapt too quickly. If
you suddenly switch from being a mother who stays at home to one
who goes out on the town every night, your child will undoubtedly
resent the change in your role. He will feel anxious and abandoned,
jealous that you are having a good time away from him.

Some children clearly wail their objections: "You never have any
time for me anymore!" or "You don't love me!" Other children resort
to tantrums or become sick the night you plan to go out. Still other
children may make thinly veiled hostile remarks to their mother's
male friends, such as, "My dad is bigger than you and he has lots of
hair on top of his head!"

But if you enter the dating world more slowly, balancing your
needs for companionship, fun, and sex with your child's needs for
attention, you can mitigate some of these problems. "I learned the
hard way," confesses Maria, a very attractive mother of three young
children. After divorce Maria got caught up in a whirlwind of social
activities. She explains:

> I was married at eighteen and had never dated anyone but
> Mike. After seven years of constant fighting and problems, we
> were divorced. Suddenly I realized I was free—free to date, go
> to parties, do what *I* wanted to do. I bought new clothes and
> cut my hair. To my surprise I found myself popular and attrac-
> tive to men. I must admit it was a thrill to feel so desirable!
> My social calendar became increasingly crowded, and my

kids complained that I was never home. It was true, but I told myself that they were well cared for by my mother and I deserved my fling. Then Carlos began having asthma attacks regularly on the nights I was out. After a particularly bad attack, I finally came to my senses and realized that my kids, whom I really love, were paying for my popularity. I got off the merry-go-round and have never regretted it. I still date and go to a few parties, but I'm not frantic anymore. I love my children and I don't want to be free from them. Although I'm single again, I'm not eighteen. I am a mother and that's what I want to be!

Especially after divorce, your child needs *you.* Of course that doesn't mean you should spend every moment with him — that would be suffocating for both of you. But neither should your children become TV-dinner orphans. As Maria discovered, balancing your needs and your children's needs is far more sensible.

2. *Limit the number of men or women in your child's life.* Not only is it wise to limit the number of evenings you spend away from your child, but it is also better not to involve your child in all of your casual dating. That's not to say that you should hide the fact you are dating from your child. Obviously, that does not make sense, but you should not expect your child to get to know all the persons you are dating. There is a limit to how many people your child can relate to in a meaningful way. Furthermore, since his anxiety increases when you date, there is no point in involving him unless your date becomes a closer friend.

Harold, a part-time father, shares his experience and offers advice:

I found that it's best to wait until you really know and like a lady before you introduce her to your kids. I used to think it was good to invite my dates to spend Saturday or Sunday with my kids and me. I wanted to see how she and the kids would get along, and frankly, combining dating and visitation was convenient for me.

But it got to be kind of embarrassing. Missy and Greg were openly jealous of my attention to my lady friends and they would go out of their way to be kind of politely rude, if you know what I mean. For example, Missy would ask, "Daddy, where's Sally? Why isn't *she* here this week?" And of course she'd say that in front of Linda.

After a few of those episodes, I decided I'd better do more of my dating on my own time. It's really fairer to my dates too. Now I'm not involving my kids until I meet someone special. At that time, of course, they would need to get to know each other before I would even consider getting married.

Many single parents have discovered that Harold's experience is similar to their own. Keeping most of their casual dating and sex life apart from their children seems to work better than constantly involving the children in relationships which are not deeply rooted. There is nothing to be gained by flaunting your dates or involving your children prematurely. Children, like adults, become "burned out" by having to relate to people who randomly wander in and out of their lives. They need more constancy and continuity to relationships. Wait until your relationship with a man or women has become *very* special before you bring your child into the relationship.

3. *Establish a couple of nights a week which belong to you!* Many parents mentioned that staking out a night or two during the week which belonged to them (without the children) was very helpful in getting the children used to the idea that some of Mother's life is separate from theirs. "When my kids could count on the fact that I would not be home on Wednesday evenings and that either Friday or Saturday night I would be out also, things went a lot better," says Helen. Often it is possible to line up babysitters for those evenings on an ongoing basis. This helps the children to feel more comfortable when you are away. Margaret confirms what Helen found to be true:

> The children really used to hassle me about going out. You'd think I was leaving for Outer Mongolia, the way they acted. But now that I go out regularly on Tuesdays and Saturdays, they just know and accept that those are my evenings out! There's no question about it. It's become my right!

4. *Don't let your dating become competitive with your teenager's.* After divorce often men and women adopt a more youthful wardrobe and style of grooming. Women commonly lose the pounds they gained during marriage and childbearing. Men start jogging in hopes of regaining their youthful vigor. It is understandable to want to be as attractive as possible — especially when your self-esteem may be somewhat low. But be careful that you don't begin to compete with

your teenagers. Remember that teenagers want *parents*, not competitors or buddies. Don't start borrowing clothes from your daughter. She will have many mixed feelings if you do. The same is true about a father and son. If you do not ordinarily wear blue jeans to go out and suddenly you appear in jeans more faded than your child's, he's bound to feel that you're encroaching on his world!

Furthermore, it is not wise to share intimacies about your dating experiences. Although your son or daughter may listen with avid interest, being involved even vicariously in your dating and sex life makes the teenager uncomfortable. It is fun to share, but be discreet and appropriate in your sharing! Don't fall into the feeling of "we're all just kids together." Both parent and child will lose.

5. *When you do invite a man or woman to be with you and your family, plan activities which are fun for adults and children.* Don't drag your child to the movies with you and your date unless the movie is appropriate for all ages. Conversely, don't invite your date to your child's birthday party unless he or she *truly* loves kids — and even then think twice. There is no point in involving your date and your children in activities which will bore or irritate them. It is better to plan wisely so that you increase the chances that your friend and your child will get off on the right foot. It is much easier to begin a relationship well than to fix one which started poorly.

6. *Don't use your child to spy and report on your ex-spouse's dates.* Your child already feels considerable ambivalence about each parent's dating. Don't put him on the spot by asking detailed questions about the other parent's choice of dates and activities. As we discussed in Chapter 10, asking your child to carry tales increases his anxiety and puts him in a difficult position. He doesn't want to hurt either your feelings or his other parent's. If he tells you his father's new girlfriend is half your age, twice as pretty, and a real pro on the tennis courts, you undoubtedly will be hurt and angry. But if he roundly condemns his father's choice of women, he is criticizing his father. He can't win!

Of course you cannot help but be interested in your former spouse's new relationship, but try to be rather neutral in your approach to your child's reporting. Remember to give yourself the same message as you would give your child: each parent is now free to involve himself with whomever he wishes.

7. *Be prepared that your child will view each new person in your life as a potential mate for you.*

I have a large family—five kids, three dogs, two cats, and heaven only knows how many gerbils! Can you imagine how a man feels when he's dated me twice and my kids come up and say, "Are you going to marry us?" If he's got any sense, he runs like hell!

If your child has seen the same man or woman several times, he may wish to know whether you are anticipating marriage. Although sometimes the question is hostile, intending to make you or your friend uncomfortable, usually the child asks in order to predict his future more accurately and to deal with his anxiety and conflict. The best way to handle the situation is to be honest. If this is your second date, tell your child you hardly know the man or woman. If you are serious, share this with your child. Make sure your child knows that nothing is definite. If you are certain that marriage will not result, tell him that. If you are as honest as possible, your child will learn that he can trust you to be direct with him.

SEX AND THE SINGLE PARENT

Some years ago in a town that isn't very small, a kindergartner delivered this report for Wednesday's "show and tell": "Uncle Charlie stayed overnight so Mommy wouldn't be lonely." Within moments, the shocked but titillated teacher conveyed this tidbit to her friend, the music teacher, who in turn enlightened the school principal. A few days later it was common (though whispered) knowledge that Amy Williams's mother was sleeping with her neighbor, Charlie Phillips.

That was less than a generation ago! Sexual mores have greatly changed in recent years. Today people are much more open and less judgmental about sexual relationships. For example, recently when a young kindergartner proudly showed her gaudy, green glass necklace, she announced, "Mommy and Ken, that's her boyfriend—brought this back for me when they were on vacation in San Francisco." This time the kindergarten teacher scarcely raised an eyebrow!

No longer are there rigid social standards for sexual behavior. Instead, individuals must define their feelings and make many decisions about their own sexual conduct. A mother we interviewed summed up the current thinking: "What is good for me in my situation might not be good for someone else. There is no one morality for everyone anymore—if there really ever was!"

Although some of the parents we interviewed knew exactly how they felt about their own sexuality, most were struggling to clarify their views. Margaret, forty-one, is a good example:

When I got married twenty years ago, it was rather simple: "good" girls didn't and "bad" girls did! And if a "good" girl slipped, she certainly didn't advertise her indiscretion! But now it's all different. I feel as if I've just emerged from spending twenty years in a cave. I'll tell you one thing, reading magazine articles about the sexual revolution is no preparation for being in the midst of it!

The lack of binding social constraints presents new problems for single parents. What do *you* believe about sexuality and sexual behavior? Would you be comfortable inviting your date to share your bed? Every date? Only a few? Just one special person? With the knowledge of your children or only if your children were away? Would it bother you to have your date's car parked in front of your house overnight? Would you spend the night at his house? Would you leave his name and phone number for the babysitter? Would you go away with a man for a weekend? What would you tell your children — the truth, a lie, or a bit of truth laced with lies? *What do you want your child to learn about sexuality?*

Of all the questions above, the last question is probably the most crucial for parents. After all, *you are a model!* Here the old adages really apply: "It's not what you say, it's what you do," or "Actions speak louder than words." Parents are constantly modeling behavior for their children, and nothing turns off children — particularly teenagers — so quickly as hypocrisy. Often it is tempting to say to your children: "Do as I say, not as I do," but we all know it simply doesn't work!

CHANGING YOUR LIFE-STYLE SLOWLY

Whether you decide to become celibate, sexually active, or something in between, without a full-time, live-in mate, your sexual life is bound to be changed by divorce. After divorce, single parents must take stock of themselves, their situation, and their relationship to the opposite sex and reevaluate their sexual values and beliefs. However, remember that no matter what you decide, you have your children and their feelings to consider.

Go slowly! Don't suddenly or drastically alter your life-style. Just because you have reconsidered and, for example, have decided that sex should be enjoyed with a wide number of sexual partners, it doesn't mean that you should proceed immediately to parade men through your bedroom. Responsible parents do not put their children through *radical* change needlessly.

If you have been monogamous in the past, it will be hard for your child to accept your sexual involvement with many people. Even if your marriage has been "open" and the child has been aware of your involvements, it still will be difficult for him to accept substitutes for his father or mother. But if you approach changes in your life slowly, your child will usually be better able to accept these changes.

Pamela now feels that she was not sensitive enough to her son's needs. "What I did to Eric," she reports, "really wasn't fair."

For several months after divorce, I dated no one. Then I met David and we went out one evening and had a marvelous time together. When he brought me home, I dismissed the babysitter and we settled down for a nightcap—which multiplied into several. Anyhow, one thing led to another and we wound up in bed together. Ordinarily, Eric is a very heavy sleeper—he almost never wakes in the night—but wouldn't you know it, he picked that night to have a stomachache! He came running into my room crying "Mommy, Mommy! I'm going to throw up!" And without thinking, I snapped on the light, totally forgetting about David lying nude next to me. Poor Eric! And poor David! They both just froze, eyeing each other!

Well, it scarcely seemed like the time for a formal introduction, so I picked up Eric and carried him back to bed. After David hastily left, I lay in bed thinking about what I should tell Eric in the morning. But the next morning Eric didn't mention the subject, so neither did I. However, he's more anxious about my going out now and acts jealous and hostile toward David, whom I really like. It would have been so much better had Eric really known David before all this happened!

Pamela is right. Had Eric known David and felt his mother's growing attraction to the man he would have been much better prepared to accept his mother and David in an intimate situation. But finding a stranger in his mother's bed was another thing! Eric's jealousy and distrust of David, and of his mother too, will now be harder to overcome.

SENSITIVITY AND DISCRETION

Most parents wouldn't (and shouldn't) think of allowing their child into their marital bed; after divorce, parents still need to use discretion about their sexual life. Even when your child seems to be adjusting fairly well to the changes in your role, there are still sound pyschological reasons for keeping sex a reasonably private matter.

If you passionately "make out" on the living room couch in front of your child, you are bound to make him feel anxious and uncomfortable — and somewhat sexually aroused. For the comfort of your child and yourself, privacy is important. One seventeen-year-old confided his feelings of conflict about his keen awareness of his father's sexuality:

> Sometimes I hate being over at my dad's. The walls of his apartment are real thin, and I can hear everything that goes on between him and his girlfriends. One lady especially gets to me. She's only six years older than I am — and what a knockout! My fantasies start running away with me. I can't help thinking it ought to be *me* with that chick instead of Dad. It makes me kind of jealous and angry with Dad, and kind of embarrassed too.

All over the world in highly disparate communities and cultures, ranging from the most primitive to the most technologically sophisticated societies, incest taboos exist. These taboos protect parents and children from becoming sexually involved with each other. In the United States, reports of actual parent-child incest indicate that this is an increasing problem. Being *directly* involved in incest, however, is only one way in which parents and children develop a sexual relationship. More often, when parents are not discreet, they and their children become involved in *indirect* sexual relationships. By flaunting your sexuality in front of your child, you are involving him in your sexual life. Your child needs you as a model for learning about sexuality, but he shouldn't be overstimulated.

Craig, another young man we interviewed, was greatly disturbed by his feelings about his mother's newly found sexuality and her covert attempts to seduce her son. He reports:

> Since Dad left, Mom is a lot different around me. She dresses kind of sexy and sometimes I think she makes sure I'll see her in her thin nightgown on the way to the bathroom. Even when

I'm in my room studying, I can hear her with her friend, Ted, laughing and carrying on. Sometimes my mind wanders — and I'm ashamed to admit it — but I get to thinking about my mom in the wrong way.

Although Craig was working hard to maintain the sexual boundaries between him and his mother, his growing feelings of attraction and arousal, which strongly conflicted with the constraints of his conscience, were beginning to overwhelm him. Adolescents who are already coping with their own budding (or fully bloomed!) sexuality particularly require a separation between their own sexuality and that of their parents. When living with parents who are married, the child or teen's sexual desire for his parent of the opposite sex is checked by the presence of the parent of the same sex. In the same way the parent's natural awareness of the child's growing sexuality is also checked. But when mother and son or father and daughter live alone together, more care needs to be taken that situations do not arise which promote either direct or indirect incest. Being sexually involved with one of his or her parents greatly complicates the child's ability to separate and mature sexually as an adult.

LIVING TOGETHER

Recently a young first-grader drew a picture of his family. He labeled the tall man standing next to his mother, "Tom." The teacher who thought she knew the members of his family was perplexed. "Who is Tom?" she asked.

"Oh," replied Barry breezily, "Tom is a guy who is living with us. We're trying to see if we can get used to him. If we can, he and Mom might get married!"

In an age of freer living and sexual arrangements, sometimes parents decide to live together either before marriage (a trial period) or instead of marriage (a long-term relationship which is simply not formally legalized). Although a large percentage of parents do remarry, some are initially reluctant even to consider marrying again. One parent asks rhetorically:

Why should I get married again? What's to make this marriage any more successful than my last one? Sure, I love James, but a few years ago I thought I was madly in love with Karl. We said "until death do us part" and after five years together we were ready to kill each other! I don't want any repeats!

Often people emerge from a disastrous marriage feeling cynical, bitter, and fearful of trying again. Some parents blame marriage itself, pointing out its flaws and proclaiming it a doomed institution. Others are unwilling to marry again because they feel that they themselves are unsuited for marriage. Marcia is a mother who feels that way:

> I know the problem is me. Living with Chuck is great, but if we were to get married, I'd start taking him for granted. Before long I'd be hollering at him and ordering him around, finding fault with everything he did or didn't do. Living together is much better. It keeps me on my toes and keeps our relationship from going stale.

For Marcia, living together provides the benefits of companionship, sex, and mutual support without the perceived potential problems and constraints of legal marriage. But what about her child? How does he perceive and react to his parent living with a new man?

For the child, "non-marriage" — just like marriage — involves a series of complex adjustments. He must discover who the new person is — his character and personality, as well as his background and values — and what his role in the family will be. In some ways, however, non-marriage may be more difficult, for it tends to be a more ambiguous union. For example, what is the new man's relationship to the child? Is he merely his mother's "friend," or is he an additional or replacement parent? What is his authority within the household? Will the union be long-lived or will it dissolve after the first quarrel or difficulty? The child must face the same questions in relation to his father's "live-in" woman friend. The child needs to know, *What are the commitments?*

Often parents who fear commitment delude themselves by thinking that the non-legalized union is not as real to the child. Therefore, if the parent and friend part, the child (and perhaps also the parent) will not feel the loss and pain as keenly as the breakup of a marriage. But, of course, this is untrue. Depending upon the degree of investment and the length of time the union has lasted, the child cannot help but feel a loss. Furthermore, unlike the divorce of his parents, if this union breaks up, the child most often never sees that person again, for the child and the friend have no legal ties to each other. When the parents have a series of live-in arrangements, the child especially suffers. No one can repeatedly invest and lose without becoming deeply distrustful of relationships.

It should be noted, however, that living together can sometimes provide both the adults and the children with a transition period, a chance to get used to each other without the anxiety of failure which marriage often engenders. Often, after family members have had time to work out secure relationships, a deeper commitment to one another can be made.

Qualifications for Marrying a Parent

So you're thinking of becoming a stepparent! At best, stepparenting is not easy, but if you are a *parent* who is considering marrying a parent be prepared for problems. In fact, it's been found that the number of problems multiply in geometric ratio to the number of children you and your potential partner bring together. Before you impetuously accept the position of stepparent, stop and consider whether or not you have the necessary qualifications for the job.

1. *Warm heart and thick skin.* To be successful as a stepparent, you will need a warm heart and a thick skin! Compassion, sensitivity, and understanding need to be your strong points, but if they are not combined with a sufficiently tough skin, you'll end up with a punctured ego. Remember that although children are loving and tender, they can also be insensitive and cruel — especially when under stress. If you take to heart everything your stepchildren (or your own children for that matter) say about you or your wife or husband, you won't survive. While they struggle with the changes in their lives they are apt to be jealous and angry with you, their new stepparent. Although you can understand their problems, you can't absorb all of their anger. Some must simply roll off your back.

2. *Wisdom and deafness.* Especially if you are a parent marrying a parent, you will need the wisdom of Solomon, for in the months and years ahead you will often be called upon to make hair-splitting judgments which would tax the finest legal minds in the country. For example, when your stepchild spends the weekend away with his other father, *who* is responsible for his household chores? *Your* child who has not gone away for the weekend? And what if your stepchild is not required to do anything at his father's house? "It's not fair!" your child will complain, "Billy doesn't have to do any work on the weekends and I do!"

If you don't have the deafness of a baseball umpire, you'll not succeed. Remember that no matter how you interpret the play, both sets of kids (and maybe your spouse too) will protest and proclaim that you are UNFAIR! Somehow though, amidst the thunder, you must continue the game. Obviously, selective deafness is a useful talent.

3. *Patience and a set of strong teeth.* Like the tortoise climbing the hill, you will need infinite patience to reach your goals. As much as you would like to, you can't walk into a new family and start changing things to suit yourself. Change is effectively accomplished only in small steps. Often in the months ahead, you may find yourself grinding your teeth in frustration, but you can't hurry the process of building a cohesive, loving family. You can't immediately make your stepchildren like you (or your children) nor can you quickly erase the feelings of jealousy, anger, and distrust. Affection and respect develop slowly, as they are earned.

If you approach re-creating a family slowly, like the tortoise, you will reach the top of the hill. "I just hope I'm not over the hill before I reach the top!" said a friend, smiling wryly.

4. *Humor and agility.* These are surely the most important requirements for becoming a stepparent, for without a good sense of humor and the ability to keep your balance, all is lost. Many times a laugh will save a tear, and catching yourself in midfall (even if you lose a few of the pieces you were juggling) prevents a resounding crash! Being able to keep life and its miseries in perspective is the greatest gift of all!

If after considering this formidable list you are not dissuaded from your purpose, undoubtedly you have two more qualities which will serve you well: *courage* and *optimism!* Or, as a mother of four children remarked on the eve of her marriage to a father of five children, "Perhaps we're both simply fools!"

Here Comes the Bride!

"Here comes the bride, all dressed in white . . . ." Before I even had my eyes opened, I heard my kids lustily serenading me. My wedding day! The second one of my life. I thought back to that first time almost seventeen years ago. So many dreams — so much hope! But there was no "happily ever afters" for Sheldon and me. I opened my eyes, shook away the cobwebs, turned my thoughts to Stuart, and I felt warm and happy — reassured by our love for each other.

Suddenly, Dawn, Michael, and Beth burst into my room singing more loudly (and more off-key) than before.

"Happy wedding day to you!"

"No," Beth interrupted. "That's not right! It's happy wedding day to *us*! Right, Mom?"

"Of course," I agreed and I gave her a hug. Obviously, "our" wedding day was a new beginning for all of us!

A wedding is a ceremony which binds two lives together in love, hope, and commitment. But second weddings often join more than *two* lives together. There are the children: sometimes hers from a previous marriage, sometimes his, and sometimes his *and* hers! Saying "I do" involves far more for a parent than it does for a non-parent. Young Beth was right. When a parent remarries, the whole family remarries.

Children invariably have mixed feelings about their parent's remarriage. Anne Simon points out: "At a parent's wedding a child becomes a stepchild. The ceremony which makes his mother somebody's new wife, or his father a new husband, makes him a relation he knows nothing about." The child's ambivalence about both *becoming* this new relation and *acquiring* a new relation also makes him ambivalent about the ceremony which symbolizes these changes in his life.

As much as you might want your child to rejoice in your remarriage, he most often cannot feel the same kind of joy and hope that you feel. A part of him continues to mourn the passing of his most treasured fantasy — the reunion of his parents. His anger and jealousy and his anxiety and feelings of disloyalty to his other parent (the one he feels is being replaced by this ceremony) keep him from being totally free to rejoice with you.

Attending the Wedding — Pros and Cons

Should a child who feels ambivalent — or perhaps outright angry — about his parent's remarriage attend the wedding? There are pros and cons to the question. Some parents feel strongly that despite their children's mixed feelings, it is beneficial for them to be present, for it helps them accept the reality of the new relationship. Others feel that their children's presence with feelings of misgivings will mar the parents' enjoyment of their special day. Both views have merit.

Gerry is a thirty-eight-year-old father of four children who is planning to marry Marissa, a twenty-four-year-old woman who has never been married. They have decided *not* to have Gerry's children attend the wedding. Marissa explains:

Gerry's kids live in town and I've spent some time getting to know them. I'm really beginning to like Sarah, the youngest one, but the older teenagers are still kind of hostile and suspicious of me. I think in time things will work out, but meanwhile there is still that tension.

This is my wedding day — the only one I'll ever have, I hope! I've always dreamed of this day — and my dream didn't include children — at least not my husband's children. And especially not children who aren't that happy about me yet. I think it is better for me to have my day unspoiled than to resent forever having Gerry's kids there.

Marissa paused for a long moment and then suddenly with great feeling added:

I know it's selfish of me, but there *is* another reason why I don't want Gerry's kids there — they remind me that this isn't Gerry's first marriage. The children symbolize the other commitments in Gerry's life — commitments before I was a part of his life. On my wedding day, I don't want to think about his first marriage! I just want to think about *us* and our wedding!

A bride — especially a first-time bride — wants this day to be perfect. She doesn't want to cope with the conflict of her future stepchildren. There is plenty of time to work out these problems. The wedding day belongs to the bride and groom. Although Gerry initially wanted his children to be with him at his wedding, he could readily understand Marissa's feelings. In fact, he admitted to having some of the same concerns himself. He realized that the tension of worrying about his children's feelings would lessen his involvement with Marissa.

Of course, some parents do not have an elaborate wedding the second time. Parents who are married by a justice of the peace in a civil ceremony often feel that there is no need for the children to be present; the brief ceremony is merely a legal formality.

Karen and Doug, on the other hand, felt very strongly that all of their children should be present at their wedding. Karen had three children who lived with her; Doug had four children. The two oldest boys lived with him, and the two younger children lived with their mother. Doug explains their reasons for not only inviting the children, but also involving them in the ceremony:

> We thought it was very important that our marriage ceremony bring all nine of us together in a deeply personal way. We knew we were all going to have to function as a family and the place to formalize that concept, we believed, was at our wedding. From the start we involved the children in the planning. And we talked a great deal with them. We discussed our relationships to each other. Since both sets of kids already had other parents, Karen and I saw ourselves as additional parents — not replacements! We tried to make that clear from the beginning. I think that really helped to reduce the anxiety.
>
> Anyhow, the day of the wedding, the children were very excited, for they had helped plan the ceremony. After Karen and I had spoken our vows, the children came forward and we all held hands and exchanged vows of commitment and belonging to each other. It was so beautiful! And as I glanced at each face around that circle — my new family — I knew we could make it work! I looked at Karen. The tears were running down both our faces. I really think that ceremony helped set an atmosphere of trust and love in our home.

By including their children so thoroughly — both in open and frank discussions prior to the wedding and in the wedding itself — these parents were able to help their children accept their marriage and share in the happiness.

REMEMBER

Your child cannot help but feel ambivalent about your dating and remarriage. You can help him deal with his ambivalence, however, by moving slowly and by letting him know that you understand some of his negative feelings. Don't involve him in all of your casual dates, but *do* involve him with the more serious contenders for the role of stepparent. By being sensitive to the feelings and needs of everyone involved, you can make the prospect of remarriage and stepparenting an exciting challenge.

12

Stepparenting

"Adjusting to a new marriage and trying to be a good stepparent is a lot like patting your head and rubbing your stomach simultaneously," laughs Susan. "It's almost impossible to do both at the same time."

Susan is right. Almost all of the parents we talked with confided that at some point they had considered giving up. And no wonder! It is difficult enough to get used to a new spouse; adding children greatly complicates marital adjustments.

"With kids present, it's not as if you can lie around basking in the glory of love," Susan points out with a grimace. "Gazing passionately at each other somehow loses its romantic appeal when a small, sticky face intrudes between you and your loved one!" Mike, her husband, nods his head in wholehearted agreement. He remembers his problems adjusting to Susan's household:

> It certainly was not easy getting used to having Susan's kids around all the time. If I'd give Susan a little love pinch, one of the kids would suddenly appear from nowhere and frown disapprovingly at me. One day, Stanford, who was then five, solemnly informed me: "Before you came to live with us, Mommy never closed her door at night." What could I say? I felt like a lecherous old man who had been found out!
>
> You know, while Susan and I were going together I thought those kids were really cute. And Susan was always telling me the funny things they said and did. But soon after I moved in,

they turned into little terrors! For a while I thought Susan had sold me a bill of goods about the kids, but she was right — they are cute. We just had to get used to each other.

OUT OF EQUILIBRIUM

In a first marriage where there are no children, the husband and wife have time to get to know each other and to adjust to each other's idiosyncrasies during a relatively unstressful time in their lives. But when children are already present, family stress is necessarily high. Right after their parent's remarriage, children clamor for attention and reassurance that they have not been displaced by the new spouse. Of course, as we have noted before, their efforts to get extra attention will take different forms depending upon the age and personality of the child and his particular set of experiences. But what Mike discovered about his new stepchildren may apply to yours: children who were previously cute and appealing often don't seem so appealing during the first few months after marriage.

Of course, most children give new stepparents a brief "honeymoon" period during which they control their seriously out-of-bounds behavior until they can assess how safe it is to express themselves more freely. If you're lucky, this "honeymoon," which started during courtship days, will endure long enough to give you a brief respite before the children begin testing the new situation. Be prepared, however, that the adjustment period will not be smooth for your stepchildren.

The stress of testing relationships, trying out roles, and discovering what will be the same as in the past and what will change throws children into temporary disequilibrium. Their lives lack the comfortable feeling of security and predictability. Until their new situation becomes more real and secure, many children will misbehave, test, and swing between emotional extremes.

Be assured that this stress will not last forever. As new patterns of living and relating are established, life within your home will smooth out — at least as much as life with children ever smooths out! In most cases, children who are initially out of equilibrium will, before long, begin to find their balance once again.

STEPPARENTS: A NEW BREED

Do you remember the first time you heard the word "stepparent," or more likely, "stepmother"? For anyone over thirty-five, it probably was in conjunction with the fairy-tale heroines, Snow White or Cinderella. Both of them had formidably wicked stepmothers who were madly jealous of their beautiful stepdaughters. The myth of the wicked stepmother probably grew out of the deep conflicting feelings of the stepmother, who was required to step in and raise another mother's children or, more precisely, her husband's first wife's children! Burdened by heavy expectations, the stepmother sometimes couldn't help but feel consumed by jealousy, anger, resentment, and even rage. When that happened, the children were often the recipients of her hostility.

But today *our* children do not automatically equate "wicked" with "stepmother," for often they personally know a stepmother—their own or a friend's. There are other differences today. Whereas in years past children most often acquired stepparents as a result of the death of one of their parents, today children more frequently gain a stepparent as a result of divorce. These stepparents are seldom replacement parents; usually they are *additional* parents.

ROLES OF STEPPARENTS

Does the change from stepparent because of death to stepparent because of divorce affect the role of stepparent? Definitely! Of course, if a parent abandons his children or lives far away, a stepparent may replace the original parent. More often, however, the stepparent becomes an additional parent or even another type of relative—something between a concerned friend and an aunt or uncle. Other relationships may also be possible. For example, we know of a fifty-six-year-old man who married a young mother and became a kind of "grandfather-stepfather" to her two youngsters. As we shall see, stepparents often assume a variety of roles in the new families created by divorce and remarriage.

REPLACEMENT PARENT

When a child has been physically as well as emotionally abandoned by one of his parents or when the parent shows little interest in the child and does not maintain consistent contact, the stepparent usually adopts a replacement role. He or she becomes the child's primary parent, replacing the one who left. This arrangement is particularly true if there are young children.

Harry, thirty-eight, is a good example. He married a woman with four young children and slowly took over the role of father. When he married their mother, these children only saw their father for a couple of weeks in the summer; now, even that contact has ceased. Harry, a relaxed man with a warm and easy nature, shares his experience:

> I knew from the beginning that if I married Lori I would be marrying a ready-made family. It would be diapers and broken bikes, baseball and dance lessons, Boy Scouts and back-to-school nights. Frankly, after years of bachelorhood, the prospect intimidated me. But my love for Lori must have given me the strength I needed! All joking aside, becoming the father of four *was* a shock—no question about it! But, you know, the rewards and pleasure have far outweighed the initial pain!

Stepparents like Harry have a tough job, for it is not easy to walk into a new family and pick up the reins. But, as Harry reminds us, "It didn't happen overnight. Little by little, however, we became a family. In fact, now when I hear the kids bellowing, 'Daddy!' I seldom think I'm not their real father. They call me 'Dad' and that's what I've become!"

ADDITIONAL PARENT

Most often when you marry a custodial parent, you become an additional parent to the children who live with you and your spouse. The children usually maintain some contact with their part-time parent and that relationship continues to be important for the children. In this situation you don't want to replace that parent, but nevertheless, as a full-time stepparent you must work out a relationship with your stepchildren which includes strong elements of parenting—particularly love and discipline. This is especially true if your stepchildren are young. Margie tells how her stepsons, Chris, seven, and John, almost six, helped clarify her relationship with them.

> At first I didn't know how to react to Chris and John, especially when they'd start to get rambunctious. They'd get on my nerves, but I didn't want to behave like a parent. I thought they'd resent it.
> Then one day Chris marched into the kitchen with John in tow and asked in his blunt way, "Now that you and Dad are married, are you still going to be Margie or are you going to quit that and be our mom?" I was floored. Here was the very

crux of the problem! Was I going to be their friend, a big sister, or a mother? I didn't know, so I threw the ball back to them. What did they think?

"Well," drawled John in that funny, old-man way of his, "I think you'd better be our mom because if you're not, we'll probably get out of hand. Right, Chris?"

"Yeah," Chris agreed, but he warned me, "You can't be our same mom because our mom is real pretty and has dark hair and you have orange hair and those freckles and you wear those funny shoes." Then he gave me an ear-splitting grin and added, "But you can be our *other* mom 'cause you make the best burritos in the whole world!"

Marge and the boys shook hands on their agreement, and Marge became their "other mother." But Marge wisely heeded John's message: she was not to usurp their mother's position (obviously their mom is the "fairest of them all"), but they were glad to accept Margie on her own terms with her own strengths — like her cooking.

As Marge discovered, young children feel safer when an adult is clearly in charge. When you live with a child — for your own sake as well as his — you have to be free to set limits and exercise your authority. Of course you wouldn't attempt this the moment you walked in, but little by little you need to carve out your own individual style of parenting. At the same time, however, you must also be sensitive to your stepchild's loyalty and involvement with his part-time parent. Some of your stepchild's needs may already be met primarily by his two original parents. The relationship with his part-time parent may be strong and special. Try not to be jealous of that relationship.

Remember that meaningful relationships are not built overnight. They take years to develop. Instead of worrying about whether your child loves *you* or his part-time parent more, or trying to compete with that parent, *give what is special about you!* Share yourself — your interests, talents, personality, and affection — with your new family. Just as you have enough room in your heart for many people, so does your stepchild. He can grow to love you and still continue to love his part-time parent.

ADDITIONAL PARENT ROLE: LIMITED

If you are married to a non-custodial parent, your role as stepparent may be that of additional parent, but it will be a much more limited role than that of the stepparent who lives full-time with the children. Like the non-custodial parent, you are not free to make major decisions involving the child. Instead, you must often live with decisions which are not entirely to your liking.

Anne Simon points out that the successful part-time stepparent must be able "to love the stepchildren in their natural habitat and leave them to grow there undisturbed." This is very profound, for without this ability, you can only hurt yourself and your stepchildren. Leslie is a good example of a successful part-time stepmother. She discusses some of the joys and heartaches in her limited role as mother:

> When Mandy comes over on the weekend looking ratty and uncared for, I have to grit my teeth not to say anything horrid about her mother. But while I bathe her and dress her in fresh clothes, Mandy talks my ear off. And she's so darned cute with those big, dancing eyes and that earnest look—so like her daddy's! I have to stop and remind myself that her mother has given her a lot of love or Mandy wouldn't be so adorable.
>
> Sometimes it is hard to have Mandy with us and then have to let her go back to her mother's. I've got to admit, there is a possessive streak in me that I have to keep in check for Mandy's sake—and for my own as well! Letting go, however, has its advantages. I get a lot of satisfaction from mothering Mandy without losing the benefits of a childless life-style. Rudy and I have a wonderful relationship. Through the week and every other weekend we are free to do whatever we like—shows, theater, skiing, or dinner with friends. And every other weekend we get to be parents again!

Leslie's attitude is beautiful. She loves and appreciates Mandy's special qualities and at the same time she is able to control her impulse to possess her stepdaughter. She and her husband have created a real second home for Mandy where she is both loved and disciplined. Leslie functions as a mother to Mandy, but in a limited way, for as much as she loves her, she realizes she does not have full control and authority:

> I can't take her to have her long, stringy hair cut into a cute, short hairdo as I would like to, and I can't let her have piano lessons once a week because her mom won't take her, but we

can do many things with her on the weekends when she is here. We've taught her to ski and ice skate and she's good at both. We have to be content with what we can give her.

Like Leslie, part-time stepparents must learn to accept the constraints of part-time stepparenting and enjoy the advantages and rewards.

SUMMERTIME STEPPARENT

If you only see your stepchildren for a few weeks in the summer, your relationship with them will obviously not be the same as it would if you were in frequent contact. Roberta found that by giving up trying to be "mother" to her stepchildren and adopting more of an "aunt" role instead, her relationship with her stepchildren greatly improved.

Before Martin and Kate came out for the summer, I had decided that as much as possible I would love and treat them just like my own two kids. But they are so different from what I had expected. They were nothing like my kids in personality and they had been raised so differently! Furthermore, I was unprepared for how much jealousy developed between my kids and Mel's kids. The summer was a fiasco and we were all relieved to see it end.

Before the next summer's visitation, I had thought the whole thing over. I remembered my own childhood, thinking about the summer I had spent with my Aunt Viola and her children. I had a wonderful time and to this day, Aunt Viola and I still have a special relationship. But it's *not* a mother-daughter one.

Before Martin and Kate arrived the second summer, I had a long discussion with my kids. I encouraged them to think of Mel's kids more like cousins or friends — not as rivals. And I decided to be more relaxed in my role — not pressuring myself to love them like a mother. I adopted a role more like my Aunt Viola had with me. That summer went far better.

Roberta found that by easing her expectations of herself, she decreased her conflict about not being able to love her stepchildren as much as her own. As a summertime stepparent, think back to your own childhood. Other than your parents, what adults played an important role in your life? What made those relationships special?

And how were they different from your relationship with your parents? Keep in mind some of those good adult relationships that you enjoyed as a child, and let them serve to guide you as you relate to your summertime stepchildren.

STEPPARENT TO TEENAGERS

"If you think being a parent to a teenager is exasperating, try being a stepparent to one!" Craig, who three years ago became a stepfather to three teenagers, gives this advice to would-be stepparents of teenagers:

> Wait! Don't do it! Take your time. Why complicate your life and theirs? In a few years, they'll be grown and out of the house. As soon as they leave, it's safe to marry their mother.

Although Craig is being facetious, his advice is practical. Unless your relationship with the teenager is very good, it may be less of an ordeal for everyone if you delay marriage until he or she has left the household.

Of all the ages of children, teenagers have the most difficulty adjusting to their parent's remarriage. Their problem is understandable. The teenager, who is already struggling to loosen the bonds of authority and begin the process of emancipation, most often resents a new parent figure — especially one who lives in the house. "No man is going to move in with Mom and tell *me* what to do," says one young man, and another adds vehemently, "I'd run away before I'd let some guy who thinks he's my father boss me around!"

Many stepparents have found that forming a relationship with their stepteenagers is tricky. Jeanne, a stepmother of two teenagers, sums up the problem she and other stepparents face:

> You just can't win for losing! If the teenagers' relationship with their mom or dad has been troubled, then they take out their resentment and hostility on the new stepmother or father. On the other hand, if the teenagers' relationship has been good, they often resent you because they don't want you or anyone trying to take their parent's place. It's really a terribly trying situation to be in.

The best advice is to go slowly — even more slowly than you would in other stepparenting relationships. Don't impose your ways and your values on your stepteenagers — especially not immediately. And don't start right off disciplining them and setting limits. Most stepparents find that it works out better if the natural parent continues to do most of the parent "dirty work"! Curfew, allowances, and permission for dates and attending other functions should also continue to be decisions which are discussed and agreed upon by the teenager and the parent who has been involved with him all along.

A teenager may be much more comfortable thinking of his stepparent as his father or mother's spouse rather than a parenting figure. Along with this attitude, however, comes a potential problem. Since the teenager is less apt to regard you as a parent (and you are less apt to regard the teenager as a son or daughter), you will need to guard against developing a sexual relationship with your stepteenager. Be aware that teenagers are experimenting with their newly developed sexuality and often lack the wisdom to set appropriate limits. Sexual intimacy between the stepparent and stepchild can cause harm to the child as well as destroy the new family. Teenagers and stepparents usually end up feeling guilty and ashamed about the obsessive sexual fantasies they have about each other or about actual sexual encounters.

What's in a Name?

Remember how you felt the first time you tried calling your in-laws Mom and Dad? Foolish, no doubt! Those names were for your own parents. But the alternatives seemed worse. Mr. or Mrs. was too formal, and Jenny or Bill lacked the feeling of appropriate respect for parent figures. Often a new daughter or son-in-law attempts to avoid the whole ordeal by not calling the parents-in-law anything. However, this rapidly becomes awkward.

Your stepchildren are in the same situation. What should they call you? If they call you by the same name as their own mother or father, they may feel disloyal and even silly. Calling you by your given name may not feel exactly proper either.

What is in a name? Does the name your stepchildren call you mean something special to you or to them? For instance, if your stepchild were to call you Mom or Dad, would that make you feel more like a mom or dad? Shirley's answer is a strong yes!

As long as Bill and Melissa called me Shirley, I felt a distance between us. My own kids call me Mommy of course, and I can't help responding more warmly to "Mommy" than to "Shirley."

I didn't say anything about my feelings but I guess they must have leaked out. Or maybe Bill and Melissa felt a little funny calling me Shirley when my kids called me Mommy. Anyhow, after a while they dropped "Shirley" and I became "Mommy." Sure, it's a little confusing at times since that's what they also call their own mother, but most often we all know which mother they're talking about. And the payoff is that I *do* feel closer to them now.

For Shirley, "Mommy" elicited warm, maternal feelings and allowed her to adopt a more nurturing attitude toward her stepchildren. Often stepparents as well as stepchildren are more comfortable when parental names are used, for "Mom" and "Dad" symbolize a relationship which we all know something about. We bring a set of associations and expectations to parental names.

Sometimes children and stepparents favor using parental names to avoid calling attention to the steprelationship. They want to be perceived as living in a "real" family. To some, a stepfamily may not seem as legitimate as a biological family. This has become much less of a problem in the past years, however, for as the number of stepfamilies has increased, the stigma which was once associated with divorce and remarriage has decreased. Most often, children and parents gradually grow to feel comfortable and even proud of their steprelationships.

However, there are many children who feel strongly against using a parental name for their stepparent. Jimmy is a good example of such a child. When he complies with his stepfather's wish and calls him "Dad," he feels disloyal to his own father. "Lloyd is *not* my real dad," says Jimmy, hotly. "Lloyd wants me to call him 'Dad' so I'll forget my real dad, but I won't!" Instead of insisting, which only intensifies Jimmy's conflict, it would be far better in this case for his stepfather to allow Jimmy to call him "Lloyd." In this way the stepfather can reassure Jimmy that he does not intend to supplant Jimmy's original parent.

Better yet, Jimmy and Lloyd might work out another name — such as "Pa" or "Pop" — which conveys the parental flavor without infringing on the name which, Jimmy feels, belongs strictly to his real father. One boy we know calls his stepfather "Chief." Others have worked out a compromise appellation; a name which is not what the original parent was called and yet which is not so impersonal as the stepparent's given name. Examples we have come across include: "Muz," "Binks," and "Scutter." These names – used only by the stepchild (or stepchildren) for their stepparent – help in the creation of the new relationship and emphasize its uniqueness, thus removing the threat that the new relationship will somehow diminish or impair the older one.

Try to be sensitive to your stepchild's feelings and preferences and *be honest with him about your own feelings.* As your relationship grows and develops, sometimes the name the child calls you will change. He may begin calling you by a parental name or he may even find an apt nickname for you. Bear in mind that what the child calls you is not nearly so important or significant as the relationship you and he develop!

Money, Money, Money

Despite the popular myth, two definitely *cannot* live as cheaply as one! And when you add children to marriage, expenses soar. Children – whether they are yours or your spouse's – cost money. But whose money? That question can become a source of conflict in second marriages. Like sexual conflict, financial conflict often masks even deeper issues and problems in the marriage.

For example, consider the following case. Prior to her marriage to Dick, the father of three children, Ann asked all her divorced friends, "Do you think it's fair for a man to have to pay for children he doesn't live with after he remarries?" Ann was surprised how unanimous her friends were in their agreement that it *was* fair! One father summed up his feelings:

My children are my children regardless who they live with! I wouldn't want another man to support my kids. I am their father and I'm damned proud of it. My children know they can count on me!

Despite her misgivings about Dick's child support obligations, Ann married Dick. Over the years, however, her resentment of Dick's children has grown. Dick's oldest son reports:

Ann really hates all three of us kids. She used to kind of pretend to like us, but now she doesn't even bother. You can tell she doesn't want to spend a nickel on us. When my sister's sneakers wore out while we were there for summer vacation, she made my sister pay for a new pair. And she constantly told us we were wasting money. She criticizes our mom and tells us that Mom is wasting *their* money. She even told us that it was *her* money, not Dad's, that was sent for child support. Well, I don't want that lady's money, even if it means peanut butter for the next ten years!

Ann's anger and resentment about child support covered an even deeper anger and jealousy about Dick's relationship with his children. She did not want to share Dick or their money with his children. Nor does she want to be reminded that she was not Dick's first love. Over the years, Dick's involvement with his children has dwindled as has his financial support of the children. Ann has her husband all to herself now, but Dick's children have lost their father, and Dick has relinquished the joys of being involved with and loved by his children.

Sending money to children whom you hardly know can be difficult, but that is the reality for the part-time stepmother. Resenting child support obligations harms your stepchildren who need the money as well as the continued emotional support and involvement of their father. Furthermore, a father who does not live up to his obligations often feels bad about himself and eventually may come to resent the wife who encouraged him to forget his children. No matter what reasons he gives himself for not sending money, he knows he is letting his children down.

But what about a stepfather who lives with his wife and her children? Should he contribute to the support of her children? Or should he separate himself from their financial needs? After all, he is not legally bound to support stepchildren. "You have to be pretty hard-hearted to ignore the needs of children who live under your own roof," says a stepfather. However, one stepfather we know did just that. His stepson, Kerry, thirteen, still feels rage as he remembers a particularly painful incident.

I lost my jacket at school, and I was scared to tell my folks. I knew my mom didn't have the money to get me a new one, because my dad hadn't sent a support check that month, and I was afraid my stepdad would hit the roof if he thought he had to pay for a new jacket. I didn't say anything, but Mom noticed one snowy morning that I was leaving with just my sweatshirt on. "Where's your jacket?" she asked. I tried to mumble something and leave, but she wouldn't let me go. Finally I told her. My stepdad overheard and got furious with me. He made me call my dad in Arizona and tell him to send money immediately. I was so embarrassed and angry that I started to cry on the phone. My stepdad was yelling at me and my mom was crying and my real dad didn't know what was going on. It was awful!

Most stepparents do contribute partially to the needs of their stepchildren—especially when they all live together as a family. Charles, stepfather and father to five children, says with a good-natured shrug and a grin, "It doesn't matter whose kids they are, when they need something, they need it! Being financially responsible and involved is one way of showing you really do care about them all!"

MOTHERS AND STEPMOTHERS

"How does your child's stepmother treat your child?" we asked a group of mothers. The question triggered a fury of complaints.

"She's so strict with him," said one mother. "What does she know about children? She's never been a mother! She expects Raymond to be a perfect angel all the time."

Another mother, extremely upset, reported, "She spoils my daughter by buying her presents and giving her treats constantly. Debbi never has to work there, so of course she thinks her stepmother is great. I'm the big ogre these days!"

Other complaints included:

"She ignores my child and favors her own over mine."

"She makes my child do all the work in the house, while her own kids get to go out to play."

"She won't let my ex-husband buy anything extra for my son."

"She acts sweet and nice to my kids when their dad is around, but when he's gone she treats them like dirt!"

Stepmothers also have their list of complaints. They say that their stepchildren's mother neglects them, doesn't discipline them or set limits; that they are dirty and untidy, and their wardrobe is insufficient or needs mending; that they are impolite and insensitive to the needs of others, etc., etc.

Although stepmother and mother may not know each other—in fact may never have even met—a definite relationship exists between them. It is a secondhand relationship, maintained and conducted by intermediaries. The child shares his perceptions of each with the other, and the stepmother also has her husband's perceptions influencing her impression of the child's mother. More than likely, stepmother and mother will end up with a skewed picture of each other — skewed negatively, of course!

The father-stepfather relationship is also not without problems — often rivalry exists between the two — but it is our observation that mothers and stepmothers often have a more difficult time working out their relationships. Why might this be true? It could be related to the fact that in our society females have had the primary responsibility for child care. Or perhaps the "maternal instinct" actually exists. In any case, there are problems and mothers and stepmothers have few precedents to guide them, for this is the first generation which has had to confront the issue of "one child, two mothers" on a widespread scale.

Because of the special problems we have observed in this area, we would like to share a few thoughts with both mothers and stepmothers. The following messages are a compilation of thoughts from mothers and stepmothers who have managed to make some peace with their respective roles.

MESSAGE TO MOTHERS

It is understandable that you are jealous of your child's stepmother. You can't help worrying that she will supplant you in your child's affections. (This is especially true if the stepmother has taken your ex-spouse.) If you are the custodial parent you may worry that you will "lose" your child to your ex-husband and his new wife. You may be afraid that your child will want to change homes and leave you. If your ex-husband's remarriage came fairly quickly after divorce, you may still be dealing with intense feelings of rejection. And even if you think you have laid most of those feelings to rest, you are bound to have a resurgence of anger about his choosing a new wife to replace you. You can't help wanting to know what she is like — how she resembles you and how she is different — but at the same time you don't want to know.

However, the reality of this new marriage remains. You must come to terms with the fact that your child *does* have a stepmother. Of course you don't have to be chummy with her, but somehow, for the benefit of everyone involved, you do have to learn to coexist.

Keeping your resentment and jealousy alive serves no one — least of all you, for if you are constantly angry, you may end up pushing your child away from you. Nobody likes to be around someone who is constantly angry.

Instead of worrying that your child's relationship with his stepmother is going to deprive you, concentrate on strengthening your own relationship with your child. Remember that your job is not to rival his stepmother; it is to continue being a good mother. If you continue to love and care for your child, as well as to set the necessary limits, your child's stepmother cannot replace you in your child's affection; she can only augment what you have to give.

MESSAGE TO STEPMOTHERS

You are in a difficult spot. You are struggling with the pressures of a new marriage, trying to relate to your spouse and his children, and attempting to adapt to the new realities of your life. Even if you knew your stepchildren very well before marriage, you and they can't help but feel distrustful of each other. It is normal and natural for you to have ambivalent feelings about them. You want to like them because they are part of your husband's life, but they also remind you that your husband was deeply involved with another woman before you. You may be afraid that you are being compared with his first wife or that your husband loves his children more than you. You can't help resenting their relationship — after all, it spans a time before you were involved in his life. It is natural for you to want either to reject and ignore your stepchildren or to go to the opposite extreme and try to possess them — rivaling their mother for their affection and loyalty. You may even feel that by possessing the children, you will possess more of your husband.

In any case, you must face the realities of the situation and deal with them. You have needs, your husband has needs, and so do the children and their mother. In order for all of you to get along in the new situation, each of you will have to be willing to understand each other's feelings and sometimes modify your own actions. You *have* married a man with children and neither rejecting your stepchildren nor attempting to possess them will contribute to a sound marriage.

A better solution is to look at the positive side of your situation. It can be a highly gratifying experience to contribute to the parenting of a child. You don't have to own a child to give him something of yourself. And you don't have to be so threatened by the existence of your stepchild that you have to push him away. Remember that some of your initial feelings will dissipate. Give yourself and the child a little time and a little understanding. As you get to know each other and begin to feel comfortable, you can work out a special relationship which gives both of you good feelings.

Hints for Positive Stepparenting

The following hints for positive stepparenting are an accumulation of the wisdom of several successful stepparents. They are sound principles that will help you ease into your new role with a minimum amount of damage to your stepchildren and to your own ego.

1. *Go slowly!* You will remember that this headed the list in dating advice, and once again it appears at the top of the list. It is advice worth repeating, however, for strong, meaningful relationships take time to build. You cannot love your stepchildren (even cute ones!) until you really know them well. And your stepchildren cannot love you either (even if you *are* wonderful) until they get to know you. Relax. Don't push yourself to love them, and don't insist that they show affection for you. Love, respect, and trust take time to root and grow properly. The blossoming of your relationship, however, will be well worth the effort, care, and patience it takes.

2. *Shield your ego.* You can't take personally everything your stepchild dishes out. In any family, children know their parents' Achilles' heel and will deliver the appropriate kick. Especially during the early months of your marriage, you may be the target of the child's hostility. Try to keep in mind that your stepchild has mixed emotions about you. He would like to allow a relationship to develop, but at the same time he is restrained by his anxieties and worries. If he likes you, will he be disloyal to his other parent? Are you planning to usurp his original parent's position? Will his mother or father become so involved in the relationship with you that there is no time or affection left for him? Your coming into the family has disrupted and changed his life. It will take some time for the child to let go of some of his initial fears and begin to relate to you more as a person than as a threat.

3. *Build memories.* A stepparent who first joins a new family is an outsider; the children may even see him or her as an interloper. Of course, as a new family member, you are not familiar with all the nuances and special meanings of conversations and gestures. Nor can you understand the "in" jokes and references to the past. You

lack all the shared memories and experiences which "glue" a family together.

But you *can* manufacture some of that cement by hearing those funny or sad anecdotes and stories. And you can familiarize yourself with your new family's past by receiving a "guided photographic tour"! Marcie said proudly, "We showed our new dad all the pictures of us when we were babies and just growing up. Now he almost remembers us when we were little!" Sharing her babyhood with her new stepfather is as important to Marcie as it is to her stepfather.

Bridging the gap of the past is important in any close relationship. Remember, however, that sharing must be reciprocal. You need to catch up on your new family's past and they need to fill in your past life in their minds. If you were married before, your past includes your first spouse just as your stepchildren's lives include another parent. Although you probably won't dwell on your relationship with your first wife or husband, you don't need to skirt around the issue either. After all, you can't tell a story properly when you leave out the central people in the story. Many of your children's stories will include their other parent. They, too, should feel free to relate these incidents without editing.

4. *Structure sharing time.* One of the quickest ways to get to know each other is by sharing feelings. Since people are often reluctant to share what they are thinking and feeling, sharing often needs to be encouraged. A family we know set up special "getting to know you" times after dinner once a week. Over dessert they would take turns responding to a topic such as, "The funniest thing that ever happened to me." This approach was adapted from "Magic Circle," a program used in schools around the country which was developed to facilitate communication and understanding among students and teachers. The possibilities for topics are limitless. Here are a few suggestions:

The time I felt the proudest.

The most dangerous thing I ever did.

A time I helped someone who needed me.

The saddest thing that ever happened to me.

One of the most embarrassing moments of my life.

The strangest thing I ever saw.

5. *Create new traditions.* When two families come together, each

brings traditional ways of doing things. Don't be afraid to blend traditions and create new ones! Your life and your new family's life do not have to be identical to the past. You are free to adapt and change as long as you go slowly. Experiment with new ways to celebrate holidays and make new occasions for celebration. Especially when two sets of children are brought together to form a new family, creating fun times for all can be a rewarding part of recreating family life after divorce.

6. *Make time for your marriage.* Particularly because you are not alone in your new marriage—the children are present from the very beginning—it is very important that you and your spouse find time to be alone together. Building a sound relationship with good patterns of communication is not easy when one is surrounded by the constant demands of children. You need some time for you and your spouse to be alone together. Such special times can be counted upon to greatly help cement your relationship. If you don't find regular times to communicate, you can easily get out of touch with each other; resentments and problems can pile up and eventually the accumulation can bury you. Set aside a weekly time for yourselves. Even a cheap sandwich in a small coffee shop can give you a break from coping with the children. Treasure your relationship together. Have fun and enjoy each other. Relationships take time and care. Don't cheat yourselves!

7. *Make time for yourself.* As well as making time for your marriage, you also need to carve out a little time for yourself to be alone. Whenever stress is high—and it almost always is in a new marriage which involves children—people need to be sure that they feel gratified and good by doing something they greatly enjoy. For each person it is something different—a shopping trip, bowling with friends, or lunch by yourself. Just be sure that you guard this precious time for yourself. Don't forget, you are important to yourself as well as to your family. Take care of yourself!

8. *Learn to communicate your feelings.* In a situation where several people are living together, it is essential to learn to communicate honestly. Don't let your angry or resentful feelings pile up. Don't nurse wounds or feelings of rejection. Let your family know how you feel. You don't necessarily have to yell at them, and you certainly do not have to point an accusing finger. But saying how you feel works miracles. Sometimes we are so egocentric that we assume everyone knows how we feel—after all, it seems perfectly obvious. Not so! It is far better to say, "You know, Sally, when you get up in

the middle of a conversation and leave the room, I get my feelings hurt," than to assume she knows how you feel. It also gives Sally a chance to say, "Well, Dad, I only leave when you start bawling me out about something. I feel like you've always got an agenda and it's never good." From there a real dialogue is possible. *Parent Effectiveness Training* by Thomas Gordon is an excellent book which teaches parents how to communicate positively with their children. Try it, you may like it!

9. *Set limits.* Whenever you live with others, you must set boundaries. Others have to know where the limits are and you also need to know their limits. If we don't set reasonable limits we constantly risk infringing upon each other's privacy. If you cannot stand having people poking around in your things, say so. You have a right to your privacy. If respect is important to you, let your stepchildren know how you feel. Tell them that "please" wins more from you than a demand. If your stepchildren's loud voices irritate you, start training them to lower their voice level. You won't accomplish your goal overnight, but you can begin by showing them how much you appreciate their trying.

Again, we cannot assume that others are mind readers. Each person differs in what he can tolerate and cope with. To live harmoniously together, all family members may have to limit or modify their life habits somewhat.

10. *Carve out your own role.* As a stepparent — whether you are replacing the original parent or augmenting the parental role — you need to carve out your own individual style. You do not have to rival your child's other parent, nor do you have to fit a predetermined role. Each of the child's parents can contribute to the child's sense of well-being by bringing his or her own gifts, talents, and individuality to the relationship. That is what makes each person and each relationship special.

REMEMBER

Stepparenting is not easy, but neither does it have to be grim. You can increase the chances that you and your stepchild can become positively involved with each other by relaxing, stepping back, and allowing the relationship to grow slowly and naturally. Review the list, "Hints for Positive Stepparenting," and remember to focus especially on the sixth hint: Make time for your marriage. If you and your spouse have a solid, loving relationship you will find it much easier to relate warmly to your stepchildren.

13

Yours, Mine, and Ours: The Blended Family

A school psychologist was evaluating a young boy who was suspected of having learning disabilities. At the end of the testing session, she handed him crayons and paper and instructed him to draw a picture of his family. "What part of my family should I draw?" he timidly asked her.

"Why, the family you live with, of course!" she responded impatiently.

The child stared at her for a moment and then he bent his head and quickly complied. He drew a man, a woman, and two children. Silently, he handed her the drawing and started to leave the room. At the door, he turned suddenly and with eyes flashing, he said angrily, "But that's only *half* my family! You made me leave out my dad and stepmom and all my brothers and sister who live in my other home!" And with that, he fled.

Like many youngsters today, Jason is part of a complex family. Both his parents remarried — each marrying a divorced parent — so Jason has a wide network of family members who are important to him. Jason, his siblings, his stepsiblings, and half-siblings are part of the new extended family — extended by divorce and remarriage.

The Extended Family of the Past

In the past thirty to forty years we have seen dramatic changes in the structure and functioning of the family. Not too long ago, people lived primarily in rural areas. Families were large, interdependent, and extended by grandparents, aunts and uncles, cousins, and other relatives who either lived under the same roof or nearby in the same town or community. In the extended family, life was a fabric with many varied and interwoven threads. Charlie, sixty-four, reminisces about family life in what his grandchildren refer to as the "olden days"!

> In some ways it was a good life. A youngster could always find an empty lap to nestle in, and if Mother said no to a before-dinner cookie, Grandma was sure to say yes! But, oh, how relatives could fuss and feud! And everybody always had to put their two cents into every decision — no matter how small. They all had their nose in each other's business — for everyone's own good, of course!
>
> But you know, despite all of that, there was real comfort just knowing you had folks to depend on. I remember when Pop got laid up for months with a bad back. Everyone just pitched in and took care of the work — and you know Pop would have done the same for anyone of them.
>
> The best thing about the old family was that you knew people could be counted on to give a hand. There was plenty of sharing and caring!

In recent years the extended family of the past has been romanticized in stories and in television series, but as Charlie points out, such a life was certainly not without problems. People frequently "got on each other's nerves" or actually clashed; and there was little tolerance for the one who wished to "do his own thing." Beneath the friction, however, there was usually a substratum of goodwill and support. In times of crisis there were people to help out, for the family was not isolated. As Charlie humorously sums up: "There was a place for everyone and everyone stayed in his place!"

THE NUCLEAR FAMILY

As mobility increased, this extended family pattern gradually disintegrated, and the responsibility for raising children fell almost exclusively on the shoulders of mom and dad. As parents moved their families to the cities, life-styles developed which were quite different from those they had known in their rural communities. Many basked in their newfound autonomy and freedom — especially the freedom from the eagle eyes of the self-elected board of advice-givers — the family elders!

With these advantages, however, new problems develop. Cut off from the larger support system of relatives and interested community members, parents and children often find themselves locked in a strangling embrace of dependency. Frequently, we tug on one another, demanding that all our needs be met by this small handful of family members. Of course, we cannot be everything to one another, but we try hard, sometimes to the point of feeling guilty when we fail. Conflict, stress, and tension rise. Unfortunately, living within the small, isolated nuclear family is sometimes like living in a pressure cooker with a stopped-up escape valve. It's no wonder that divorce rates have risen dramatically over the years.

THE NEW EXTENDED FAMILY

Beth's button nose wrinkled as she concentrated on the task of counting the members of her family:

> I have a mommy and a daddy, a mom and a pop, a granny, a grandma and a grandmama, two grandpas, and a grandpapa, two sisters, one brother, one stepsister, two stepbrothers, one new baby, and a whole bunch of other relatives. I also have one dog, three goldfish, and two stephamsters. I really have a big family!

When divorced parents marry divorced parents, the children acquire more parent figures, more siblings, more relatives of all kinds—and even more pets. As we can see from Beth's accounting, divorce and remarriage have the potential of greatly expanding the family. In fact, divorce—which has been perceived so negatively— can sometimes solve some of the problems of the nuclear family. We're certainly not advocating wholesale divorce, for it definitely has its own pains and problems, but when it is handled sensitively and sanely by both parents, it does have the potential for creating new options and alternatives for family members. Parents often understand and appreciate how divorce can free *them* in ways that seemed impossible when they were married to their former mate. They may also see how the new extended family sometimes offers them relief from the responsibilities of parenting, but rarely do they examine how this enlarged family circle can provide options and alternatives for their child.

Let's look at some of the positive possibilities offered by the extended family. Most children of divorce have two homes—two places where they belong. They have a greater number of people involved with them who can model a variety of life-styles, values, and individual talents. The ability to see many alternatives in life gives us more power to set and achieve our goals. Furthermore, a child's definition of himself may no longer be so tightly tied to his place in the family, for the role he plays in one family may be quite unlike the role he assumes in his other family. For example, the baby in his mother's family may be the oldest in his father's family. He may develop a greater appreciation of his individuality and his unique traits. One father we know said proudly of his son:

> In the past two years since the divorce, Kevin has really changed. He no longer insists that things can only go one way — *his* way — but instead he seems much more able to roll with the punches and still have a lot of control over the situation. Maybe he's just growing up but I think he's learned more than most kids in two years.

Margaret, eleven, is one of a growing number of children who are gaining by being a part of two families. "When I'm at Mom's, I'm the oldest," Margaret says with pride. And then she adds impishly, "I like being the oldest because I get to boss Doug and Mike!" At her father's house, Margaret is the youngest girl. She likes that position, too. "It's the first time I've ever been a little sister," she says thoughtfully. "Pat and Pam are twins and they are fourteen. They teach me new dances and let me listen to their records. And they even take me shopping and tell all their friends that I'm their new little sister!"

Being both a big sister *and* little sister gives Margaret a chance to try out two very different roles. In addition, Margaret receives a great deal of attention, not only from her stepsisters, but also from her new stepmother. For Margaret there are definite advantages to being a part of two families, and although it requires that she shift gears each time she goes back and forth, there is considerable reward for her flexibility.

Typical Problems Faced by Blended Families

If, like Margaret, your child is able to function well in both homes, relating to all the various people in his life and adjusting to changes in expectations and roles, he stands to gain considerably. Of course, some children have difficulty adjusting to the demands of two changed households — especially immediately after the remarriage of their parent. All too often parents are insensitive to the problems their children are facing.

As parents, it is easy to forget that our child's life is *twice* as complex as our own since we are closely involved in only *half* of his family network — our *own* half! Since we don't shift homes, it is easy to overlook the enormity of the adjustments involved. In fact, some parents we interviewed seemed insensitively myopic when it came to viewing their child's life. They were only marginally aware of the problems and struggles their child had as he attempted to adapt to new expectations and fit into new roles in each of his families. Let's examine a few of the typical problems children encounter as they attempt to work out their new roles in the context of the new family settings.

YOUNGEST, MIDDLE, AND OLDEST CHILD

Consider the complexities and changes that children face when they are a part of a network of families such as this one described by a social worker who is counseling Alisa and Alan's mother.

Alisa, eight, and Alan, five, are Paul and Nancy's children. Two years ago their parents were divorced, and soon afterward, Paul married a woman with two children — Bradley, nine, and Jeffrey, six. Three months ago Christopher was born. Meanwhile, Nancy's boyfriend, Sam, has moved in with her and the children. Sam has three children who spend every other weekend with Sam and his new family. Those children are Kate, four, Kelly, seven, and Karen, ten.

All told, there are eight children in this network of families. Although each set of parents only relates to some of the children, Alisa and Alan must relate to *all* of them! It's no wonder these kids are having problems. It's a lot of changes in just a couple of years and they haven't had much help in adjusting.

One of the most difficult problems for these youngsters is finding their places or roles in their families. For example, consider Alan, Jeff, Kate, and Christopher — each is the baby of his or her biological parents. However, in the blended family their positions shift. When Kate goes to visit her dad, Alan is shoved out of the baby position. Or if he goes to his father's house, he takes the role of middle child, for the newborn is clearly the baby of that family! Alan's stepbrother, Jeffrey, has some of the same problems as Alan, for both have learned the role of "baby" in their original families.

The oldest children also have problems. Alisa and Brad rival each other for position of "top dog." Despite the fact that Alisa is a year younger than Brad, she competes strongly with him (and often wins), but she knows better than to compete with ten-year-old Karen when she comes to visit. Although superficially Alisa and Karen get along, their relationship is an uneasy one, marked by much covert hostility and jealousy.

In these new extended family networks, each child has to discover where he or she fits into each family and under what circumstances. He also has to learn to be flexible enough to give up that place when stepsiblings arrive or go home. In the nuclear family, often there are problems resulting from the "pecking order," but at least the order remains the same. In the extended family network, power struggles are more complicated and often require sympathetic parental intervention to prevent the development of antagonisms.

STEPSIBLING RIVALRY

Sibling rivalry, of course, goes beyond vying for oldest or youngest position in the family. Ever since the days of Cain and Abel, sibling rivalry has been recorded as a universal problem of families. Every child wants to be the "one and only" child in the family — uniquely special to his parents. Of course he resents any competitors! When a new baby is born, a child feels quite ambivalent. His parents expect him to grow to love the little intruder as much as they do, but the child is deeply worried. What if the baby supplants him? What if this newcomer takes attention and love away from him? What will his relationship to his parents be now that a new baby has arrived? After each addition to the household, the child has to test whether his special relationship with his parents still exists or whether it has been changed by the presence of other children.

In the nuclear family, children often hotly vie for their parents' attention and love; but in the blended family, rivalry can become an even more complex problem. Why is there often such intense rivalry between stepsiblings? To understand, let us review briefly what divorce and remarriage mean to a child. When his parents divorce, the child seethes with fears which may never become conscious but which nevertheless influence him profoundly. He is shaken, scared of abandonment, and he questions how lovable he actually is. After divorce, when he discovers that his parents (or at least one of them) still love and care for him, his trust in himself and his parents is again strengthened. Then his parent (and often both parents) remarries and once again he is plunged into despair. What if the new spouse monopolizes his parent's love and leaves him emotionally abandoned? And when additional children enter the picture as stepsiblings, the threat of loss is doubly sharp. The child greatly fears that his parent's stepchildren will usurp the special relationship which he needs for himself.

For the child who is present only part-time, this worry is intensified. For example, if his father's stepchildren spend more time with his father than *he* does, he feels he is bound to lose out. After all, he is not even around to protect his claim. The stepchild also worries. He may want to form a close relationship with the new parent, but he fears that he can never become as special to him as his stepparent's natural offspring.

It's no wonder that, at least initially, both sets of children regard each other with distrust, suspicion, jealousy, and even rage. These feelings cannot be wished away or swept under the carpet. They *do* exist, although they may not be expressed openly—at least at first. Right after a remarriage most families experience a honeymoon period during which all the children seem to get along beautifully. This is a time when each child is busy taking the measure of the other. He is sizing up the new situation, watching how his parent and the stepparent are reacting and treating their children and stepchildren. He is trying to determine how much the new child (or children) in the family threatens his own place in his parent's heart. Claire tells how she and her husband, John, coped with their children's problems following remarriage:

Right after John and I were married, all the kids seemed to get along fantastically. John's kids were with us on weekends, and, of course, mine live with us full-time. They don't see much of their real dad. Well, things were going great and we were congratulating ourselves for handling everything just right. But as they say, "pride goeth before a fall." It started with minor incidents of tattling and complaints, but before long there were actual fist fights! We were totally unprepared for the amount of jealousy our kids were feeling.

Finally, John and I made all of them sit down together for a big meeting. Bit by bit the children began expressing how they felt. They yelled at each other and even at John and me. Some were crying. It was a real wild scene! I'm not sure anybody ended up agreeing on anything, but do you know what? The next weekend went a lot better! I guess just getting all those feelings out in the open helped.

John and Claire were taken aback by their children's arguing and fighting, but they discovered an important truth: *conflict, even though it is unpleasant and painful, is not necessarily a negative experience to be avoided.* Quite the opposite! Only by confronting their feelings and trying to find ways to resolve conflict can children, stepchildren, and parents really work out a positive—and eventually loving—relationship with one another.

INEQUITIES

Stepsiblings watch each other and their parents very carefully. They are *hyper*sensitive to every nuance and gesture, and they scrutinize the interactions between parents and children. Although their jealousy and distrust are understandable, the problems remain difficult to deal with. Often "fairness" becomes an overriding issue. Unfortunately, as many parents and stepparents have found, there is simply no way in the blended family for things to be always worked out fairly. Peggy gives us an example of one of the problems she faced:

Jake, my twelve-year-old, had been begging us for boots. The ones he wanted cost a small fortune, and we didn't feel we could spend the money. Imagine how Jake felt when recently Barry, his thirteen-year-old stepbrother, showed up wearing the very boots Jake had been wanting! At first, I was furious with Barry. I knew he didn't really want those boots. It was just a way of showing up Jake. But what could Karl and I do? Run out and buy expensive boots for Jake? And then how would his younger brother feel? Keeping things fair can be a nightmare—especially when you don't have the money.

The truth is Barry's mother does have more money than we do. After all she gets support money from Karl, plus her job pays plenty. And in addition to supporting Barry, we're supporting four of my kids!

This kind of inequality does exist in blended families, and it is very difficult to cope with. There are no simple answers. Obviously, however, we cannot spend our lives "keeping up with the Jones' " — even when the Jones' are our children's stepsiblings. Often, hard as it is to accept, inequalities have to be borne. Life is not always fair!

In the case above, Peggy decided to get the two boys together and really hash out the problems. Both boys were initially sullen and noncommunicative, but gradually they thawed. "Before it was over," reports Peggy, "they were really yelling at each other. It was the best thing that ever happened for it sure cleared the air!" One of the important issues which came to light during this session was the degree to which Barry was jealous of Jake. "I knew that Jake was jealous of Barry because Barry always had the best of everything, but I had no idea that Barry was even more jealous of Jake!" Although Barry had more *things* than Jake, Jake had Barry's father as his full-time stepfather and to Barry that was the ultimate injustice.

You cannot always level inequalities, but you can help your child accept some "unfairness" by being sensitive to his outrage, talking with him, and hearing his feelings. Often by venting anger and jealousy, your child can make some peace with inequalities. As the heat of emotion abates, you and he (and perhaps his stepsibling) can look at the real issues underlying jealousy and evaluate the situation more clearly.

CHORES, RULES, AND DISCIPLINE

Another thorny problem! With children coming and going in a household, it is difficult to establish rules and procedures which apply to all of them. What is the role of the children who do not live full-time in the home? Are they full-fledged members or are they guests? Are they responsible for some household chores? Should they take out the garbage, wash the dishes, and sweep the floor? Do all the rules which apply to the set of live-in children apply equally to the children who are with you part-time? Do you feel free to discipline your stepchildren? In the same manner as you would you own?

"I come down more heavily on my own children than I do on my stepchildren," confesses one mother. "I just feel freer to yell and get mad with my own than I do with the others. I know how mine will react, but I'm never sure of my stepkids' reactions."

Your child and your stepchild need you to be fair with them. In fact, as the following example shows, your stepchild may even push you into making a truly fair parenting commitment.

Sonny, my stepson, had spent all weekend needling and provoking my son, Ricky, who is the same age as Sonny. When
Ricky came to me crying because Sonny had thrown his baseball mitt high in a tree, I lost my temper, called Sonny into the
house, and whaled the tar out of him. Afterward, I was ap-
palled at what I had done. Sonny already resented me and I
knew he would blame Ricky for telling on him and getting him
into trouble. In the past, I had been careful not to be too hard
with Sonny.

Imagine my surprise when later that afternoon I overheard
Sonny telling Ricky about how I had spanked him. Sonny's
tone was just plain boastful. "Boy," he said proudly, "your dad
doesn't kid around when he gets mad! He sure gave me a whip-
ping!" And then, in a really buddy way, the two boys pro-
ceeded to swap stories about what a mean guy I am. And you
know what? Ever since that spanking, Sonny has not only
gotten along well with Ricky, but he is great with me. I guess he
needed me to show him I cared!

Parents can feel torn between their children and their stepchildren
at times. Being fair to both is a real challenge. You and your spouse
need to sit down and talk about your approaches to division of
labor, rules and regulations, and discipline so that at least the two of
you provide as united a front as possible. If the children find they can
play you off against each other, all of you are headed for trouble.
After you and your spouse clarify your own feelings about some of
these issues, you are ready to sit down with the children and stepchildren and thrash out the problems. Don't try to solve all the problems
yourself. Insist that the children be involved in the problem-solving
process, for if they are, they will have more interest in making those
solutions work.

PREFERENTIAL TREATMENT

Most stepparents realize that problems can result from treating
their own children and their stepchildren differently. They are fully
aware that every parent-child interaction is being watched and
weighed. In fact, some stepparents are so afraid of showing preferential treatment to their own child that they overcompensate by being
"nicer" to their stepchild. They may find themselves seldom scolding
or setting limits for their stepchild — often excusing him from chores

and other work. Although such stepparents are usually only trying to avoid undue conflict with their stepchild, they may also be using this special treatment to cover their resentment, dislike, or lack of love for him.

Sometimes stepparents indulge their stepchildren in order to court them — trying to win their affection. Needless to say, this doesn't work very well, for your children and stepchildren are both bound to be upset. Your own children may accuse you of not loving them and of preferring your stepchildren. "Mary's your *new* daughter and you think she's perfect, so you don't need me anymore!" may be the response. And your stepchild will not be comfortable with the favoritism either, for he may interpret it as an attempt to buy his favor. Of course, if you always take your own child's side in an argument, your stepchild, quite legitimately, may accuse you of being unfair: "You always take Mike's side because he's your own son! You don't like me!"

You can help your children and stepchildren overcome their fears of favoritism in two important ways. First, try very hard to avoid obvious displays of preferential treatment. This isn't always easy — but *try*. Second, you can help them by getting them to look at some of the undercurrents of their distrust and worry. Ask the children, "Are you afraid that I like one of you better than the other?" Even if they say, "No," you have opened a topic which you know is of deep concern to all the children: which child do you and your spouse love best? Whom do you favor? Debating or trying to give evidence that you are not favoring one child over the other rarely helps, for the child is not looking at these issues from a rational standpoint. He is responding from an emotional level of fear and anxiety.

Of course, as we discussed in the previous chapter, you cannot help but love your own child best — at least initially. That's reality. After all, you've been your child's parent for some years and you are deeply involved. Don't lie to your stepchild by telling him you love him as much as your own child. Both of you know that cannot be true — especially soon after remarriage. Instead, point out to him that just as he loves the people he knows best — like his own parents — you also love those whom you've been close to over the years. Remind him that love grows as people become involved and care for each other. By being sensitive to his feelings and by treating him as fairly as you can, you convey to your stepchild a real sense of caring for him.

END-OF-VISITATION BLUES

As stepsiblings become attached to one another and find they really enjoy being together, another problem may crop up. When it is time to part at the end of visitation, they may become sad and disappointed. Megan shares her feelings:

> I hate it when it's time for my stepbrothers and sisters to go back to their mom's house. It's so lonely after they go. We're all close in age and we have lots of fun together. I wish we could be together all the time.

Parting is often painful and sad. Megan isn't the only one in her family who feels that sadness. Her stepsiblings share her feelings. For children who see their other parent once a week (or perhaps less often), the sadness of leaving is often coupled with vestiges of the old anger of separation from their parents. It hurts to leave the people you love — even if you are returning to more people you love!

One little girl who was tearfully departing after a weekend with her dad and his family asked angrily: "Why can't all my family live together?" Of course Kimberly knew it was impossible, but to her it felt like the perfect solution. If everyone would just move in together, she wouldn't have to miss one family while she was with her other family. Kimberly's father tells us how he felt about Kim's tears:

> At first it used to break me up when Kimberly would cry and get mad like that, but lately I've realized something. Kimberly is a darned lucky kid! She cries because she loves being with us. And yet she loves her mom, her brothers, and her stepdad too. It may hurt Kim to leave us, but she really has much more love in her life than most kids!

Although there is some momentary pain in parting, children like Kim are fortunate when they have many who love them.

Some children handle leaving differently — they get mad instead of sad. Ken discusses how his children and stepchildren reacted to the end of visitation:

> It didn't matter how great the weekend had been, about two hours before it was time for my kids to go back to their mother, my kids and my wife's kids would pick a fight with each other. It could be about any little thing — they weren't choosy! By the

time I'd load them in the car, they were usually in tears and glad
to be returning to their mother's.

Finally, it dawned on me. Fighting was the way both sets of
kids were managing the sadness of leaving. My kids were saying in effect: "I don't care about leaving. I don't like this dumb
family anyhow!" And my stepkids were saying practically the
same thing: "It doesn't matter if you go, I don't like you anyway!"

Turning "sad" into "mad" is a common way children deal with
these feelings. But losing touch with what you really feel is never
good. Although sadness is painful, it is real. Ken's children and
stepchildren needed their parents' help to deal more appropriately
with their feelings about leave-taking. Ken reports how he and his
wife handled the situation:

The next weekend we called the kids together right after Sunday lunch. We pointed out to them that their fights invariably
occurred on Sunday evenings and we told them what we
thought. Of course they vehemently denied it! But it's interesting that those fights have become a thing of the past.

In addition to talking, Ken and his wife also instituted a going-
home ritual with the children. About an hour before it is time for
Ken's children to leave, the family gets together for a small party to
celebrate the end of the weekend. "We have sandwiches, chips, hot
cocoa, or punch, and ice cream. And we use small, decorated paper
plates and cups to make it kind of special as well as easy to clean up,"
explains Ken. "The mini-party sure has helped combat the going-
home blues!"

Remember that pain and sadness should not always be avoided.
We grow and mature by being in touch with our feelings and finding
new ways to deal with those feelings. The children in Megan's,
Kimberly's, and Ken's families are lucky to love one another enough
to feel sad and angry about parting.

THE NEW BABY

"Our new baby belongs to all of us!" announced Alana joyfully as
we peeked into the bassinet. The new baby in the divorced-divorced
family is special, for that baby has the same relationship—half-
sibling—to each set of children. As in any family, children have

ambivalent feelings about the arrival of the new baby. But for divorced-divorced parents, children are even more concerned and worried about the newest arrival. One mother's experience poignantly sums up how children feel when confronted with the new baby.

> The day I came home from the hospital with the baby, my husband met me with all the children — his and mine — in the car. Of course they were all delighted to see the new baby — all but my two-year-old who sat rigidly quiet on the back seat, his thumb firmly in his mouth. Not only would he not look at the baby, he wouldn't respond to me either. I asked the other children, "What's wrong with Johnny?"
>
> Laura, my husband's very sensitive four-year-old, put her arm protectively around Johnny and answered, "Johnny is thinking that new babies are better than old babies. He thinks maybe old babies are just thrown in the garbage can!"

Laura hit on Johnny's feelings precisely. In fact, Laura and perhaps all the children were having some of the same feelings of worthlessness and rejection. Again, these feelings are present in all new baby situations, but in the blended family, they are more acute. Since the baby is the product of the new spouse and the child's parent, the child of the former marriage (the "no good" marriage) worries greatly that his parent will favor the new baby and forget about him.

Unfortunately, in some families this is exactly what happens. The new baby does become the favored child, and the other children in the family are very much aware of the baby's special spot in their parent's and stepparent's hearts. If the baby of the new marriage becomes the favorite, what happens to the children of the former marriages? They feel left out, even more keenly jealous and displaced than most children feel after the birth of a new child.

This does not have to happen, however. Many parents who are sensitive to their children's feelings of rejection manage to include both sets of children in planning and later caring for the new infant. *But*, in doing so they do not lose sight of the fact that their children have strong needs themselves. They make sure that not all the time in the day is devoted to the new baby. If their other children are young, they find a few moments throughout the day and especially before bedtime to hold them and fuss over them when the baby is not present. Older children and even teenagers get a little extra personal attention from parent and stepparent. By taking time to focus on each of their other youngsters, these parents smooth out potential problems and in the long run save themselves much trouble, for the attention and reassurance they give all the children in the family decrease feelings of sibling rivalry.

Although technically the baby has the same relationship to the mother's children as to the father's children, in reality the children who live with the baby full-time become more involved and have a closer relationship. Twelve-year-old Beth tells how hurt she was by her baby brother's initial rejection of her:

> I'd looked forward all year to seeing my dad and stepmom's new baby. I couldn't wait for summer vacation. But when I finally got there and held out my arms, Jimmy burst into tears and clung to my stepsister. He wouldn't have anything to do with me. I tried not to show it, but my feelings were hurt. Of course, by the end of the summer he loved me too, and it was real hard to leave him. He's so cute!

Of course, Beth's relationship to Jimmy could not be as close as her stepsister's—after all, her stepsister lived with the baby full time. Fortunately, however, most babies quickly get used to new people—especially young people who want to play and cuddle. In situations like this, it is helpful for the parent and stepparent to send snapshots of the baby—preferably not in the arms of a stepsister or brother. That only increases jealousy and envy.

The new baby can be a joyous event in the family. When parents are understanding and sensitive to their children's anxieties and worries, the new baby can become a kind of bridge between both sets of children.

GRANDPARENTS AND OTHER ASSORTED RELATIVES

"Come see my grandchildren!" said Rachel proudly as she led us to the hallway. The hallway was a gallery of photographs! As she went down the line of pictures carefully framed and arranged on the wall, she told us all the names and ages of her sixteen grandchildren. We noted that two of the children she had identified as siblings looked very different from each other. "Oh," she said matter of factly, "those are my son's stepchildren—my daughter-in-law's kids from her former marriage." When Rachel tells people that she has sixteen grandchildren, those two are included as part of the total. And when birthdays, Christmas, and other special days come around, neither

Rachel nor her husband makes any difference among their grand-children.

In another family we know — a blended family of eight children — an aunt plays a central role in the children's lives. She, too, accepts all the children within the family and treats them equally, although some of the children have no blood relationship to her. "I'm just happy to have so many nieces and nephews to enjoy!" she says, smiling broadly. And the lives of her nieces and nephews are greatly enriched by her involvement with them.

Although many relatives may initially be reluctant to accept all the members of your blended family, it is a goal worth fostering. Their ambivalence about the new family unit often stems merely from its newness and the fact that they are not yet acquainted with all the new members. Generally you may need to take the initiative, but establishing a strong kinship network for your family is well worth the effort. Your children (and you too) are enriched by the love and involvement of a variety of people in your lives.

A FEW TIPS

How can you help your children and stepchildren work through some of these common problems and emerge feeling good about themselves and the other members of their new families? How can you reassure them that no one will be displaced but that there will be a special place in the family for each one of them? Here are a few tips:

1. *Be empathetic.* Getting used to changed households and ac-cepting steprelationships is difficult. Let your child know that you appreciate how greatly he is struggling to find his way. Realize how many problems and issues he is coping with: What is his role in each family? How does he fit in? What are the expectations of him? How will he relate to his original parent, his stepparent, stepsiblings, and to other relatives? Who will discipline him? How? What will the atmosphere be in each of his homes?

Your child needs to know that you value your relationship with him and that, despite additions to the family, he continues to be unique and special to you. Be sensitive to his feelings and his worries that others are rivaling him for your attention and love.

2. *Encourage open communication among family members.* Re-member that jealousy and hostility are normal feelings for young-sters who are presented with competitors for your attention. The

more freely a child can talk to his parents, be heard, and be responded to honestly and openly, the more quickly and smoothly he will make the adjustments required of him. Children who can openly air their feelings don't tie up precious energy suppressing emotions or diverting them into hostile behavior or physical ailments. They have the energy free to work out their conflicts and anger in direct, healthy ways.

Of course that doesn't mean that you should allow your children and stepchildren to attack each other with baseball bats! Wise limits to expression must always be set. But do encourage family members to talk to each other honestly about their feelings. Try to get issues out in the open where they can be solved before they grow too complex and intense. Often just by providing an atmosphere of acceptance, letting your youngsters know that their hostile, jealous feelings are normal and natural, you lower the tension and conflict between them.

3. *Be as fair as you can, but accept the fact that total equality is impossible.* "Fairness" is a problem in every family, but in the blended family it often becomes a focal issue. Where you can, try to smooth out gross inequalities. Don't buy something for one child and ignore another; but realize, however, that you cannot make everything even. Some children in the family have more than one parent involved with them. Those children receive attention, love, and things from more than one source. Help your child recognize the realities that exist.

Although the issue of fairness and equality do, in fact, have some legitimacy, most often these issues mask the child's deeper concerns: Am I still important? Do you love me? Am I special to you? Do I belong to your family? As each child becomes more secure, the issue of fairness will diminish.

BUILDING FAMILY COHESIVENESS

"How do I stitch this his and her family together?" moaned a mother who was tired of coping. "Every time I think we're beginning to function like a real family, some little crisis comes along and we split right down the seam again!"

"I thought that old story about the woman who yelled to her husband, 'Bill, come quick! *Your* children and *my* children are beating up *our* children!' was supposed to be a joke. Now it's my reality!" wails another mother.

How is it possible to recreate family life after remarriage? How can children who come from different families, with different backgrounds and experiences, learn to cooperate and pull together? "Is it really possible?" asks Harry, an overwhelmed father who is coping with seven children from three different unions.

Yes, Harry, it is possible—but it's never easy! A great deal of thought, sensitivity, and inventiveness must go into making a cohesive family out of members who were not originally bound together. What can you do to make the quality of your new family life enjoyable and meaningful for all members? This is one of the questions we have asked parents in blended families. The following list of suggestions is made up of their responses as well as some of our own ideas that we have found helpful. As you read the list of ideas, think of your own individual situation and ask yourself, "How can I tailor this or that suggestion to fit my family and its needs?"

Suggestions for Building a Blended Family

The following are just a few suggestions. Discuss with your spouse which ones you might want to try first. Think of other ideas as well. Activities like these take a bit of time and commitment, but they will help the family become more cohesive.

1. *Ideas that promote togetherness and a feeling of comfortableness about being in a blended family.* Your major challenge is to build the idea of "family" in the minds of all the members of your blended family. The following ideas will help each member feel that he is a part of a new and vital unit.

Plan activities which encourage children and parents to work or play together—baseball games, acting out plays, Ping-Pong, cleaning out the basement, putting up a basketball hoop, planting a vegetable garden, etc.

Plan other activities which encourage cross-family cooperation between children—shopping trips, doing chores, caring for animals, etc. This is most effective when two children (one from mother's side and one from father's) must complete a task together.

Plan special rituals which are part of the new, combination family (as Ken and his wife did with their end of visitation parties). For example, on the weekends that kids are all together, go out for donuts, or make special Sunday morning brunches. Or perhaps Dad and all the kids will prepare one meal for Mom (insist that the kitchen be left clean!).

Buy sweatshirts or T-shirts all alike which announce to the world, "We are a family!"

Create shared experiences and take lots of snapshots of the blended family working, playing, and being together. Place them in an album so they are readily accessible to the children. You will find that they all love to peruse the family album, looking at pictures together and saying, "Oh *yeah*. Remember when we did. . . . ?"

Plan vacations together — especially camping trips and visits to relatives. This gives the children some common experiences and builds the memory bank that helps cement families together.

If possible, wait until the kids are together before making major decisions. For example, don't buy a new puppy the week some of the children are missing. The same is true of a car or other important purchases. You want to make all the children feel included.

Be matter-of-fact about relationships when you introduce the children. You don't need to avoid mentioning the word *step*, though neither do you need to overemphasize the steprelationships. Often it is enough to say, "I'd like you to meet our children," or "These are Tom's and my children." Publicly and pointedly sorting out who belongs to whom makes the children feel uncomfortable "like a freak show at the circus" (one child complained) and does not contribute to family cohesiveness.

In informal situations, feel free to refer to your combined family by both last names. For example, we often receive mail addressed to "The Anderson-Buttles Family," and friends commonly refer to our family that way.

2. *Ideas that promote caring and sharing minimize rivalry and competition.* In order to promote cohesiveness, you must create an atmosphere in your home which encourages the children to begin caring for one another. These thoughts may help:

Initially, encourage activities and games which foster cooperation and team effort; play down games and activities which especially involve one-to-one competition such as cards, chess, tennis, etc. Later, as the family becomes more cohesive, competitive games are less apt to cause ill feelings.

Keep rivalry at a minimum by being sensitive to the issue of fairness. Although there is no way to equalize everything in a combined family, try not to give gifts which are disproportionately large or small. Also be aware of how much attention and special treats each child in the family is getting.

If some of your children do not have an extra parent (or set of parents) who are giving them presents, remind the other children who have two families that you must give more to the ones who have only you to provide for them.

Buy some toys and games which belong solely to the combined family and are not used unless all members of the family are together — Monopoly, badminton, etc.

Help children remember each other's birthdays and help them purchase or make appropriate gifts (even if you have to subsidize them). Have children team up to buy more expensive gifts.

Encourage your weekend children to bring some of their games, toys, and other possessions to share. Don't always expect your live-in children to do all the sharing. Sharing can be a very sensitive issue until the children become more involved with one another.

If children are the same size and wish to share or swap clothing, encourage them to do so. But don't insist. Be sure both children really feel good about sharing.

If one set of children is older (particularly if they are teenagers), try not to burden them with required care of the other youngsters. Especially at first, be sensitive to the resentment the older ones feel when they are "saddled" with younger ones. By the same token, don't require that the younger ones take orders from the older ones. They greatly resent being ordered around! Later, as relationships build and fondness for each other grows, the older ones may enjoy playing an almost-adult role with their younger stepsiblings. And the younger children may begin to enjoy and look forward to the attention and special times they have with their older stepsiblings.

3.*Ideas that promote the specialness of each individual.* Each child in the family needs to feel assured that he is worthwhile and that his uniqueness is appreciated. The better a child feels about himself, the less threatened he is by siblings and stepsiblings. He does not have to constantly vie with others, nor does he have to fight for a place in the family. He feels secure in his specialness.

Be sure to provide drawer space and shelves for each weekend child so that he will have a place for clothing and his own special possessions. He may wish to leave some things behind in a safe place. His storage space should be strictly off limits to the children who remain in the home.

Have "special nights" with two children. You, your spouse, and a child of each parent (or one from your union if he's old enough) go out together. The two children must choose where to go and what to do. (Better set up guidelines ahead of time!) Some suggestions are bowling, roller skating, going to a movie, having dinner, lunch, or dessert at a restaurant.

Make or buy individual placemats or special napkins marked with the child's name or initials, so that when he sits down to the table, his place is marked with something personal.

Encourage each child to develop hobbies, talents, and special interests. Some children have obvious gifts like musical or artistic abilities. Help them develop these abilities. Other children may need guidance to find something they particularly like to do — collections, magic, or volunteer work are some possibilities. Children can be encouraged to develop skills like chess, sports, photography, etc. All children feel special and more confident when they know they have some special capabilities.

4. *Ideas that promote open communication.* Nothing is quite so effective in promoting personal growth and interpersonal relationships as an atmosphere of open communication. Fears, frustrations, and other feelings need to be aired and solutions to problems need to be found. The following ideas should provide a good start.

Talk to one another! Don't let resentments and hostilities build up until they explode. Try to encourage the children to work out their differences at the moment and set a good example by doing the same. When children see that it is safe to "blow off" a bit, they are able to release anger appropriately and have more energy to solve problems than when they let hurt and jealousy fester.

Talk about differences and similarities among family members. It's fun to find out that you have some qualities which are more similar to a non-biological relative than to one related by blood. Encourage children to appreciate the similarities and differences among themselves.

Start family councils. They are an excellent way of promoting harmony. Whether or not the children live with you full-time, family councils can be used regularly to air grievances, make family decisions, divide up chores and work, etc. Remember to include a compliment time at the end of each family council. It's a nice way to end since much of the family council often is spent on problems. "What I especially like about you" or "Thank you for what you did for me this week" are positive ways to end a family council.

Set up a communication box. This is similar to a suggestion box but with individual cubbyholes or drawers (a sewing or tool box works very well). The children and adults can scribble messages to one another. These can be criticisms, suggestions, or compliments — and they remain private between the giver and sender. No child should peek in another's box.

5. *Ideas that promote a kinship network.* Encourage your relatives and your spouse's relatives (and where possible, those of your ex-spouse) to accept, and eventually even love, all the children in your blended family. By doing so you provide an important support system for yourselves and for your children. It is enriching for children to be involved with a variety of people — both young and old. Here are a few tips:

Encourage grandparents and other relatives to become involved with *all* the children. Be sure to provide them with a list of birth dates. Encourage children and stepchildren to send birthday and special occasion cards to their relatives.

If grandparents (or others) are initially reluctant to include stepchildren in gift giving (or if the increased numbers may be overwhelming), encourage them to send group gifts.

Try to send grandparents and other interested relatives snapshots of your blended family regularly. This will help them become familiar with all the new faces. Also send school photographs of all the children in the blended family. Grandparents often like to show off their grandchildren.

Arrange for children to visit relatives. Where possible, send a "his and her" pair. That way grandparents (or other relatives) have a chance to get to know the new member and the stepchild has his stepsibling for support in an unfamiliar situation.

REMEMBER

By using some of these suggestions, and better yet, by discovering or inventing some of your own solutions, you can do a great deal to promote family harmony and a feeling of solidarity and cohesiveness. Don't be impatient. It's a big job. Of course you can't force involvement and caring, but you certainly can foster them.

14

Re-Creating
Family Life
After Divorce

As we gathered material for this book, we talked with countless numbers of parents and many of their children. Some of the parents were considering divorce, some were involved in divorce proceedings, and others were already divorced. The last group included some parents so embittered that future happiness was only a dim prospect and others who were confidently building new lives for themselves and their children. From the latter group we gained much hope and inspiration. We've shared with you bits of their wisdom in the hope that you might be able to emerge from the experience of divorce with enough love and understanding to create a new and viable life for yourself and your children.

Many parents have continued to parent responsibly and effectively during and after divorce. Although their own personal solutions do not always fall within the framework of current conventions, their life-styles work well for them. The following stories are some of our favorites.

BECKY

"You see that red roof over there?" Becky, seven, hopped along the sidewalk in front of her father's house (careful, of course, to avoid stepping on the cracks or lines). She pointed to a house on the next street. "That's where Mommy lives," she informed us. "Jacob and I live there too on Mondays, Wednesdays, Fridays, and Sundays." She ticked the days off on her fingers. "But on Tuesdays and Thursdays and Saturdays, we stay with Daddy. Today's Tuesday, isn't it?"

Before we had a chance to confirm that fact, Becky rushed on. "I'm the only one in first grade who knows all the days of the week by heart. I can even say them backwards!"

And with this justifiably proud announcement, Becky turned a cartwheel and landed expertly in her own front yard. We later learned from her father that standing on her head and doing cartwheels is Becky's most newly acquired skill. "We see more of Becky's sneakers than we do of her face these days," her father told us with a chuckle.

In between cartwheels and headstands, Becky eagerly, if somewhat breathlessly, shared some observations about her life:

> Jessica is my best friend. She moved in next door to us at my mommy's house—where that scary, big dog used to live. Jessica has a baby sister named Tish and a daddy who eats dinner at her house 'cause he's a sleep-in-their-Mommy's-bed kind of daddy.
>
> My daddy isn't that kind of daddy. He has his own house and his own bed, and we take turns living with him and then Mommy. Jessica's daddy doesn't even know how to cook, but my daddy does! Jacob and I sleep at Daddy's house, but Daddy never sleeps at my mom's house. Jessica's family is different from mine.

Becky was fascinated by the differences between Jessica's home and her own life-style. While she sat on the back porch dunking her cookies in her glass of milk, she shared a few more tidbits about Jessica's life. Finally, Becky was quiet for a brief reflective moment, then she added:

> You know why we are different? It's because of the divorce. I don't really remember it, but Jacob says *he* does. He says he remembers when Mommy and Daddy used to live together. At first I didn't believe him 'cause he's always telling me whoppers and then I believe him and they're not true and then I get in trouble. But Jacob showed me a picture of Mommy and Daddy holding us and anyway Mommy says he's really telling the truth, so I guess he is—this time!

Becky paused a moment to take a breath and rescue a piece of cookie which was floating in her milk. Then she continued:

You know Bennie at my school? You know, he's that boy who cries all the time even when he just breaks a crayon. Well, he was trying to sneak in front of me to go down the slide, but I'd been standing in line and it was *my* turn so I gave him a shove and he started crying. And then you know what?

Becky jumped up from the step where she had been sitting, placed her hands dramatically on her hips, and narrowed her eyes as she remembered the offending incident:

Well, Bennie said, "I hate you, Becky. You think you're so special because you're divorced!" And that's not even true so I pushed him just a little bit more and I said, "You're so dumb, Benjamin Harrington! You don't know anything! Mommy and Daddy are divorced, but I'm not!"

THE ARRANGEMENT

Mark, seventeen, stretched out his long legs and leaned back balancing the wooden chair on its two hind legs. The chair groaned ominously. "Mark!" cautioned Sheila, sharply. Looking a bit sheepish, Mark quickly settled his chair on the floor again.

Although Mark and Sheila interact like typical teenage siblings, they are related neither by blood nor by marriage—at least not legally. "It's a bit confusing," Sheila started to explain, but she was interrupted by several of the other teenagers in the room who were all attempting to explain the situation to us. Despite their explanations we remained confused.

"Wait a minute!" boomed Mark in his best big brother voice: "Let Susie explain. After all, she's the one who started everything."

Fifteen-year-old Susie blushed as all eyes turned to her. She paused, looked thoughtful, and began to explain:

Well, when I was seven, my parents were divorced. Then my dad got married and instead of being an only child, suddenly there were three more kids in the family! Mark was nine, Kathy who is exactly the same age as I am (we have the same birthdays) was seven, and Greg was six. I lived with my mom, but I spent every other weekend with my stepbrothers and my stepsister. Kathy and I became especially close.

Kathy and Susie smiled warmly at each other. Then Susie continued her story:

Then the next year my mom remarried and my family got even larger. Three more kids! And they were all about the same age as the rest of us. In fact, Carla is just two months younger than Kathy and me. Carla, Ted, and Sheila would come over on weekends to visit their dad — my stepdad. Well, I didn't want to miss their coming over, so it was arranged that they would visit on the weekends that I wasn't over at my dad's place.

Kathy and Carla became my best friends, but I felt bad that they didn't know each other. Well, they kind of did — through me! I kept telling each one all about the other. Then on my tenth birthday, Mom said I could have a slumber party, so I invited both Carla and Kathy. And that was how it all began, right?

The others nodded their assent. Then Ted, sixteen, took up the story:

Susie and Carla and Kathy became the Three Musketeers. They wanted to be together every weekend. About that time Mark and I found out that we were on the same Little League baseball team.

"But you've got to tell about the first time we were *all* together." This time it was Greg jumping in to keep the story straight.

"I remember that," interjected Sheila. "It all started because my mom wanted to go out of town. She was going to get a babysitter for us, but we decided it would be more fun to stay at Susie's house."

"Yeah," agreed Susie, "and that was the week that Mark, Kathy, and Greg were visiting. At first my mom was horrified, but we finally talked mom and my stepdad into the idea."

"I remember that weekend," chimed in Mark, "it was a blast!" Several laughed as they remembered the famous weekend. Then Susie continued:

Sheila's right. That's how it all began. After that weekend we kids came up with a brilliant idea. We decided we wanted to be together *every* weekend, so we talked our parents into letting us rotate from my house to Kathy's to Carla's. At first they thought it was a crazy idea since Mark, Kathy, and Greg weren't even related to Carla, Ted, and Sheila, but we kept begging and they agreed to try it. We made a schedule and some ground rules that applied to all the homes, like chores to be done, curfew times, and things like that. We've been doing this for five years now. It's fantastic! Our parents have more kids and we have each other *and* more parents. I think we get along with our parents better than our friends do with their parents. Maybe it's because we get breaks from each other. You know, we only see our parents every third weekend!

Mark, Kathy, Greg, Sheila, Ted, and Carla all grin and nod their heads in agreement with Susie. They all seem to like their "arrangement."

"My Kids Have Three Grandmas"

Terri, slightly built with a cap of tousled auburn curls and a sprinkling of freckles across her nose, looks more like sixteen than twenty-six. "I know," she says with a good-natured grin, "No cocktail waitress ever wants to serve me." Although Terri looks young, she certainly is not immature!

"I had to grow up fast," Terri explains, "because, as my aunts used to say with pity, 'Poor Terri — she's a product of divorce.' I was never sure exactly what they meant by that, but I always envisioned something defective coming off General Motors' assembly line!"

With her keen humor and her seldom failing sense of perspective and goodwill, Terri is one of the most thoughtful young mothers we know. As we talked, her children — Shana, four, and Andy, two — darted in and out of the living room in hot pursuit of Fluff, a small, white ball of cat. Between their squeals of delight and the cat's anxious meows, Terri filled us in on her childhood:

When I was eight years old, my father left my mother to marry Jill. I adored my father and when he left us, my love turned to hate. He and Jill moved to Texas and although they invited me to visit them, I was stubborn and refused.

After Dad left, Mom became extremely depressed — and not just your ordinary teary depression, but the kind where a person doesn't move for hours. Those months were awful for my brother and me. We might as well have had our own apartment, for we were practically on our own. We learned to cook, wash our clothes, and sometimes we even signed Mom's name to our school excuses when we were sick. Finally, after Mom tried to commit suicide, our aunts moved in to take care of her and at the same time they packed us off to Texas—against my will!

Poor Jill! Looking back, I realize now how awful it must have been for her to be suddenly saddled with us—especially me since I was so hateful. Even more than my dad, I blamed Jill for my mom's emotional breakdown and for my unhappiness. But Jill just acted as if she couldn't see how sullen I was and just went right on treating me warmly. Well, despite my resolution to hate her, I couldn't hold out and within a few weeks I grew to love Jill. When it was time for Jimmy and me to move back with Mom, I was really sad to leave.

Although I missed Dad and Jill, I was very glad to be home with Mom. Of course, things weren't all rosy when we returned, but she had definitely changed. She was much more like the mother of my earlier childhood—she laughed freely and had lots of energy again.

Soon after we got home, Mom took a job with a data processing company. She started on the bottom rung, but boy, did she climb—all the way to vice-president of the company in just five years! The more successful Mom became, the less she hated Dad and Jill. In fact, last year she told me that the divorce was probably the best thing that ever happened to her. It made her pull herself together.

You know, divorce gave me the best of two worlds. I spent summers and some holidays in Texas with Dad and Jill and their children. Taking care of my half-brother and sisters gave me good practice for my own! Most of all, I loved being pampered by Jill. She's just a born mother! But living with Mom also gave me a great deal. I learned to be independent and self-confident. She was always behind me encouraging me to do the things I wanted to do. And she appreciated my "kookiness"!

As Shana and Andy rounded the corner again, Terri swooped them up and hugged them tightly. For a few moments she was silent, lost in thought. Then she looked up and with a twinkle added impishly:

My poor, misguided aunts! They were so wrong. I didn't need any pity. In fact, in many ways I feel I'm to be envied, for my childhood was filled with plenty of love and belonging. And now, there's an extra bonus. My children have three grandmas.

Jill is as much a grandma as Bill's mother and mine. And guess who came to spend part of their summer with us? My half-brother and sisters. They love romping and playing with their niece and nephew. The love Jill gave me I now give Michael, Jennifer, and Morgan. The circle is complete!

A Father for Jeanie

Dark hair swinging and black eyes crackling with excitement, Jeanie ran into the high school counselor's office. "Mr. Black! Mr. Black!" she shouted to him from across the room. "Look, I've got it!"

Mr. Black hurried over to Jeanie, took the legal paper she was waving wildly, and looked it over. A wide smile spread across his face. "Jeanie!" he exclaimed, hugging her warmly, "I'm so happy for you! I know how much being adopted means to you." Jeanie could only nod, for tears were dripping down her radiant face.

For years Jeanie had wanted to belong legally to her stepfather and carry his name. She explained to us why it meant so much to her:

I can't tell you how much I love my stepdad. Mom and he got married when I was eight years old and my sister, Luisa, was four. My own father left my mother and us when I was five years old. Life for Mom was terribly hard for a long time. She had hardly any money and she was always trying to keep us from knowing how bad things really were. She used to work in a hotel kitchen. She worked so hard and wouldn't get home until real late. We'd wait at my grandmother's until Mom would pick us up. She tried to be cheerful around us, but I can remember hearing her cry lots of times at night.

And then my stepdad came into our lives. I think I loved him right from the very beginning because he made my mom so happy. When they got married he told everyone at the wedding, "I'm a real lucky guy! I got three pretty ladies for the price of one!"

When I was nine, Carmen was born and I started having problems in school. I got real shy and couldn't keep up with my work. Mom was worried, but Dad just kept saying, "She'll come out of it. Jeanie's got lots on her mind." One day he took me to the park to talk to me alone. He asked me if I thought that he loved baby Carmen better than me because he was her real father. I burst into tears because he had guessed what was wrong with me. "Jeanie," he said hugging me, "you, and Luisa, and Carmen are all my daughters. I love each one of you." Then he showed me his fingers and asked, "Which finger could I do without?" I knew what he was getting at.

That's how understanding my dad is. By the time I was in the eighth grade, we had two more kids in our family, Roberto and Teresa. I asked Dad if he could adopt Luisa and me so we'd all have the same last name. He explained that it was expensive and would involve a lot of legal business, but he'd see what he could do. And now, finally, after all these years, Luisa and I are Romeros — just like my dad and mom and all the other kids in the family!

The Blessing

"He's here! Grandpapa is here!" several of the children exclaimed, excitement making their voices even more shrill than usual. They tumbled out the door, each wanting to be first to greet Grandpapa. Standing in the doorway, we watched our brood of ten hugging and kissing their grandfather. Only our little Briana was not part of the confusion and joy. She watched wide-eyed from the doorway safely perched on her daddy's shoulders.

We were apprehensive about Dad's visit. I hadn't seen him for nearly two years — and that last trip was so awful. He visited right after the separation. Actually, "visit" is hardly the right word — he almost wouldn't talk to me. He was sure I had ruined my life. And marrying Hal with all his kids hadn't helped Dad's opinion of my sanity. But I guess most of all we worried about how he would relate to all the children. Of course he knew my children well, but how would he react to Hal's children who were strangers to him? Although we hoped he would be a grandfather to all of them — would he?

Later — much later — that evening when all the kids were tucked into bed and the last cry for a drink of water had subsided, the three of us sat down together to enjoy a cup of coffee and visit. We chatted and joked for some time — trying to keep the conversation light. Then Dad suddenly became serious.

You know, there's something I want to tell you. I've made many trips to Denver over the years, but I didn't want to make this one. I felt too much pain from the last time I was here. But on the phone you seemed so eager to have me come that I couldn't refuse.

While I was on my way here, I couldn't help thinking about all those other trips to Denver. I thought about the happy occasions — especially the births of my four grandchildren and the adoption of the fifth. I also remembered the last time I had seen you, Gail. After that visit I went home with a broken heart. You probably remember that I left the day after I got here.

Dad paused for a pensive moment, lightly biting his lip. He took a new breath and continued:

You — who I used to think of as my sensible little clown . . . you who used to be so merry, so full of laughter — you couldn't hide how tired and worried you were. The children were upset and it was hard for you to comfort and care for all of them. You know, that night I went back to my motel room and cried. I knew how much pain you were in and yet I felt totally at a loss to help you, so I flew back to California the next day.

And then you wrote that you were marrying Hal, who already had five children. So what was I to do? Rejoice? I couldn't! All I could think of was how overwhelmed you were the last time I was here and then add five more children to the picture. I couldn't imagine what that many children would be like. Then this year you phoned to tell me that I had a new granddaughter, Briana. I didn't know what to think. "They're crazy," I said to myself. But, of course, I wanted to see my new granddaughter.

He paused again, lit his pipe and tamped it for a few moments as he looked thoughtful. His eyes began to tear but a look of satisfaction crossed his face as he continued:

You know, I don't think I've ever been so touched as I was tonight. When we sat down together at dinner, and I saw the table set for the Sabbath — the white tablecloth, the freshly baked bread, the candles, and most of all, those bright, beautiful faces around the table — well, you saw me weep. But this time it was for joy. And as you lit the candles and I said the blessing over the wine, I truly did feel blessed. I never dreamed

I would see all of you so happy. And I was surprised and delighted by the way everyone held hands around the table and gave thanks silently in the Quaker way. How wonderful to blend your traditions. You and Hal are something else!

You have given me so much—eleven grandchildren who all call me "Grandpapa!" What a wonderful blessing! I know I will quickly come to love each and every one, for they are all so special!

And true to his word, he has.

Bibliography

Bird, Sarah. "Parents Who Kidnap Their Own Children." *National Observer*, July 4, 1977.

Bohannan, Paul (ed.). *Divorce and After.* Garden City, N.Y.: Anchor Books, 1971.

Despert, J. Louise. *Children of Divorce.* Garden City, N.Y.: Dolphin Books, 1962.

Fraiberg, Selma. *The Magic Years: Understanding and Handling the Problems of Early Childhood.* New York: Charles Scribner's Sons, 1959.

Gardner, Richard A. *The Boys and Girls Book About Divorce.* New York: Bantam Books, 1971.

Ginott, Haim G. *Between Parent and Child.* New York: Avon Books, 1969.

Gordon, Thomas. *Parent Effectiveness Training.* New York: Peter H. Wyden, 1970.

Howard, Stephen J. "A Rational Approach to Custody." *Marriage and Divorce*, May-June, 1974.

Kahn, Robert and Lawrence Kahn. *The Divorce Lawyers' Casebook.* New York: St. Martins Press, 1972.

Klatskin, E.H. "Developmental Factors." In *Children of Separation and Divorce*, edited by Irving R. Stuart. New York: Grossman, 1972.

Krantzler, Mel. *Creative Divorce: A New Opportunity for Personal Growth.* New York: M. Evans and Company, 1974.

LeMasters, E. *Parents in Modern America.* Homewood, Ill.: Dorsey Press, 1970.

Mann, Peggy. *My Dad Lives in a Downtown Hotel.* New York: Avon, 1974.

O'Neill, Nena and George O'Neill. *Shifting Gears.* New York: Avon Books, 1974.

Satir, Virginia. *Peoplemaking.* Palo Alto, Cal.: Science and Behavior Books, 1972.

Simon, Anne W. *Stepchild in the Family: A View of Children in Remarriage.* New York: Odyssey Press, 1964.

Stuart, Irving R. (ed.). *Children of Separation and Divorce.* New York: Grossman, 1972.

Index

Abandonment
  by non-custodial parent, 173–79
  children's fears of, 9, 15, 29–31, 69
Children
  discussing possibility of divorce with, 13–35
  effects of marital conflict on, 6–7, 14–15
  egocentrism, 17–18, 24–25, 61
  fears and concerns about divorce, 16–20
  questions about divorce, 21–26
  reactions to divorce, 55–74
    clinging, 65
    fantasies, 68–69
    regressive behavior, 65–67, 69
    testing limits, 61–63
    reactions to post-marital conflict, 165–69
Child snatching, 163–64
Child support, 50–52, 159
Chores, 104–8
Conflict
  marital, 6–7, 14–15
  post-marital, 158–65
Counseling
  for children, 58, 71, 72–74
  for parents, 7, 40–41, 58, 65, 79–82
Custody, child, 38–53
  courtroom decisions, 39
  definition of, 41–42
  guidelines for decision making, 43–50
  joint custody, 50

Dating, 183–94
Emotional divorce, 6–7, 20–21
Expenses, ways to cut, 110–12
Failure, post-marital feelings of, 5, 9–10
Family
  extended, through divorce, 223–43
  extended, traditional, 221–22
  nuclear, 222–23
Financial responsibility. *See* Child support
Goal setting, 10, 97–102
Guidelines, for parenting after divorce, 8–11
Joint custody, 50
Mourning, 56–61
Parent
  custodial, 75–90
    neglect, 170–73
    role problems, 178–82
  long distance, 139–55
    children's reactions to geographical separation, 139–41
    consequences of, 145–46
    maintaining parent-child relationship, 147–55
  non-custodial, 119–38
    fears and concerns of, 122–24
    maintaining parent-child relationship, 128–31
    role of, 133–36
  stepparents. *See* Stepparent
Reality, importance of facing, 9–11, 15–16

257

Remarriage, 144–45, 196–200
Single parent family, 91–117
Stepparent, 201–19
  role of, 203–9
  suggestions for, 216–19
Therapy. *See* Counseling

Visitation
  by long distance parent, 152–54
  decision making, 43–50
  sabotage by custodial parent, 159
  suggestions, 113–16, 136–38
  worries, 132–33